Completely Unbiased Endorsements

You should definitely read this book. I mean, I didn't read it. Who has time for that? It's 326 pages. You think I'm going to sit down and read 326 pages? I've got a four-year-old and a newborn. But my sister wrote it, so it's good for sure.

DENNIS MONESTIER (AUTHOR'S BROTHER)

Students, you should buy TWO copies of this book. One to read at home and one to read at school. I'm not just saying this because Tanya will make money off each purchase.

GRAZIANO MONESTIER (AUTHOR'S FATHER)

My wife is blunt. I often have to keep her away from customer service representatives; she's been known to make them cry. But, in this case, the bluntness works to your advantage. You are never going to find anyone else to give you the real inside scoop on law school.

DAVID COOMBS (AUTHOR'S HUSBAND)

I'd buy it. Then again, I'd read anything she writes....

TYLER MARTIN (AUTHOR'S FORMER RESEARCH ASSISTANT
AND RESIDENT SUCK-UP)

Sh*t No One Tells You About Law School

Sh*t No One Tells You About Law School

Tanya J. Monestier

PROFESSOR OF LAW
UNIVERSITY AT BUFFALO SCHOOL OF LAW

CAROLINA ACADEMIC PRESS
Durham, North Carolina

ISBN   978-1-5310-2475-8
e-ISBN   978-1-5310-2476-5

Library of Congress cataloging-in-publication data is available at www.loc.gov.

Carolina Academic Press
700 Kent Street
Durham, North Carolina 27701
(919) 489-7486
www.cap-press.com

Printed in the United States of America

For my dad, Graziano Monestier, who inspired me to write this book.* Not for the reasons you think. My dad believes that I have too much "free time" as a law professor and that I should earn some extra money with a side hustle. He has suggested multiple times that perhaps I could be a Starbucks barista.

Instead, I wrote this book in the hopes of getting him off my back.

---

* This book is also dedicated to my mother, Oriana Monestier. But my dad is a bit of an attention seeker, so after consultation with my mom, we decided it would be best if Dad got the spotlight and Mom got tossed into a footnote. She doesn't mind. I promise you. Oh, and I should mention that the book is also dedicated to my brother, Dennis, because if I don't mention him, I'll never hear the end of it. Not that he will read it. He hasn't read a book since *Tales of a Fourth Grade Nothing*. He fully owns the fact that he hates reading. Books are "too long" and "too boring" for him.

Contents

Contents

Contents

Contents

Contents

Foreword

by Mindy Lahiri

I know I am a fictional character,[1] but I was nonetheless honored when Prof. M. reached out to me to write the foreword for her book. I'm not a lawyer or a law student or anything, but even *I know* that this book is hella fresh. As I read the book, I felt that Prof. M. was my sister from another mister. And not just because we're both obsessed with pizza. But because we are strong women who tell it like it is. There's no uncertainty where you stand with us. We are an open book.

What I liked most about the book was that it was easy to read. I don't want to read a book in my spare time that is a snooze fest. I'm too busy for that (after all, I am an ob/gyn!). You can pick it up, read for ten minutes, take a donut break, and then pick up where you left off. It doesn't hurt your head to read, which is my main criterion for selecting a book. "Criterion" is a weird word, isn't it? Sorry, off track.

Prof. M. also doesn't try to scare you about law school. I've seen some of the other books, and they convinced me not to go to Princeton Law School. I'm obviously a proud member of Gen Z (or whatever generation is younger

---

1. There are a lot of fictional characters that give great life advice. Take for example James Bond ("Shaken, Not Stirred"), Jerry McGuire ("Show Me the Money"), Forrest Gump ("Life Is Like a Box of Chocolates"), and the Dalai Lama ("Know the Rules So You Can Break Them Effectively").

than that). So, I scare easily. I am more snowflake-y than a snowflake and I need to be treated with kid gloves.

I loved her stories about her Italian family, especially her dad. He's legit hilarious. I want to get a t-shirt printed that says "Mathematics Is Not an Opinion." In yellow, of course. And her brother, Dennis...I totally want to do shots of tequila with him. He seems like he knows how to have a good time. I hear that Papa M. once locked him out of the house because he came home at 7:00 in the morning. That dude can party.

I also think it's super cool that Prof. M. is a *real* person and not some stuffy, tweed-wearing, scary automaton like most law professors are. Or I think they are—you've all seen *Legally Blonde*, right? She makes learning fun and talks to you in "real people" language. She does not use words like "ipso facto" and "prima facie" like other law professors do.

I love, love, love that Prof. M. is obsessed with shoes. Now that's a woman after my own heart. She tells me that she even has a pair of yellow heels! I mean, that's next-level serious about shoes. She is also a really good dresser. Classic, but trendy. It's a hard to find that combination nowadays, so good on her. I feel like I'm meandering here, but that's what you get when you ask a fictional character to write a foreword.

Break time. I need a snickety-snack.[2] Going to grab my morning Bear Claw. BRB.

Where was I? Oh, I hear that Prof. M. is an amazing professor. Like my dad, Tarun Lahiri, who is also a professor. My mom had a good line about my dad that I also think applies to Prof. M.: "Your father doesn't have office hours because he teaches it *right* the first time." Her classes are fun and engaging. But maybe a little...intense. I Zoomed into one of them and needed a nap afterward.

Prof. M. is also very scholarly when she needs to be. She writes about super academic (read: boring) stuff in addition to writing for law students. There's not a lot of people who can do that. To use an analogy, it's like she's comfortable in both a ball gown and Lululemon leggings.[3] So few of us can pull off both looks.

---

2. I got that expression from Dennis. "Snickety-snack" makes it feel like there are fewer calories than just a "snack."

3. Who are we kidding? Prof. M. would never wear Lululemon leggings. *$100 for a pair of fricken leggings...where do they get off?* The latter is one of her favorite expressions.

In conclusion, I really think you should read this book. She shoots straight from the hip (total old person expression—what does that even mean?). She gives great advice, but gives you agency. I know, I used the word "agency" (correctly!). You are the master of your own destiny, you are the heroine in your own novel, you are the McDreamy in your own medical TV drama. Make your choices count. And follow her advice.

Author's Note: In case you didn't figure it out, *I* wrote this pretending to be Mindy Lahiri, a fictional character from *The Mindy Project*.[4] Mindy Kaling, Fox, Hulu, Universal, and any other person or entity associated with the show: I do not intend to infringe on any right of publicity or violate any intellectual property rights associated with a fictional character's name. Please don't sue me.[5] I love Mindy.

---

4. If this comes as a surprise to you, maybe law school is not your calling.
5. I do not have an indemnity agreement in place.

Introduction

Success is not an accident. Success is a choice.

STEPH CURRY

Welcome to my book! So exciting (for me, I mean). First off, I want to talk about the title of the book. I went back and forth on the title. Initially, the publisher had "concerns" about the title because this is an "academic book" by an "academic publisher." They suggested a variation of the title: "Stuff No One Tells You About Law School." *Borrrring.* They were worried that professors might not recommend the book because there was *a swear word* in the title. Bust out the fainting couch. Eventually, I convinced them that students and professors alike would not be offended and that the unusual title was, in fact, a selling point. They reluctantly acquiesced. No guts, no glory. Thank you, Carolina Academic Press, for being so #brave.

No academic success book can possibly cover every topic related to law school. This book will focus on the topics I know something about and not the ones that I have no real experience with—such as "How to Make Friends in Law School" and "Be Sure You Exercise." I did not have many friends in law school, so I can't really help you there. And it would just be hypocritical for me to recommend that you exercise. Walking up a flight of stairs gets me winded. Accordingly, my focus is going to be on stuff I *do* know about. Stuff like how to read for class, how to take notes, how to outline, and how to approach exams. This all seems like pretty basic law school stuff. But I think you'll see that my "take" on this is a little different (oooh...foreshadowing).

Before we talk about you and your law school experience, let's talk about me.

1. I Did Not Speak English Until I Was Five

You know what they say about when you "assume." You make an a** out of you and me. People are nonetheless prone to making assumptions. Students make assumptions about me. I went to an excellent law school. I graduated #1 in my law school class. (More on that later.) I had a prestigious clerkship. I summered at several premier law firms. All of this is in my faculty bio, so it is natural that when students meet me, they bring with them certain assumptions.

They assume that I am from a highly educated family and that I grew up with all the resources in the world. They assume that my family sat around the dinner table talking about Kant and Descartes. They assume that I have read *War & Peace* in its native Russian. They assume that I was a highly scheduled child, who balanced piano, French lessons, and ballet.[1] All these assumptions could not be further from the truth.

My parents are both immigrants from Italy. They moved to Canada in their early twenties with (literally) $50 in their pockets. They both grew up in small villages in Northern Italy. They have no formal education. As was typical at the time, they both quit school after the 5th grade. At the age of 11, they went to work: my mom in a silkworm factory, and my dad in construction.

When they moved to Canada a decade later, they did not speak a word of English. When I was born, I did not speak English for the first five years of my life. I learned English only after I started kindergarten. I didn't even know that until fairly recently. I also learned that I wasn't breastfed, which for some reason was jarring to me. *Mom, you gave me formula?* Yes, it was the 70s.

My mom stayed at home to raise me and my brother. And my dad became a tile setter. He and my godfather (no, not that kind of godfather) started their own company: Pro Tile. Imaginative, I know. Dad would leave the house at six-o'clock in the morning, after drinking his *caffè corretto*.[2] He'd be wearing

---

1. I actually did take ballet lessons for a short while. Until my dad concluded that I wasn't "very graceful" and that he "did not see a future" in it. I was six.

2. With grappa. No, he did not have a problem with alcohol. This is actually "a thing" in Italy.

his construction clothes and carrying his gray lunchbox which invariably contained a mortadella and Friulano cheese sandwich, and two pieces of fruit.

Growing up, we sat around the dinner table talking about the food on the table (potatoes are overcooked, rapini have too much garlic) and planning the next dinner. Food was, and still is, a big topic at my house. I kid you not, most of our family arguments revolve around food. My parents' favorite television show is *Blue Bloods*, and it is solely because of the Sunday dinner scene in every episode.

When we weren't talking about food, we were probably gossiping about so-and-so's kids or some extended family drama. *Did you know that Maria dropped out of university? I heard that Gino and Dario are not talking anymore. Gino was offended that he didn't get invited to Dario's daughter's wedding.* The conversations were not exactly highbrow.

As a child, I did not have any scheduled activities or play dates. *Do your homework and play or watch TV. But turn off the TV before your father comes home.* When dad came home, we had to greet him at the door to welcome him home. Anyone from a European family will probably relate. The rest of you will probably think it's weird.

I do not play an instrument, which is probably for the best because I am not highly musical. I was in choir in elementary school and my teacher, Mrs. Black, kept telling me to pipe down. My dad once got it in his mind that he wanted me to play an instrument. I kid you not, that instrument was... *wait for it*... the accordion. A man came to the house a couple of times to give me lessons. And I guess my parents eventually figured out that I was not going to be an accordion virtuoso.

Birthdays were pretty ordinary. There would be cake at the house and Zio Decimo, Zia Velia, Lisa, Stephanie, and Robert (the godparents and their kids) would come over. So would Tom,[3] Rose, Michael, Anthony, and Claudio (the

---

3. Tom was like a second father to me. A much softer version of my father. Tom passed away of brain cancer eight years ago. He is always in my heart. My favorite memory of Tom: When I was eight years old, my dad decided to send me to sleepaway camp because he thought it would "build character." I did not want to go. I was a very shy child and had never been away from home. Tom and my mom put me on the camp bus and followed behind in the car to make sure I got there okay. When we all arrived, I was bawling. I wanted to go home. Tom started crying too. He begged my mom to take me back home. But my mother knew that would not fly with my dad. So, I stayed at the camp for the two full weeks and hated every minute of it.

neighbors and their kids). There were no McDonald's birthday parties. I'm not bitter—really, I'm not.[4] There were no loot bags. There were no themes. There was an Italian bakery cake, candles, and singing. That's it.

In my career, I always kept my personal life separate from my professional life. When I taught, I never shared information with students about myself, my background, or my upbringing. To be clear, it was not because I was embarrassed. It was because I did not think it was relevant. In recent years, however, I have come to rethink that position. I have realized that where I come from has profoundly influenced who I am. It is not irrelevant. It is part of my story.

2. I Have Lived the First-Generation Experience

My parents, particularly my father, always emphasized the importance of education. For my father, it was important for me to get an education so that I did not have to do the kind of back-breaking work that he did. I saw my dad struggle with shoulder, knee, and back problems for 30 years. That sh*t leaves an impact. I felt that my parents had come to Canada to give me a better life and that I had to make the most out of the opportunities that were given to me.

While my parents provided emotional support, they couldn't provide concrete assistance with my schoolwork or guidance on academic matters. So, I went at it alone. I learned from a very early age how to learn and how to succeed in school. And succeed I did.

At every stage of my academic career, I was at the top of my class. I was #1 in my Father Serra Elementary School class. I was #1 in my Bishop Allen Academy High School class. There were no rankings at York University, but I graduated with the highest distinction, so I think that counts as #1. I was #1 in my Osgoode Hall Law School class (what we, in Canada, call the "Gold Medalist" and what you, in the U.S., call "the valedictorian").[5] And I graduated with First Class Honors from Cambridge University. Again, they don't rank, but we'll also call that #1. The point, other than bragging, is to tell you that I know how to "do" school.

The pride that my parents felt in those accomplishments was immeasurable. On one occasion, I received the Italian-Canadian Business and Professional

---

4. I am.
5. I got a real gold medal that is currently hanging in my parents' living room.

Association Scholarship. There was a reception in my honor at the Four Seasons hotel in downtown Toronto. The Minister of Education was in attendance, as was the then-President of York University, Dr. Lorna Marsden. The President was chatting with my dad and asked him where he had gone to school, assuming that he had completed post-secondary education. My father, without missing a beat, said to her, "Fifth elementary, Prodolone, third floor." She was confused and asked him what he meant. He explained that he completed the 5th grade in the town of Prodolone, Italy—population 750—and that his classroom was on the third floor. The President seemed a little stunned. Later that week, I received a personal letter in the mail from Dr. Marsden, where she included a hand-written notation saying, "I really enjoyed getting to meet your father."

On the day of my law school graduation, my dad marched up to the front of the auditorium and sat down in the front row, which had been reserved for honored guests. My mother followed along, embarrassed by his brazenness. An usher told him that the spots were reserved and that he could not sit there. My dad said, "My daughter is graduating with the Gold Medal today, and I'm going to sit here and watch her graduate." The usher let them sit front and center. As an aside, my parents threw a giant party at a banquet hall for my graduation. Like 100 guests, sit-down six-course dinner, speeches, DJ, and open bar. I think at that point, they weren't sure if I'd ever get married,[6] so might as well take the chance to celebrate when you can.

As I made my way through my academic career, however, I was always acutely aware that I wasn't like other students. My parents weren't doctors, lawyers, and teachers, as it seemed everyone else's parents were. My parents weren't able to help me with complicated math, book reports, or history and geography assignments, though they did buy me the full set of World Book Encyclopedias to help me out.

I learned how to be self-sufficient and teach myself. This was the most valuable skill I learned growing up, and the skill that I want to help impart to you. It is, in fact, the reason I went into teaching. My dad still shakes his head every time he thinks about the $250,000 law firm salary I turned down 15 years ago.

Many of you reading this book will relate to my story. For you: I understand the pressure and expectations that come with being the first in your family to undertake post-secondary education. I understand what it's like to struggle

---

6. My parents describe me as "difficult." When I eventually did get engaged, my dad told my now-husband that there was a "no return" policy. Thanks, Dad.

and feel like you don't have anyone to ask for help. I understand what it's like to feel like you are an outlier in your own family. I understand what it's like to feel less than other students because you don't come from the same background that they do. This understanding gives me a unique insight into your world. Much of my experience and background makes me well placed to understand you, your struggles, and your challenges. Because of that, I hope you take to heart at least some of the advice that I'm giving you in this book.

Here is a message I recently received from a first-generation student who saw himself in my story:

> I can honestly say that you are the only professor, or even teacher, I have ever had that has really represented my background. To me, it was really important. I specifically remember in your review session when you mentioned that you were the daughter of immigrants, a first gen student, and your parents came from a working class/blue collar background. To me, that was like an "oh sh*t" moment because my background is exactly the same. First, I thought to myself, okay no more excuses. Here is a highly educated legal scholar who comes from a similar background, so no more feeling like my background is an obstacle to my success in the legal field. Second, I finally felt like I could take advice from a professor at face value. With other professors, I tend to take advice with a grain of salt because their law school journey usually looked different than mine. So not only did I feel represented, but I also felt motivated because I could see that your hard work has paid off ... You have truly helped me work towards fulfilling the notion of the 'American Dream.'

3. I Graduated First in My Law School Class

In case you missed it, I graduated first in my law school class. First out of almost three hundred students. I received A's or A+'s in every class I took in law school—except Evidence.[7]

I usually received the top grade in every class I took. I got the highest grade in Family Law, Criminal Law, and Wills & Trusts—things that are not even re-

---

7. Damn you, Professor Morton! I took Evidence my final semester of law school. When grades were released, I saw that I got a B+ in the course. I was pretty upset about a B+ ruining my pristine law school transcript. A few days later, I got a call from the Dean informing me that I had graduated first in the class. I was obviously thrilled. But the B+ still nagged at me and I wanted to appeal it. I exercised extreme self-restraint and decided not to appeal the Evidence grade. Even *I* realized that would be obnoxious. But the B+ bothers me to this day.

motely in my wheelhouse. I tell you this because you don't need to be a "tax person" or even a "numbers person" to do well in Tax Law. You don't have to be at all interested in the subject to do well. Doing well is not about liking the course or the professor. It is about assimilating everything you learned, even if it's boring or you disagree with it, and then giving it back to the professor on the exam.

When I went to law school, there were no "how to" guides.[8] I had to figure out law school on my own. Because of that, I know what it takes to do well in law school. And I hope to share that information with you, so you don't have to go through trial and error. In law school, there isn't much room for trial and error. Your grades are very important, and if you bomb your first semester, there is a good chance that it will have some sort of impact on your academic career. Now, don't get alarmed. Your grades are not everything, but they are very important.

I want to be clear on one thing. I was not the smartest person at my law school. I was actually nowhere close to the smartest person at my law school. I know that, and I'm okay with it. But I knew what needed to be done and how to do it. Doing well in law school is not about being the smartest person in the room. It is about doing things the right way to maximize your potential for success.

4. I'm a Good Teacher (I Think)

The publisher told me that I have to tell you why I am an authority on the topic of success in law school and why you should listen to me. I feel like I've already bought some street cred by telling you about my background and my academic performance in law school. Can you say *superstar*?

But I'll also tell you that I think I'm a pretty good teacher. I've been teaching for well over a decade now. And whether I teach in a classroom or through a book, it's all teaching. Students tell me that I have a way of explaining things that resonates with them. I can take complicated things and make them simple. I can get students to understand the "why" behind things.

If you are potentially going to follow advice from an academic support book, I think it is important that the person authoring it should be a good teacher. It's weird because I've looked up some academic support book authors, and they

---

8. This is partly because I went to law school a while ago, and partly because I went to law school in Canada, which is not as saturated with legal books as the U.S. is. I digress.

have terrible Rate My Professor reviews.[9] Is that petty of me? I don't know. In any event, that would make me think twice about following their advice.

Also, and I'm sure this will piss some people off, I would be skeptical about following advice from someone who did not graduate at or near the top of their class. Being a good student is a skill. One that is best learned from someone who has demonstrated that skill in practice, not in theory.

Let me provide you with some cherry-picked student evaluations from my Contracts, Sales, and Conflict of Laws classes telling you how great I am. Hopefully this convinces you that I am a trusted authority and that you should believe everything I say.[10]

> Professor Monestier is the greatest teacher I have ever had. And I used the word "teacher" intentionally because that's why she's my favorite—Professor Monestier never misses an opportunity to teach. Most professors, when they cold call and someone gets it wrong, they just move on to someone else—not Monestier. If she calls on someone and their answer is not quite right, she will pause the entire class to make sure that everyone is clear on the answer to the question she asked. It sounds small, but very few professors do it and it's so thoughtful and helpful. It feels like she really cares about our learning and wants to take every chance she can to ensure we understand the material. Also, she never misses a chance to make us feel appreciated! If you explain something correctly during class, she'll refer back to your answer for the rest of the class, which really just makes all the studying worth it. I absolutely love Professor Monestier, because I absolutely love learning and she makes it feel so easy and so rewarding.

> Professor Monestier is truly the best professor I have ever had. She fair, she is considerate, she is organized and straightforward. Best of all, it is clear how much she actually cares about the long-term success of her students. She is also approachable and helpful and has made me feel so comfortable asking any questions. She takes the time to answer them thoroughly. Again, Professor Monestier is the best professor I have ever had. Her class is the class I look forward to most every week. I appreciate the format and structure of her

---

9. A student recently brought to my attention that I have a nasty Rate My Professor review, where the reviewer surmises that I have "no friends" and I sit at home reading Contracts books all the time. *Can you say harsh?* You Millennials/Gen Zs are kind of mean.

10. JK. One of my first pieces of advice is for *you* to independently decide what advice to follow.

to say thank you for everything. Throughout my academic career, I have always heard from students promoting college to high schoolers, or promoting grad school to undergrad students, that they will meet a professor that will change their lives for the better. I was always skeptical of that…because school to me has always been a chore. But I just wanted to let you know that you were that professor for me. You have changed my life for the better as a student and as an individual.

I loved every single class (not just subject) that I have taken with you, and you may not know it, but you have helped me a lot outside of the classroom as well. You have always challenged me and it has made me a better student and person all around. You have taught me how to think on my feet with all the cold calls you threw at me 1L year. You have taught me how to critically think and question decisions of others. You have taught me how to be professional and address my peers with confidence. You taught me technical skills as well such as how to outline which I have been able to carry over to everything else I have drafted since. I would try to always speak with you after every couple of classes in regard to some legal doctrine we discussed, and to you that may not have been a lot, but for me that was the most I have ever talked to any other professor by a long shot. I think the professor I have spoken with the most aside from you is Professor Coombs and I have only talked to him on two separate occasions. (And if he wants another student to help him work on his drive aside from Richard, I do love golf haha). I get a lot of anxiety when I step into the school so it took a lot to be able to volunteer in class and approach you after, but you made it very doable. It is no surprise to me how you won professor of the year and it would be no surprise to me if you were to win it again.

I just wanted to take some time before school starts back up to let you know how appreciative I am for all that you have done for me inside and outside of the classroom.

Break out the Kleenex.

5. I'm a Good Writer (I Think)

I'm not sure how far the publisher wants me to go with this whole "why you should believe me" thing. I'm erring on the side of caution (total legal expression) and giving you more information rather than less. It also gives me an opportunity to brag more.

I think I'm a good writer.[12] This means that you will find the contents of this book manageable. You will probably not have to read paragraphs over and over again to understand what I mean. If you do, there's one of two things happening: (1) either I did a bad job of explaining myself, which can happen...unlikely, but possible; or (2) you don't belong in law school. The latter is a joke. Sort of.

I have never written any sort of academic support article. The articles I write would probably be considered boring by even the nerdiest among you. I say that with affection as I, too, am a total nerd. Here are the titles of, and citations to, some of my previously published work:

Registration Statutes, General Jurisdiction, and the Fallacy of Consent, 36 CARDOZO LAW REVIEW 1343 (2015).

Sounds like a page turner, I know! But this is one of the most impactful pieces of scholarship I have produced. It was used by a court to strike down a piece of legislation. That's a big deal. Trust me. It's also been cited in dozens of cases.

Transnational Class Actions and the Illusory Search for Res Judicata, 86 TULANE LAW REVIEW 1 (2011).

Ooooooh, so many big words that non-lawyers would never use ("transnational," "illusory" and "res judicata"). This article was a beast to write, but it's good. Very academic-y. This might not mean much to you, but it was initially accepted for publication by a *really* fancy law review. That really fancy law review then screwed me over. Long story short, I ended up publishing with another law journal. I'm still bitter though. Like McDonald's birthday party bitter.

Amazon as a Seller of Marketplace Goods Under Article 2, 107 CORNELL LAW REVIEW 101 (2022).

Now this is something that might seem somewhat interesting to you. It's about Amazon and whether they should be liable for defective and dangerous goods sold by third parties on their website. Specifically, it is about wheth-

---

12. My 10th grade English teacher would beg to differ. She told my mom at a parent-teacher conference that my writing needed work. *Really, Mrs. Benevides? How many books have you written?*

er Amazon is liable under Article 2 of the Uniform Commercial Code. To be liable under Article 2, Amazon needs to be a merchant "seller" within the meaning of §2-314 of the statute. Being a merchant seller normally means that you must have title to the goods in question, which Amazon doesn't have with respect to third-party goods. Have I lost you yet? The article is published in *Cornell Law Review*, which is amaze-balls.

Whose Law of Personal Jurisdiction? The Choice of Law Problem in the Recognition of Foreign Judgments, 96 Boston University Law Review 1729 (2016).

There's a whole bunch of stuff here you won't understand yet: "personal jurisdiction," "choice of law" and "recognition of foreign judgments." When a U.S. court chooses to recognize (give effect to) a foreign court judgment, it must assess whether the foreign court had the power (jurisdiction) to render the judgment. In doing so, it must decide whether to assess jurisdiction using U.S. law or foreign law. This means there is a choice of law problem within a foreign judgments problem. Kill me now.

There's a lot of other stuff I've written, including a ton (OK, maybe not a ton) about Canadian law. I will have you know that the Supreme Court of Canada has cited my work on multiple occasions. In one judgment, the Supreme Court of Canada cited three different articles of mine. That's unheard of. When it happened, I told the Dean about it, but he didn't really seem to care. He was basically like, *Oh, that's nice.* I assume it was because it was the Supreme Court of *Canada*—which, to you Americans, is obviously inferior to the U.S. Supreme Court.[13] I went ahead and made a big deal of it on my own. Cause why not? I told a colleague about it who sent out an email blast to everyone. I mean, I could have sent the email myself, but that just would have been tacky.

I feel like I might have lost my ultimate point here, so let me regroup. The point is that I generally do a very good job of communicating in writing. I have persuaded judges of my position and have started important conversations in academia. It's at least worth considering what I have to say.

---

13. When one of my colleagues was cited in a dissenting U.S. Supreme Court decision denying certiorari (i.e., not a real decision), the school practically threw a parade in his honor.

6. I'm Decidedly Middle Age

When I started teaching, and for some years after, I fancied myself the young, *cool* professor. I don't actually think I was ever cool. But I could pretend. Plus, my comparison group was law professors who had been teaching for 30 or 40 years—so I had to be cooler than them, right?

In any event, over the past couple of years I have come to realize that I am decidedly not cool and decidedly not young. Some people say I look young. Last year the photocopier repair guy asked me what exam I was studying for. Definite highlight of my day. But looking young and being young are two different things.

What clued me in to the fact that I was getting old? It didn't happen all at once. It was gradual. One morning really solidified it for me though. I was lying in bed and it was raining. My first thought was, *Awesome. The rain will be good for the grass. And we'll save money by not having to run the sprinkler.* That is definitely an old person thought.

Then I got to thinking about all the other little things that have crept into my life in recent years that bring me further and further from my youth. For those of you wondering whether you've crossed into "old person" land, at least in comparison to the typical law student, the following list might be helpful.

1. I buy multiple Fiber One products. They are delicious, low-calorie, and good for you.

2. I know the difference between a Hibiscus, a Hyacinth, and a Hydrangea. So does my husband.

3. I make weekly trips to Home Depot. And not only do I not mind going to Home Depot, I actually enjoy it.

4. I have no idea what words the "cool kids" are using and/or what they mean. I know "lit" was popular a few years ago. There's something I heard about "tea" recently. And "fire."[14] But it's too much effort to get up to speed.

5. I DVR the news every night. And two for one, I have a DVR.

6. I have been known to call and complain about my Verizon cable/phone/internet bill. *How can we get this lower? Are there any bundles or discounts?* My dad's favorite hobby is calling Rogers (the Canadian equivalent to Verizon)

---

14. *That's fire? That's *the* fire? She's on fire?* Who the f**k knows?

going to tell you how I think you should do things, and what things I've seen successful students do. But ultimately, the choice is yours. Do not outsource responsibility for how you approach law school to an academic support book. You do you.

Fifth, I want to provide you with proof that some of the things I'm saying really work. It's one thing for me to tell you that you should outline every day. It's another thing to hear this advice straight from the horse's mouth (the horse being a student who implemented this technique after *not* implementing it initially). You will find real emails, evaluations, and comments in here.

Sixth, I want to tell it like it is. I am a direct person. It's who I am. It's a good thing and a bad thing all in one. I don't like pussyfooting around something. I am not aiming to spare your feelings here. I am not aiming to inspire you. I will not praise you for getting into law school.[18] There are other books for that. I am aiming to be accurate, blunt, and realistic.

Seventh, I occasionally use mild or redacted profanity. You've probably guessed that based on the title of the book. That, in itself, probably makes this book different. On the one hand, it seems a little undignified, even to me. On the other hand, profanity has a history of being used effectively to underscore a point and is decidedly part of the human experience.[19] For those of you who are offended by the language, I'm sorry.[20] My mother-in-law is a sweet, old-fashioned woman who would never ever swear. The closest she has come to swearing is "Gee willikers!" and "Gosh donnit." I guess she's not getting a copy of this book for Christmas.

Eighth, I want this book to be somewhat fun to read. I often insert small digressions, examples, stories, and footnotes[21] to make it more interesting. You may think this is to up the popularity of the book. And it is. But there's also a pedagogical[22] reason. Students are more likely to remember things if

---

18. Congrats. You and thousands of other students.

19. https://www.nytimes.com/2021/05/04/books/review/nine-nasty-words-john-mcwhorter.html.

20. Actually, I'm sorry/not sorry. If you can't handle some redacted swear words, you might want to reconsider your chosen profession.

21. I may have gone overboard with the footnotes. Just ignore them if you don't want to read them. Just like you'll ignore the footnotes in the cases you read.

22. Fancy word alert.

they are "sticky."[23] When I teach, I try to make doctrinal material sticky. In this book, I have tried to do the same thing.

I think it's also fair to tell you what this book is *not*. This book is not a play by play on every aspect of law school. It does not start with "The Common Law System" and then move to "How to Read a Case," "How to Case Brief," and "How to use IRAC." There are other books for that. Instead, I focus more on what the other books don't tell you about law school that you might be curious about. Every chapter is freestanding, and you can jump around the book as you choose. With that said, a portion of the book does focus on the study techniques I think work best. My advice about notetaking, outlining, and studying is not universally shared, so this book will likely deviate in many ways from the common wisdom.

I sincerely hope that some of what I say in this book is helpful to you. If it's not, such is life. At least the book only cost, what, three Starbucks Mocha Frappuccinos?[24]

---

23. That's an actual term in the science of learning. I can't take credit for it.

24. I constantly equate monetary value to food. My food of choice is Big Macs. For example, if I see a sweater I like that costs $30, I ask myself, "Do I like it more than six Big Macs?" I realize that it's not an either/or, but it's nonetheless a helpful reference point.

Sh*t No One Tells You About Law School

ONE

Before Law School

Be brave enough to be bad at something new.

JOHN ACUFF

Before we get started, you may have noticed that each chapter of this book starts with an inspirational quote. I have to say that I'm not an inspirational quote person. I will never, ever, be one of those people whose email signature line reads "Character is what you do when no one is watching."[1] But I know that inspirational quotes are sort of a *thing* nowadays. I think you guys call them affirmations. So, I've decided to pander on this, and only this. The quotes have been carefully curated for maximum affirmation impact and so that you "feel seen."[2]

1. Have Fun

Let's cut to the chase—law school will be hard. It will be demanding of your time, it will have little regard for your personal life, and it certainly will not care that your college friends are in town and want to go bar-hopping the night

---

1. I find those quotes so cheesy, but that's just me. You do you. On the character quote specifically, I am left wondering: Do you really need to telegraph to the world that you have "character"? After all, you've just said that character is what you do *when no one is watching.* Just a little ironic, I think.

2. In case it was too subtle, this was intended to throw shade at your generation. Sorry, but I gotta have some fun writing this book. It's not like I'm writing it for the money.

before your first LRW[3] memo is due. The time before law school should be spent wisely. And by wisely, I mean having fun. Okay, let me walk that back a bit. You should have fun *and* do some other stuff to get ready for law school. You should get your life in order, financially and logistically, and you should maybe do a bit of preliminary reading. But other than that, have fun. You won't regret it.

The summer before law school, I went to Italy to visit my grandparents and my very large extended family. I hung out at the beach during the day, ate pizza Margherita at every opportunity, and went to "la discoteca" at 11:00 at night. By the way, 11:00 p.m. is considered *early* by Italian standards. I did not worry about the impending doom of law school; I just sort of tuned it out. I think it was my form of denial.

In any event, I might have taken it too far. I ended up extending my Italian vacation by a week, so I missed orientation. Back in "those" days, orientation wasn't really a big deal. It was more of an opportunity to meet other students and get your bearings. I showed up the first day of law school with a killer tan[4] and not knowing anyone. Everyone else already seemed to have a friend group. I later learned that there was a rumor going around that I arrived late because I had been "waitlisted." *The shame.* When I kicked a** in law school, I quickly put those rumors to rest.

In retrospect, I regretted not going to orientation. Not because of the waitlist rumor, but because it would have allowed me to make friends (maybe)[5] and get the lay of the land a bit better. With that said, I had an amazing time on my *last hurrah* vacation, so I can't say that I regretted my decision too much.

Okay, I know, this book is not about me. It's about you. Fair enough. Bottom line: Do all the carefree things you usually take for granted. Hang out with your friends and family. Enjoy a vacation or staycation. Sleep. Binge Netflix. Consider the summer before law school "you" time and make the most of it.

---

3. LRW stands for Legal Research and Writing, a required first-year class at every school (though it may be called something different at your school).

4. That was before the days of SPF. Now I slather on SPF 60 like it's my full-time job.

5. I'm not really one to have a lot of friends. I guess you could say that I'm not a "people person." Surprise, surprise.

2. Get Your Sh*t Together

I know I just said that you should spend your summer having fun. And that's true. But you should also spend part of your summer getting your sh*t together.

Figure out where you are going to live. Fill out all the paperwork you need to fill out. Buy your books. Invest in a new computer if yours is crap. Figure out where things are (the bookstore, the gym, your classrooms). Go to the doctor and get your yearly physical. Ditto for the dentist for your bi-yearly cleaning. Buy school supplies. The more of this sort of stuff that you do ahead of time, the better. You do not want to be spending three hours at the DMV updating your car's registration when you should be reading for class.

More than that, being proactive about getting your life in order will put you in a good frame of mind for when you enter law school. You will feel like you've controlled the things you can control. There is nothing worse than entering a new endeavor and feeling discombobulated from the outset.

3. Be Prepared for an Onslaught of Information

You will get bombarded with a whole bunch of information the first few weeks of law school. Actually, it will probably start a few weeks before you officially begin. You'll get a trickle of emails that will quickly become a flood. You will get emails about events, about forms you need to fill out, about your classes, about tuition payments, about technology, about your login information for Westlaw and Lexis, about everything under the sun. It will be hard to keep up. But try anyway.

You may want to develop a system to keep track of this information. Simply relying on memory is not a good plan. Perhaps you have a file folder. That's what we used in the prehistoric days before electronic files were invented. Perhaps you have a notebook with different tabs. Perhaps you have some sort of electronic filing system. I really couldn't care less how you do it. Just keep track of it.

If you don't, you will start dropping the ball in all sorts of ways. *I didn't know we were supposed to do computer training. I assumed that the professor would remind us of the deadline. I wasn't tracking the mentor-mentee lunch.* You don't want to start law school feeling like you already suck at keeping track of things.

4. Get in the Zone

I'm sure you've heard the saying, or some version of it, "The race is not for the swift, but for those who endure to the end." Think of your law school journey in the same context. Oh, it's a race alright, but not the type of race you expect it to be. It's more of a marathon than it is a sprint, and oddly enough, you only start training for it once it begins.

Envision an athlete preparing for a marathon. She will do months of strength and endurance training, and she will most likely change her diet, train with a coach, and make improvements in her time and efficiency, so that she is in top form by the time race day approaches. Now, envision yourself as the athlete. Only this time, you're training for the race at the same time you're running it. You will have to alter your study habits or learn new ones, you will have to improve your strength and endurance, and your coaches—your law professors—will give you guidance on how to get in top-tier shape. The tricky part is you're figuring out each step as you go. Take comfort in the fact that everyone else is running the same law school race, and they too are training as they go.

What's unique about your race is that it is three years long and results are based almost exclusively on a few game days (your final exams). I'm mixing and matching sports references, aren't I? As you can probably guess, I'm not exactly sporty. I tried out for track in high school once and, well, it didn't work out. I thought eating a tuna fish sandwich at lunch that day would give me needed protein. It didn't. I also tried out for the rowing team at Cambridge. I figured, *Rowing? It doesn't seem that hard…you just row. Is rowing even a sport? It seems more of, like, an activity.* Trust me, it's hard. And it *is* a sport.[6] Sorry…where was I? Okay, your race is three years long and your performance is gauged at fixed mileposts. Dammit, did I just introduce a different sport?

The point I was trying to make is that you need to be savvy and strategic about how to succeed. You need to seriously tap into your inner Tom Brady.[7] You need to make good choices, always stay on top of things, learn from your mistakes, and show up. As TB has said, "If you don't play to win don't play at all." F**kin' eh.

---

6. I probably dodged a bullet there anyway because rowing practices were at 5:00 in the morning. That wouldn't have worked with my sleep schedule.

7. Nobody should be allowed to be *that* athletic and *that* good looking.

TWO

Law School Is a Mindf**k

If you realized how powerful your thoughts are,
you would never think a negative thought.

PEACE PILGRIM

1. Be Forewarned

In this chapter, I chronicle the ways that law school will mess with your head. And it will. Of course, there are exceptions to every rule. There will be a cohort of you reading this book who are entirely well-adjusted, low-stress, level-headed, and reasonable people. You will be in the minority, but you will exist. My husband, David, is like that, so I know. For the Davids out there, law school won't be that much of a mindf**k. But, for most of you, it will.

Being aware ahead of time that law school will mess with your head, and the ways it will do so, is helpful. If you are prepared for something and know it is coming, it is not as daunting when it happens. Forewarned is forearmed. My husband is retired military, so I've now taken to using military words and expressions such as "cover your six," "recon," and "intel."

My goal here is not to tell you "Don't feel that way" or "It's not so bad." Both would be bad advice. You *should* feel that way. And it *is* pretty bad. But the mind-f**kiness is part of the law school experience for everyone. Feel what you need to feel, but do not get mired in that feeling to the point where it affects your performance and your sense self-worth.

I'm going to discuss various aspects of the law school experience that tend to be particularly taxing, both emotionally and mentally. Where possible, I also suggest ways to deal with what you are experiencing. I have tried to present things in the order that they will appear to you in law school. I have started with things like how to cope with conflicting advice, and how to manage the avalanche of new terms being thrown your way. I then progress to things like the Socratic Method, the class gunner, and the 100% final exam. The end of the chapter is a little different. It focuses broadly on more emotional reactions to law school, such as Imposter Syndrome and feeling like you are treading water all the time.

2. You Will Get Conflicting Advice

There is an expression that I'm sure you've heard: "Opinions are like [you know]."[1] My opinion is just that—my opinion. There's nothing special about it. It is not "right." It is not better than anyone else's. Do not take anybody's opinion, including and especially mine, as gospel.

You will get a lot of advice in law school. And it *will be* conflicting. You will get advice from professors, administrators, other law students, practicing lawyers, family, and friends. You will hear things about "this course" or "that course" and "this professor" or "that professor." Please take all of this with a grain of salt. Try to figure things out for yourself. Don't assume other people know any better than you do, and don't do things just because other people tell you to do them. Spend the first few weeks of law school getting oriented and figuring out what *you* think.

You will feel pressure to do what other students are doing. This is normal. Try to resist doing something only because you see other students doing it. I remember my first weeks in law school. It felt overwhelming and daunting. A girl in my class, Kelly, had five different color highlighters. She would spend hours in the library making her textbook into a rainbow. Yellow for the facts, blue for the holding, green for the dissent. She seemed very confident that this was the way to approach reading a case. I began to doubt myself. *Was my "pencil" method inadequate? Should I try the rainbow approach?* I ultimately decided against Kelly's method, and it worked out just fine for me. But I had what we now call FOMO. I felt like I was missing out on the right way to do law school. Fortunately, I found my own path and didn't end up doing things "just because" other students were doing it. When you're in doubt about what

---

1. If you don't know the expression, then my response is: *Seriously?*

to do, pause and think about Kelly's rainbow highlighters...are you doing this because you think it's the right thing to do, or because Kelly is doing it?

One of the biggest sources of frustration is when *professors* give you conflicting advice. You would think that "the school" could get its act together and professors could get on the same page when it comes to advice. You would think. But law school is a strange place. Professors have opinions, and lots of them. Every professor is going to have a different take on what you should do and why you should do it. This is particularly stressful for students. Professors are considered authority figures, so when Professor Green says one thing and Professor Black says another, it's hard to know what to do.

Let me give you an example. Almost every professor I know tells students not to take verbatim notes. *You are not a legal transcriptionist! You should spend your time in class thinking, not writing down every word that comes out of the professor's mouth.* I tell my students the polar opposite. Write down everything you can.

You can see why students are confused. They just want to be told what to do, and they will do it. They can't do it when it's literally impossible to follow both pieces of advice. What do you do when you get conflicting advice?

First, consider the source. If the conflict is between, for instance, what academic support is saying and what your Civil Procedure professor is saying, you might want to consider going with the latter. Not because their advice is inherently better, but because they will be grading your assignments and exam. With that said, sometimes the advice that you get from academic support will be better than the advice you get from your doctrinal professors. *Seriously?* Yeah, I know. It's confusing. So, the source thing only gets you so far.

Second, and more important, evaluate the why. Try to get to the bottom of why the professor is saying what he is saying. It is easy for professors to stand at the front of the class and declare, all professorial-like, "You are not a stenographer!" I mean, it's true. And when they say it, they make it sound like taking lots of notes is a bad thing. Something you should be embarrassed about. *I don't want to be a...stenographer.* But these professors rarely go further than that. They don't explain how taking very few notes in class is going to help you on the exam you are taking in four months. Beware of grand proclamations. Instead, give more weight to the professors who seem to have thought about the advice they are giving you and explain why they are giving it to you.

Even still, you need to independently evaluate the "why." Just because a professor explains why she thinks it is a good idea to do such and such doesn't make it a good idea for you to do such and such. I know a professor, for example, who believes that students perform better on exams if they handwrite their class notes. There is some empirical evidence to support this. Many students have glommed on to this advice because it comes from a professor who has been teaching law for 30 years, and the professor has provided evidence to back it up. On its face, it seems totally reasonable to follow this advice. I would nonetheless encourage you to independently assess the advice in light of your own knowledge and circumstances, and not to blindly follow advice because it is what your professor said.

On the notetaking issue, for example, there are tradeoffs to consider. First, you will not be able to get down as much information if you take notes by hand, which means you might miss capturing some material. Second, you will have to re-type your handwritten notes into an outline, which is going to eat up some time. You need to evaluate whether the benefits associated with taking notes by hand outweigh the potential burdens. There is no definitive answer here. *You* must make the judgment call. Do not farm out the decision to your professor. Or, worse yet, to other students who don't know any better than you do.

3. The Vocabulary Is Daunting

As a 1L, you are going to be inundated with a new law school vocabulary: *prima facie, stare decisis,* OCIs, biz org, shepardize, Black's, the Restatement, moot court, etc. You will be overwhelmed because you won't know what half this stuff means. Rest assured that it is completely normal to feel overwhelmed by this new vocabulary as you start law school. It's a bit like learning a foreign language.

You will get freaked out when one of your classmates uses a word you don't know. It might make you feel nervous and insecure, like somehow you missed something. Or it might just make you feel plain stupid. Either way, remember that your classmate probably learned the word the day before. I promise, you will figure out what this stuff means. In the meantime, don't panic. Law school is like a special club where no one tells you the rules and everyone pretends like they belong.

One particularly stressful aspect of the law school vocabulary challenge is figuring out what your professors are saying. Your professors will sound, well, like professors. They will use words you don't know. And they will phrase things in a complicated way that you don't understand. They are not doing this on purpose. They just don't remember what it's like to be a law student. They don't remember that a 1L who has been in school for, like, two weeks doesn't know what the "dispositive" issue means, or what "the correct doctrinal approach" refers to.

As professors, we have developed law-speak over the years. For us, it seems totally natural to talk this way. This means that law students must do a sort of simultaneous translation in their head. When the law professor says, "The court erred in its application of the statute of frauds," the student must translate this into: "The court applied the statute of frauds wrong."

Professors often *speak* the way that they would *write* a law review article. They don't speak like normal people. You're lucky if you get a "normal person" professor. In time, you will get better at understanding exactly what your professor is saying. Until that happens, though, try not to worry too much about it: it's them, not you. Okay, it's a little bit you. But it's also a little bit them.

4. The Gunner Will Both Annoy You and Make You Feel Insecure

I was not familiar with the term "gunner" until I started teaching in the United States. In Canada, we call them "keeners." Same difference. There is usually at least one in every law school class. They are the students who sit in the front row,[2] put their hand up all the time, ask crazy and far-fetched questions, and stay and talk to the professor after class, every class. You know exactly who I'm talking about. There are two types of gunners: the smart gunner and the not-so-smart gunner. The latter will just annoy you. The former will annoy you too. But he or she will also make you feel insecure.

The gunner, let's call her Maggie, will have read every footnote in the case and will ask the professor about them. You, by contrast, did not even notice that there were footnotes in the case. Maggie will also have dreamt up hypothetical variations of the facts. You could barely wrap your mind around what happened in the case. You were not able to proceed to the let-me-make-up-hypothetical-variations stage. Maggie will know the answer to every question the professor asks. You, on the other hand, don't even understand the question, much less know the answer. Maggie will occasionally argue with the professor

---

2. I sat in the front row in every class. But I had none of the other characteristics I describe, so I don't meet the definition of gunner.

or try to sharp-shoot him. You would rather die than attempt to do that. I think you get the picture. You will encounter your fair share of Maggies in law school. How do you deal with the overwhelming sense of anxiety that Maggie provokes in you?

First, realize that no matter what it seems like in class, Maggie is probably not as smart as you think she is. And not as smart as she thinks she is. Maggie may get an A in the class. But she may not. I have seen plenty of Maggies struggle when the rubber hits the road.

Second, Maggie's apparent stand-out performance in class is meaningless. Your grade will come down to how well you perform on your exam. Whether you put up your hand every time the professor asks a question and whether you have brilliant and insightful commentary on the case is not going to matter to your final grade.

Third, on some level, you should feel sorry for Maggie. Being a good lawyer requires emotional intelligence. Maggie clearly doesn't have this in abundance. Otherwise, she would realize that she is monopolizing the class conversation and acting as though this were a private tutorial between her and the professor. These things matter in the long run.

My ultimate advice, as always, is to *do you*. Don't worry about Maggie. Don't be intimidated by her, although I know it will be hard. I do, however, give you full permission to be annoyed by her.

5. The Socratic Method Is a B*tch (And How to Cope)

Wikipedia, the bastion of scholarly insight, defines the Socratic Method as "a form of cooperative argumentative dialogue between individuals, based on asking and answering questions to stimulate critical thinking and to draw out ideas and underlying presuppositions."[3] Okay, that's super helpful. English, please. The Socratic Method, in its pure form, is supposed to be a dialogue between the professor and the student aimed at pushing students' reasoning and critical thinking skills. Today, I would say that the Socratic Method has morphed with "cold calling," and the two terms tend to be used interchangeably, though they are different.

The Socratic Method/cold calling is the predominant method of instruction in American law schools. But it doesn't have to be. There is nothing inherently

---

3. https://en.wikipedia.org/wiki/Socratic_method.

better in the Socratic Method than other forms of instruction, such as lecture. I went to law school in countries that do not use the Socratic Method, and I turned out just fine (I think). So why has the Socratic Method endured? Why are professors so resistant to change? And, the biggest question, is the Socratic Method really the best way of teaching and learning the law?

Let's start with why the Socratic Method endures. My personal guess is because of tradition. Your professors were schooled using the Socratic Method and don't know any different. They may not be able to imagine a universe where the mode of instruction is something other than the Socratic Method. They may also believe, rightly or wrongly, that the Socratic Method is the best way to teach students and that it hones skills that the lecture method simply cannot.

There is probably another reason professors employ the Socratic Method: because lecturing is boring. I don't want to stand in front of the classroom for over an hour just talking at a bunch of silent students typing frantically. I want to have a dialogue, even if it makes you uncomfortable—because it's all about *me*. The Socratic Method is preferable from the professor's perspective because it is more interesting and engaging. It enables us to gauge more readily what students know and don't know. It's also satisfying for us to see a student do a really good job or bring up points we didn't expect them to bring up. The Socratic method is *dynamic*.

That still doesn't mean it's the best way of teaching or learning law. As someone who did her initial law degree in Canada, the Socratic Method strikes me as a highly inefficient way to learn. I could spend 15 minutes with you just to get at one point, or I could just tell you what the point is and ask if you have any questions. The Socratic Method is a bit of a time suck. Not only that, but from a student's perspective, it's as scary as hell.

I am not against the Socratic Method. I use some form of cold calling in my classes, but I also do my fair share of lecturing and explaining. I also think that some of the stated rationales in favor of the Socratic Method are less than compelling.

One of the biggest things students are told is that the Socratic Method helps your public speaking skills. The exact expression your professors will use is this: "The Socratic Method helps you think on your feet." Let's deconstruct. To some extent, this rests on a conception that being a lawyer involves extensive public speaking. Not every law job requires amazing public speaking skills. Some law jobs involve you sitting in a cubicle doing tax work. That's not to say that law students shouldn't aim to improve their public speaking skills—because you will have to speak *at some point*. But you're not all looking to be Perry Mason, Alicia Florrick, or Harvey Specter. (I've tried to spread out my generational references to appeal to different audiences.)

More importantly, does the Socratic Method really help you "think on your feet"? I don't think so. It largely involves recalling minute details of a case, or maybe not-so-minute details, in front of a large audience that is watching your every move. It requires thinking through a topic that you just read about for the first time the day before. And now you're expected to have insightful critiques of it. How can you have well-developed thoughts on the "American Rule" when you just heard about it for the first time yesterday?

It is true that law practice will require you at times to think on your feet (e.g., in court, in a meeting with a partner, etc.). But the difference there is that you are likely an expert in what is being discussed. If you're in court, it is your case. You wrote the briefs, you know the facts, you know the law, you've spent dozens of hours thinking about the case. You are ready to think on your feet. That is a far cry from being quizzed on the fine points of *Hadley v. Baxendale*.

Also, some students need time to process and think through things. They can't simply do it on the fly. This is not a character flaw. This is a characteristic. I personally fall into the category of people who often needs time to process. I was the student who left class feeling confused and who needed time to sit with material and really think about it. Slowly. And at my own pace. I would have been *terrible* at the Socratic Method.

I do think the Socratic Method can cause more harm than good. I have been noticing this more and more in my classes. Students are so concerned with not embarrassing themselves and "looking stupid" if called upon that they over-prepare for class and under-prepare after class. And they often sit in class terrified that they will be called on next, which means that a lot of what is being said is like *wah wah wah*.[4] In other words, I see that fear of the Socratic Method is causing students not to learn. This is problematic. A tool that was intended to promote learning may be hampering learning. Unfortunately, it is not likely that law school professors will abandon the Socratic Method/cold calling anytime soon. You have to accept that it is just a part of law school.

With that said, remember these things:

---

4. Charlie Brown reference.

First, a cold call does not telegraph how well you will ultimately do "on your feet" in the real world. It is not even close to the context in which you will be required to speak in the real world. So, when your professor invariably tells you that this is what cold calling will help you do, smile and nod politely. But make a mental note that this is not true.

Second, over-preparing for fear of cold calls ultimately works to your detriment. Focus on preparing for the exam, not for cold calls. Try not to sit there in fear of being called on. If you're called on, deal with it then.

Third, taking time to process things is completely normal. If it feels like other people are amazing in class and see things that you never would have seen, just remember that you will get there too—maybe just a little slower. But who cares? All that matters is that you know the material for the exam, not that you know it when asked to recite it at the drop of a hat in class.

Trigger warning.[5] Every law student will have at least one cold call which sticks out in their mind as The. Most. Horrible. Experience. Ever. You're lucky if it is limited to just one. It is inevitable that you will have a disastrous cold call, or one that feels disastrous to you. What do you do after you have completely bombed a cold call?

Well, for starters, you might want to hit the bar with your friends that night and commiserate about it over a beer or two. Please drink responsibly. In short order, this will be a story you tell to make people laugh, and not one that makes you want to cry by yourself in a corner. But, in the immediate aftermath, it's going to feel raw.

Screwing up a cold call is not as big of a deal as you think it is. It's kind of like having a pimple that you think everyone is staring at, but really, no one notices but you. It is unlikely that the disastrous cold call registered with the professor—unless it was out-of-this-world disastrous. When I say out-of-this-world disastrous, I mean something like this (true story):

Professor:	Can you tell me what happened in *X v. Y* case?
Student:	Sorry, can you repeat that? I was sleeping.
Professor:	Excuse me?
Student:	I said I didn't hear the question. I was sleeping.

---

5. I'm told that your generation requires these. Okay, that was a little harsh. In all seriousness, though, research shows that trigger warnings are actually harmful. *See* https://www.newyorker.com/news/our-columnists/what-if-trigger-warnings-dont-work.

There's no recovering from that cold call. As you might guess, that student didn't make it past his 1L year.

But if it is just a run-of-the-mill "um," "well," "can you repeat that?" and "I'm not sure" cold call, then chances are, your professor will not commit it to memory. At least three or four times a semester, a student approaches me after class or sends me an email apologizing for doing "such a terrible job" in class. On every occasion, I am hard-pressed to remember what I asked and what they said. Frankly, I'm focused on me and making sure *I* did a good job. I'm not focused on your personal performance in class. I am not saying this to make you feel better; I'm saying it because it is true. Your professor will not remember that you flubbed a cold call. Seriously.

Also, fellow students probably won't remember your bad cold call, though they will be more attuned to it than a professor is. But whatever anyone thinks about your performance in class doesn't really matter. You could completely mess up every single time you're called on in class and still get the CALI award[6] in the class. Nailing a cold call is sort of meaningless. It's like getting the highest score on the bar exam—who cares?

Finally, and I know this is hard, practice some self-compassion. This is new age-y stuff that I usually think is bullsh*t, but in this case, it is true. We are our own worst critics. Let yourself off the hook for a bad cold call. Move on. Don't ruminate. Don't play it over and over in your mind. Don't apologize to the professor for it. Don't make it into a bigger deal than it is. Don't define your self-worth by a cold call that means nothing.

6. The Curve Is Hard to Wrap Your Mind Around

All law students know that courses are graded on "a curve." But many don't understand exactly what this means, or why law schools have taken this approach to grading. In high school and college, your grades were based on your own individual performance. For instance, if you got 100% on a test, that would equate with an A (or an A+ if your school gives A+'s). If you got a 60%,

---

6. This stands for the Center for Computer-Assisted Learning Instruction. The "CALI Award" is given "to the highest scoring student in each law school class at many law schools." https://www.cali.org/content/cali-excellence-future-awards. There's no money that goes along with this, only bragging rights. At my law school in Canada, the highest grade in the class got the course "prize" which *was* a monetary award, sponsored by a law firm. *Cha-ching!*

this would translate into something like a C (every school is different, so this might be lower than a C). The point is that you were judged on your own merits and not in comparison to anyone else in your class. Consequently, if everyone in the class got between 90–100%, then everyone would get an A. If everyone got in the 60% range, then everyone would get a C.

Law school is different. It does not assess you in absolute terms, but rather in relative terms. How did you do in comparison to your classmates?

Let me describe this in a more concrete way. A professor will grade your exams using whatever metrics they choose. Usually, they will assign a raw score to your exam. Let's assume that the raw score is out of 100. The highest raw score is 70/100 (70%) and the lowest raw score is 20/100 (20%). The 70% will receive an A (usually) and the 20% will receive a low grade (maybe a D or an F). Everyone else will fall into line accordingly. Now where a professor draws the lines between an A, B+, B, etc. is usually up to them. Sometimes there are parameters that they are expected to follow (e.g., no more than x% of the class can receive an A or an F; the class mean needs to be a 3.0/4.0). But usually, there is a lot of discretion afforded to the professor.

Let's boil down what this all means. This means that a student who got a 70%, which normally wouldn't be a particularly good grade, could get an A and the CALI award in the class. It also means that a student who got a 48% could end up with a B. Yes, you could have a "failing" numerical grade and get a B! This is because the percentages are somewhat meaningless. They are just a way of ranking students (i.e., putting them in order of highest to lowest exam performance).

At this point, it looks like the curve is awesome! But let's also spell out the flip side. If everyone in the class does well, say in the 75-95% band, not everyone can get an A. In this context, a 95% would be an A and a 75% might be a C- or a D. *What the coconut?!* (That's an expression my four-year-old niece uses.) Again, you have to remember that the numbers don't mean much. If you got a 75% when everyone else in the class scored higher than you, then this puts you at the bottom of the curve. Given that professors must follow some grading parameters, they are literally not able to give you a B.

Why in the world would law schools grade like this? Several reasons. Unlike math, where there is a right and a wrong answer, there are many shades of gray in law. Law school is about how you can best analyze a given fact scenario or solve a problem. In this respect, some answers *are* better than others. Grades signal to the outside world where you ranked in a cohort of your peers. This is more valuable information than where you ranked in absolute terms according to the metrics imposed by one particular professor.

Curves are also designed to ensure consistency between sections and to rein in the discretion of an individual professor. You've all had an easy professor who gives out A's like they're candy. And you've all had a hard professor who thinks that no one *ever* deserves an A because there's "always room for improvement."[7]

Let's assume that Section A has Easy Professor and Section B has Hard Professor. This would mean that you would likely fare better with Easy than with Hard. This seems profoundly unfair. Whether you get an A shouldn't depend on which section you are assigned to. By having a curve, we temper the potential inconsistencies between sections. Easy can't give everyone A's. And Hard can't give everyone C's. The curve makes them give out lower grades (in the case of Easy) and higher grades (in the case of Hard).

I realize it is hard to wrap your mind around the scenario where you do well but don't get the grade that you believe is commensurate[8] with that performance. This sometimes happens. But in my experience (cue the sanctimonious music), the curve tends to work out in most students' favor. I don't often encounter a situation where I think to myself, "I feel like this is an A exam, but I have to give it a B because of the curve." Usually, students end up benefiting from the curve. Professors must give higher grades than they think a student "deserves" because the curve obligates them to do so.

What is my advice here? Don't worry about the curve. It's nothing you can control and not something you should concern yourself with. Just do your thing—work hard, study hard—and let the chips fall where they may.

7. You Will Feel Like You're Treading Water

From Day 1 of law school, you will feel like you've been thrown into the deep end of a swimming pool and are treading water. If you don't have a good plan for tackling law school, this treading water will soon start to feel like you're drowning.

At first, logistical and unfamiliar stuff will take up a lot of your time (e.g., getting your email up and running, figuring out who to contact for what,

---

7. You might already be able to guess which camp I would fall into.
8. Oooh, another law word!

buying your books, sorting out your schedule, fussing with the course management software, etc.). After the first few weeks, this will subside and now you will face a deluge of schoolwork. Initially, it's not so bad. There are readings for every class, but they are fairly short. There are no assignments yet. And professors are going over the material slowly and in depth. Eventually, this will change.

You will still have readings for every class, but the readings will get longer and harder. You will now have assignments for some of your classes. Certainly, you will have assignments in LRW. You may have quizzes and midterms for your doctrinal classes. And the substantive material will get more and more complicated as it starts to build on itself. And professors will expect that you have all that material in a repository in your brain. By October, you will be in treading-water mode.

The first thing to realize is that this is a completely normal feeling. Every law student will feel this way for pretty much the duration of law school. There are some weeks and months that are better than others.

Treading water is a manageable state of affairs but can quickly proceed to you being underwater if you don't get your ducks in a row. I know, there's *way* too many water references here. You need to be diligent about time management. You need to pre-plan how you are going to tackle law school and stick to the plan. Or, if the plan isn't working, you must recalibrate the plan. You can't let things slip. You can't wait until the last minute to complete assignments or to study.

Feeling like you're treading water is not fun. But it is normal. And I hate to break it to you, it's pretty much how you're going to feel when you get out there as a lawyer in the real world.

8. The Intimidation Factor Is Real

Law school is an intimidating place. From the second you walk into the law school building, you will feel intimidated. You will see photos of important people on the wall and think, "Do I really belong here?" You will see trophies and awards behind glass cases and think, "That'll never be me." You will see your school's courtroom and think, "Am I just kidding myself? What makes me think I can do this?"

You will encounter professors who use words you don't understand. They will have degrees from Harvard and Yale and Stanford. They will make obscure historical references and try to relate to you by quoting movies from the 1970s and 1980s. They will set the stage for who you think you should be—an ideal you feel like you can never achieve.

You will feel intimidated by your peers. I don't just mean Maggie, the gunner. I mean everyone. It will seem like they have their sh*t together, are getting straight A's, and already have summer jobs lined up. Don't even get me started on "dress up" days. Occasionally, there will be an event at the law school which requires students to dress up like lawyers. On those days, everyone will look so lawyerly. And you will feel like you're playing dress up.

You will also feel intimidated by "the law" and by the profession. You will have grown up watching lawyers on TV and hearing that being a lawyer (or a doctor, of course) is the job you should aspire to. Now that you're here, you are sure someone in admissions made a mistake letting you in. More on that in a second.

Law school is an intimidating place. Professors are intimidating. Other students are intimidating. The profession is intimidating. But just because these things are intimidating does not mean that you have to be *intimidated*. Deep, huh?

9. Almost Everyone Has Imposter Syndrome

If you don't know what it is, you don't have it. Move on. This section is not for you.

I had Impostor Syndrome when I was in law school. And, I'm not going to lie, to some extent, it never goes away. I did very well in undergrad and earned a full scholarship to law school. You would think that that would make me feel like I belonged in law school. Not so. Instead, it made me feel more pressure. I thought, "Well, undergrad was different. Sure, I did well there. But this is *law school*."

I had heard the urban legend of "Look to your left, look to your right. One of you three won't be here in a year." One of my first weeks in law school, all 280 1Ls (we called them "first years") were in the large appellate courtroom. We were doing some sort of legal writing lesson. I remember looking around the room and thinking just how many students were there and how smart they must be. I said a little prayer then and there: *Please, God, let me get B's. That's all I want. To do okay.*

I meant it. I had no high aspirations. I was not aiming to be at the top of the class or get a fancy law firm job. I just wanted to get by. In some ways, it's still shocking to me that I ended up graduating first in my class. It must also have been shocking to others in the class. I remember one kid saying, "I'm surprised you did so well. You never say anything in class."[9]

The whole time I was in law school, I suffered from Impostor Syndrome. Getting good grades did not really help. After my first year, I was ranked at the top of my class (#humblebrag), and I still did not feel like I belonged in law school. *It was probably a fluke. It won't happen again next year. It's not because I'm naturally smart, it's because I just worked harder than other people.* I never got to a point where I felt confident that I belonged in law school.

My Impostor Syndrome probably stemmed from two things: the high expectations that I always put on myself, and my status as a first-generation law student. The two are also certainly inter-related. As I told you already, my parents are immigrants from Italy with a very limited education. I was the first person in my entire extended family to go to university.[10] And the first to go to law school. I don't have any lawyers in the family. Tile setters, bricklayers, plumbers, carpenters, electricians: Yes. Lawyers: No. If you need "a concrete guy," my family has you covered.[11] If you need a will drawn up, not so much.

Being in law school, where it seemed like everyone else's parents were professionals, made me feel like this wasn't the place for me. Like I was an interloper. I mean, my classmate's mother was appointed to the Supreme Court of Canada. Yes, *the* Supreme Court. I think you can see how I might have felt out of my element.

I think the causes of Impostor Syndrome are manifold[12] and will be different for everyone. But I do think it strikes first-generation students, and students who are historically underrepresented in the legal profession, particularly hard. Maybe it's because these students feel like they are carrying the weight of the world on their shoulders. Maybe it's because many of these students don't have role models to emulate. Maybe it is because students from some of these backgrounds lack the resources, connections, and professional acumen

---

9. This was from the weird kid who sat in the front row, had his hand up all the time, and ate tuna fish from the can in class. *So gross.*

10. I mean ever. There was no one on either my mom's or dad's side of the family that had been to university.

11. We also have a butcher, a knife-sharpening guy, and a shoe-repair person. The Italians reading this will relate.

12. Law word alert!

that students from more privileged backgrounds seem to have. Whatever the reasons, the bottom line is that there are many students who feel like they don't belong in law school.

Now, I don't think it is helpful for me to say, "Just get over it." Or, "Of course you belong in law school." Not because it's not true, but because you won't believe it. I didn't. No amount of someone telling you something will make *you* believe it is true.

Some of the literature says that you should practice self-affirmations and question your assumptions. Maybe this will be helpful, but I doubt it because you're going to find a way to talk yourself back into feeling like an impostor. Let me give you an example:

Student (to herself): I feel like such an impostor. I don't belong here.

Student (to herself): I heard I'm supposed to question my beliefs. Okay, well I'm in law school because the admissions people think I'm good enough to be here. They're smart and I should trust their judgment of me.

Student (to herself): But what if I just barely got in? I'll never know. So, I'm here, but I might be at the bottom of the class.

Student (to herself): But I did well in undergrad. I have no reason to believe that won't be the case here.

Student (to herself): Everyone says that law school is different and what worked in undergrad won't work here. Any success I had before was before. This is now. Plus, that was just a fluke. I took really easy classes.

You get my point, right? It's hard to talk yourself out of your beliefs. I wish I had a magic pill for Impostor Syndrome. Wouldn't it be great to pop a Xanax and have it disappear? Unfortunately, there is nothing I can say that will make the bad feeling go away. Accept that this is *how you feel*, but that your feelings are just that: feelings. They are not reality and they do not need to determine your actions. This is some serious Jon Kabat-Zinn sh*t.

Here are five concrete things I would add:

First, a lot of students have Impostor Syndrome. A lot of high-achieving students have Impostor Syndrome (i.e., the students you would not expect to have Impostor Syndrome). And since misery loves company, know that you are in good company.

Second, Impostor Syndrome is not all bad. I think it's what made me work so hard and achieve what I have achieved. When you feel like you are not as good as everyone else, you work harder to catch up to them. And when you think your good grades were all just a fluke, you never let yourself slack off.

Third, like I said, you will not be able to convince yourself out of feeling like an impostor. Instead, focus less on how you *feel* and more on what you *have to do*. In other words, try not to be in your head too much.

Fourth, eventually, the Impostor Syndrome does subside. I don't know anyone that went through their entire life feeling like they were an impostor at everything they did.

Fifth, fake it till you make it. You've all heard this expression before. But it really works. If you act like you belong, eventually you will feel like you belong.

My dad is a big proponent of *if you act like you belong, no one will question you*. Except, it's in a totally different context. You see, pre-pandemic, one of my dad's favorite hobbies was going to Costco to load up on the free food samples.[13] Why does he do this? Because it combines his two favorite things: food and free. But the problem is that my dad does not have a Costco membership card. It's not a problem for him, though. Because he acts like he belongs. He whips out his wallet, flashes something at the 16-year-old kid manning the door, and walks in confidently. So next time you're feeling like you don't belong, break out your non-existent Costco card and walk in like you own the place.

10. Your First Grade in Law School Will Probably Freak You Out

Law schools are moving more and more to providing formative assessments. *What the what?* A formative assessment is a smaller assessment during the semester designed to get your feet wet and provide you with some feedback on your performance. You might have quizzes, assignments, a midterm, etc. where you receive feedback and a grade or score for the assessment. Leave it to lawyers to call a f**king quiz by some indecipherable term.

---

13. He is also a big fan of the Ikea lunch. He specifically goes to Ikea just to have lunch. *It's so affordable. And I like the little meatballs.*

You may get a good score and be pleased with your performance. If you are in this category, then my advice to you is not to get too cocky. Doing well on these smaller assessments does not necessarily mean that you will do well on the final exam, though it can be a signal that you will. And it doesn't mean that you can rest on your laurels. If you do well, be pleased, keep the news to yourself, and keep working. This advice is more for the students who don't do well, or as well as they wanted, on these smaller formative assessments.

I've seen a range of emotions over a bad score, and none of them are good or healthy. For instance, I have given small quizzes or assignments worth three raw points.[14] I've seen students who get a 1.5/3 have full-blown meltdowns over the score. Tears and hysterics. I've seen students get very angry at me over a bad score ("This is *your* fault. Obviously, if everyone did this bad, it's on the professor and not on the students.") I've seen students pull the "Do you know who I am?" card. These are the students who say, "I am an Honors student. I have never gotten a grade lower than an A in my life." I've seen the existential-crisis students: "I'm such a failure. Law school is not for me. I'll never pass the bar and get a job." I've seen students try to stage a full-on revolt. I've had students go to the Associate Dean to complain about getting a bad grade on a virtually meaningless assignment.

None of these are healthy reactions. Before I talk more about this, I want to say that I get it. I get how devastating it is to receive a bad grade, even if it counts for very little. I once got a B+ on an 11th grade Geography paper and sat at the top of my parents' staircase crying for hours. But I was 15 at the time.

As young adults,[15] law students need to be encouraged to develop a thicker skin. By this, I am not discounting the emotional turmoil and self-doubt that a bad grade engenders. But I am saying that you need a little bit of perspective. Zoom out. Are you really going to have a full-fledged meltdown because you wish you had scored 8/10 instead of 6/10? Do you really think that your grade on an LRW outline is something you're going to think about in five years?

Students are not used to being told that they are anything less than stellar. No one likes to hear that they "need improvement" or that they didn't perform well. Me included. But you are in law school *to learn*. You would be foolish to think that you're already at the point where your work product is amazing. Let

---

14. In other words, the assignment will be worth only 3% of the final grade. That's like basically what you get for putting your name on your exam.

15. You know you're old when you refer to students as "young adults."

me suggest the following concrete advice for you in dealing with a bad grade on a low-stakes assignment.

First, assess how "bad" the grade is. Did you get an average grade, and you just think it's bad in comparison to how well you performed in the past? Or is the grade objectively bad? It helps to have a sense of "how bad" this is on the spectrum of bad.

Second, be upset. But then get over it. You have a right to whatever emotions you're feeling. Be upset, cry, eat ice cream, vent to your parents, whatever. But then, move on. Don't carry the emotional baggage around with you.

Third, do not beat up on yourself. Students tend to beat up on themselves when they get a bad grade. They think, "I'm not lawyer material," or, "I'm never going to get this." The blame game is not helpful and will just keep you focused on the past rather than the future. Focus on what you *should do* with the grade or feedback you've received, rather than what you think the grade or feedback signals about you.

Fourth, do not blame your professor. I'm sure this is self-serving advice. But please don't blame your professor for your bad grade. Your grade is *on you*, not on them. Take personal responsibility for not doing as well as you wanted, and then figure out how to do better.

Fifth, do not compare yourself to others. Students talk and you will undoubtedly hear that Leo got a 10/10 and Aliyah got a 9.5/10. You are not Leo or Aliyah. You are you. Focus on the grade and feedback you were given and make something out of it, so that next time, you can be like Leo or Aliyah.

Sixth, get some perspective. Law school is a very insular universe, and it is sometimes hard to see outside its four walls. But you have to. You must get some perspective on how bad this grade/feedback is in comparison to real-world problems. You got a 6/10 on a quiz. So what? People have way bigger problems out there.

Finally, do something. The whole point of formative assessments is to give you feedback so that you can perform well on the final exam. Do not look at your score and comments, put your tail between your legs, and then sulk. Figure out why you got the score you did and how to fix it. Be proactive. Do not expect the professor to tell you how to do better. *You* need to figure out how to do better.

THREE

The Logistical Stuff

I'm not telling you it's going to be easy.
I'm telling you it's going to be worth it.

ART WILLIAMS

1. Get Organized

O rganization and time management are really important in law school. If you don't get a handle on your time, it is hard to be successful in law school. After you get your schedule for the semester, you should craft a tentative plan for what your days and weeks will look like. I recommend that you revisit this plan after the first week or two and keep the plan fluid. Do not be wedded to a schedule that looks good on paper but doesn't work for you.

In devising your schedule, consider the following:

1. It might make sense to put pen to paper so you can visually see what you need to do every day.
2. Not every day will look the same.
3. Try to end your work at a reasonable hour and carve out breaks and leisure time.
4. Make the most of dead time: the one or two hours between classes. If you use that time productively—instead of, say, getting a coffee with your friends or playing on your phone—it can ease your workload considerably.

5. Your time management plan needs to account for outlining after class.

6. Do not leave anything until the last minute. Violate this rule at your extreme peril.

7. Recognize that you will have to build in time for completing assignments and studying for quizzes and exams.

The worst thing you can do as a law student is to scramble to get through the day. This is a virtually guaranteed recipe for failure.

Let me give you an actual study schedule I worked out for my Research Assistant. She is taking Wills & Trusts, Constitutional Law, Remedies, Family Law, and Evidence. It's a tough schedule for sure. On Tuesdays and Thursdays, she is in class pretty much from 9:00am to 5:00pm. Here is the plan I worked out:

Monday:	Read Wills in the morning; 2:00 Wills class; after class, read Evidence and Remedies; do Wills outline.
Tuesday:	Class all day; after and in between class, work on outlines.
Wednesday:	Read Wills in the morning; 2:00 Wills class; after class, read Evidence and Remedies; do Wills outline.
Thursday:	Class all day; after and in between class, work on outlines.
Friday:	Work on outlines.
Saturday:	Work on outlines.
Sunday:	Read for Con Law and Family for entire week.

This schedule may not mean much to you. But I wanted to include it here to illustrate a couple of things:

➢ The schedule is different every day, though there is some consistency on M/W and T/Th.

➢ The schedule has different reading approaches to different classes. On Sunday, my Research Assistant will read for Constitutional Law and Family Law for the whole week ahead. For Evidence, Wills & Trusts, and Remedies, there is a different plan. She will read for Wills & Trusts in the dead time before class, so the material is fresh in her mind. And Evidence and Remedies are pretty intense, with minute details, so she will read both of those the day before class.

➢ The schedule includes a lot of time for outlining. Two entire days, plus time on other days.

➢ Outlining days can be used for assignments and other things that come up.

There is no magic to scheduling. Just be organized, deliberate and try your best to stick to the plan. If it doesn't work for you, adjust the plan as you go along.

I recently heard of a "trend" called Time Blocking.[1] It's writing down what you are going to do for blocks of time during your entire day:

9:00-10:30	Read for Contracts
10:30-11:45	Go to Torts
11:45-12:15	Lunch

And so on...

I'm not sure how or why this is a "trend." I just call this *scheduling*. But if it helps you to think that Time Blocking is a cool thing that all the kids are doing on TikTok, great. For the rest of us adults, this goes in the least-novel-trend-ever category.

2. Study Aids Are Probably a Waste of Money

1L students ask me all the time whether they should buy a study aid for Contracts. Some of you might be thinking, "Wait, I don't even know what that is." A study aid is a book, aside from the textbook, that essentially gives you the black letter law in a fairly straightforward manner. There are a lot of different study aids out there for every subject imaginable. For instance, there's Nutshells, a Short and Happy Guide, the Understanding books, Emanuel's, etc. There are probably more than a dozen study aids available for each subject.

---

1. My husband tells me he was required to do this at his first duty assignment. Then he would hand in his Time Blocks for the entire week, along with a notation of whether he completed the task. I sometimes wish law schools were run more like the military. I guess in some ways they are—like overspending on stupid sh*t and having so many layers of administrative red tape.

Students are inclined to think that a study aid is the magic key to doing well in law school. After all, if someone is giving you the law on a silver platter, *why not* buy it? Makes sense. But I'm here to break it to you: Study aids do not contain the magic keys to the kingdom and can end up confusing you more than if you didn't look at one to begin with.

You will probably find that a number of professors caution against using study aids. Some do this for bad reasons (i.e., they believe that they are the best teacher ever and why in the world would you need a study aid). Some do this for good reasons (i.e., they believe you're going to end up chasing your tail if you go down the study aid rabbit hole). I'd like to think I'm in the latter camp. But, if I am honest, I'm also a little bit in the former camp. Let me explain why purchasing study aids might not be the best plan.

First, as I mentioned, there are many study aids per subject. In your 1L year, you are probably taking Criminal Law, Torts, Contracts, Property, and Civil Procedure. If you have, say, ten study aids out there per subject, that means you have 50 options to cover your bases. That is a lot to choose from. Some are better than others. What are you going to do? Buy 50 different study aids? In other words, even if you buy study aids, it's a shot in the dark whether they will be effective for you.

Second, a study aid will necessarily be written by someone who is: (1) not the professor; and (2) not the author of your textbook. Is it really that helpful to have a third party thrown into the mix? What I mean is that the study aid author will teach the material in a different way than your professor and your textbook. It may be hard for you as a 1L student to bridge the gap between what the professor or textbook is saying and what the study aid is saying.

Third, study aids *will* contain information you didn't cover in class. Sometimes you may not recognize that you did not cover the material and therefore work to learn information you're not responsible for. This may end up causing problems. Anytime a student writes something on an exam that we did not cover in class or that was not in the book, I am immediately suspicious. It alerts me to the fact that they are doing their Contracts learning on the side and that I should scrutinize the answer carefully.

Fourth, study aids are sometimes wrong. I know that it is hard to believe that something in *a book* written by a law professor is wrong. But it is true. I found one pretty egregious error last year in a study aid for Contracts. When I first noticed it, my immediate reaction was, *Wait, have I been teaching this wrong for the better part of a decade?* Panic set in. I went to a more authoritative source—a Contracts expert from a top-ten school. That source confirmed that the way I had been teaching it was correct and that the study aid was wrong. *Phew. Crisis averted.* I don't know how widespread it is to have incorrect information in study aids, but I can say for sure that it happens.

With all that said, I am not anti-study aid. Study aids can be useful if used the right way. They are a good way to make sure that you understand the material at a holistic level, or to track down one particular aspect of the doctrine or material that eludes you. But study aids should *supplement* your in-person learning, not *supplant* it. As long as you understand the difference, study aid away.

One final thing. Given how many study aids there are and that you don't know which ones will work for you, I do not think you should purchase them. Your library will, or should, carry the main ones. Whenever you need to consult a study aid, just check one out, look up what you need to look up, and then return it to the library. Old school.

3. Don't Spend Forever Reading for Class

Law school involves a lot of reading. So much reading, in fact, that you'll probably need to up the prescription strength of your eyeglasses. I deliberately say glasses because your eyes will dry out too much reading regularly with contacts.

Especially in your 1L year, a lot of this reading will go over your head. This will induce panic in many of you. Maybe even mini-existential crises.[2] *How can I be a lawyer if I don't even understand cases?*

Law professors will say, "Read the case two or three times. Or until you understand it. Look up every word you don't know in Black's Law Dictionary." *Two or three times? Look up every word in Black's? How in God's name will I be able to get this reading done, much less the reading for my other classes? And when am I going to find the time to outline?* While the advice you're given by these professors is well-intentioned, it is not realistic. There is not enough time in the day to read cases multiple times. As Trevor Noah would say, "Ain't nobody got time for that."

I think you should read each case once—but read the case slowly and carefully. Look up words that seem to be important and that you can't figure

---

2. Yes, there are a lot of these in law school.

out from the context. Take marginal notes and/or maybe do a very mini-case brief. Do not be anywhere near a phone, television, or the internet.[3] You need to really read, not just pretend read. If your brain is half doing something else, like checking the football scores or thinking about the photo you want to upload to Instagram, you are pretend reading.

There is something else I'm going to tell you that other professors won't. As a 1L, and even as a 2L and 3L, you will not understand everything in a case. You'd be lucky to understand 60% of the case. Don't try to kill yourself getting from a 60% understanding to a 63% understanding to a 65% understanding. There's this thing called the law of diminishing returns. Look it up if you don't know it.

Additionally, don't forget that much of the case will be *irrelevant* for teaching purposes. The case is in your textbook to illustrate one or two principles of law. If the case is under the "Misrepresentation" chapter of your Contracts textbook, focus your attention on the aspects of the case that deal with that. If there is a paragraph on how undue influence or duress plays out in the case, that is probably not important. In short, always remember why you are reading the case.

Instead of wasting time reading and re-reading and re-re-reading, your time is much better spent outlining after class, once you've heard what the professor had to say about the case and once you've had a fulsome discussion in class. More on that coming up. I know this advice going to feel foreign to you, especially when almost all professors emphasize reading over and over again. But I think it is far more helpful to re-engage with the case after you've talked about it in class. Shift the time that you *would have* spent on the second and third reads to outlining after class. The time spent that way will pay off in a way that multiple read-throughs will not.

4. Case Briefs Are Overhyped

I'm going to give you some advice that other professors will consider sacrilegious: *Do not brief cases before class.* Cue the angry emails from my colleagues.[4] I beg of you, don't. Even though every professor will tell you to. You should

---

3. The internet is not really a thing you can be near. But I couldn't write, "Don't be near a computer" since you'll probably be working on your computer. So what I'm saying here is find a way to block the internet if you don't think you can resist the urge to meander onto it.

4. Law professors are such a weird bunch. I absolutely guarantee I will get multiple emails from professors on the history and benefits of case briefing. Can you say "delete"?

certainly take some notes on the cases, underline or highlight important stuff in the textbook, write down the legal rule, etc. But I do not think you should be doing a full case brief before class. Why?

First, it will be wrong, or largely wrong. No 1L law student will get the correct take-away from a case entirely on his or her own.

Second, because of the time you invested in your case brief, you will feel committed to it, even though it is wrong and/or doesn't contain the full analysis that the professor wanted you to get out of the case. This is referred to as the sunk cost fallacy.[5] This means that you will insert your inaccurate or incomplete case brief verbatim into your outline, rather than feel like you wasted all that time.

Third, and most important, law school exams don't reward case briefing. You are not *ever* going to be asked to case brief on an exam. You will be asked to apply black-letter law to a given fact pattern. A traditional case brief does not even remotely help with that exercise.

It is much better to take some basic notes on a case, go to class, take copious notes on the class discussion, and *then* create a case brief. The case brief should focus on what the professor considered important. There is no need to go through the Facts, Procedural Posture, Holding, Reasoning, Dissent, etc. if the professor didn't go through all this.

At least in courses like Contracts and Torts, I suggest that you use the case briefs as a mini-fact pattern. There is nothing super-special about the cases. They simply illustrate a principle of law and its application. They are just a handful out of hundreds or thousands of cases that the authors of the case book could have chosen to make the same point.

For example, let's say that you're looking at a case dealing with the doctrine of promissory estoppel. In my view, you should capture the basic facts, and then how each of the elements plays out:

1. Was there a promise intended to be relied on?

2. Was the promise detrimentally relied on?

3. Was the reliance reasonable?

4. Would it be an injustice not to enforce the promise?

---

5. *See* https://www.behavioraleconomics.com/resources/mini-encyclopedia-of-be/sunk-cost-fallacy/ ("Individuals commit the sunk cost fallacy when they continue a behavior or endeavor as a result of previously invested resources (time, money or effort).").

This is much more valuable than randomly cutting and pasting passages from the judgment.

Some of you will be skeptical about briefing cases after class because *what if you get called on?* Potentially getting called on is not a good enough reason to spend hours doing case briefs before you've had an opportunity to discuss the material in class. If you've read and taken some marginal or other notes, you should be fine on your cold call. And if not, so what? Eye on the prize. You need to prepare for the final exam, not one individual cold call. Your time is your most precious commodity. Use it wisely.

5. Take Verbatim Notes in Class
(And Ideally, Use a Computer)

At the beginning of law school, students struggle with pretty much every decision, including whether to take notes by computer or by hand. To the outside world, this seems like an inconsequential decision, like "Should I have a ham and cheese sandwich or a chicken salad sandwich for lunch?" But to a law student, it feels like a decision that can be make or break. It feels like you're choosing between an A and a C. But unfortunately, you don't know which choice is which.

You will get advice from everyone and their brother[6] on this. Professors, academic support, other students. The advice, unsurprisingly, will be conflicting. And some advisors will be very adamant that *they* are right,[7] which will make you feel bad about making a decision that conflicts with what they are saying.

---

6. Where did that expression even come from?

7. I know a professor who does not let students use a computer in class because he believes that the research unequivocally shows that students fare better taking notes by hand. Although it is his right to do what he wants in his classroom (it's called "academic freedom"), I think this is misguided. While some studies show that the way you take notes makes a difference, other studies say the opposite. For example, a recent study by a law professor at Ohio State concluded that there is no difference in academic performance between those who take notes by hand and those who use a laptop. She writes:

Based on prior research, one would have expected my computer users to perform worse on the final examination than students who only took notes by hand. In fact, there was no difference between the grades for computer and longhand note-takers even when I controlled for their LSAT score, undergraduate GPA, and fall GPA....

...A simplistic statement that laptop users should not take verbatim notes appears to be an insufficient way to help students take more effective notes. Some students may take effective notes using handwriting. Other students may take effective notes with computers. The technology itself does not dictate the outcome. The student's note-taking effectiveness affects the outcome.

First of all, do not feel any pressure to go in one direction or the other. Do not worry about who gave you what advice, what the academic studies say, what the 3L on law review says. Take it all in, weigh the options, and then make the decision you think is best. If that decision doesn't work out, it is very easily reversible.

I have heard good arguments in favor of taking notes by hand and good arguments in favor of taking notes by computer. I, myself, have done both. For my first year in law school, I took notes by hand. Then, I went home every night, and typed those notes into my desktop computer, creating my outline. I did this because I did not have a laptop my 1L year. Very few students did. My 2L year, however, I got one. For my 2L and 3L year, I took notes on my laptop. I found that it was much faster and more expedient than taking notes by hand.

Some people are not fast typers, and some may feel like they just take better notes by hand. Then, by all means, take your notes by hand. But bear in mind that you're going to have to type them all up later, which will add some time on the back end.

One argument in support of taking notes by hand stems from the notion of encoding in the science of learning. It has been shown that the process of hearing something and then writing it down on paper encodes the concept better in your brain than simply typing what you hear. That may be true. But I personally don't believe that deep learning occurs in the classroom. I believe that learning happens on your own, by yourself, after class. For me, the extra encoding effect of handwriting during class is negligible in comparison to where and when the real learning happens — during the outlining and study process. Let me bottom line it: Focus less on the modality of taking notes, and more on the note-taking process (i.e., what exactly you should be writing down in class).

You'd be surprised how many questions this issue can generate: *Should I take down every word the professor says? Should I just jot down the important points? Should I mainly be focused on listening or note-taking? Should I take notes in the margins of my briefs? Should I take notes on some sort of special paper or with a special computer program?*

In law, we are always teaching our students that answers are murky, there are two sides to most issues, and one needs to assess facts with care. A professor's reflexive "no-laptop" policy fails to hold us to these high standards.
Ruth Colker, *Universal Design: Stop Banning Laptops!* 39 Cardozo L. Rev. 489, 492 (2017), available at http://cardozolawreview.com/wp-content/uploads/2018/08/COLKER.39.2.pdf.

I think you should take comprehensive notes in class. You should write down as much as you can. You should try to be a stenographer. Other professors will absolutely recoil (good word, huh?) at this advice, but I stand by it. My view is that you should try to capture as much of the class as you can on paper and then figure it all out *after class.* If it's on paper, you can piece it together later. If it's not on paper, it is lost forever.[8] There is an old Chinese proverb that states that "the faintest ink is more powerful than the strongest memory." Lest you think that I am more learned than I actually am, I confess that I didn't know about this proverb until I heard it on *Mad Men.*

My brain isn't able to simultaneously take down information, organize it, and decide what is important. When I was in law school, I needed to take time with the material after class to systematize it. At that point, I could cut out duplicative points, reorganize the material, and put it together in a way that made sense. I was not able to make those judgment calls in class. And, truly, in my experience,[9] very few students are able to do so either.

I may not have sold you yet on the transcription approach. It seems like a lot of work. And the point of law school is not to transcribe what is coming out of the professor's mouth. It is to learn the law. All this is true. But learning takes time. And you can't learn something you haven't adequately memorialized. You may *think* you are going to remember nuances, exceptions, and glosses, but I guarantee you, you won't. If it is not down on paper, you will not magically remember it and then apply it on an exam.

Let me give you an example. Last year, when I taught the statute of frauds, I discussed the detrimental reliance exception in the context of the common law.[10] A student asked whether the exception also applied to Article 2 sale of goods transactions. I explained that courts were divided on this issue. As a class, we then went through arguments for and against applying the exception under Article 2. Because this discussion was in response to a student question, very few students wrote it down. Thinking that this would be a gimme, I crafted an assignment question involving this issue. More than half of the students did not spot the issue, even though we had talked about it at length in class. Not one of them had put this in their notes because (1) they thought they'd

---

8. This is referred to as the "storage" function of notetaking.

9. Ever notice how "in my experience" is a bit of a trump card we professors routinely play?

10. I realize that this is literally gibberish to you at this point. Bear with . . .

remember it, and (2) it wasn't part of the planned class discussion. Remember that everything in the book and everything that comes up in class is fair game for examination. You don't want to be missing out on easy points like this.

Now that I've given you my overview of why I think you should take detailed and comprehensive notes, I want to give you some pointers on the nitty-gritty. Again, take it or leave it as you deem appropriate:

1. Use a new document for each set of notes. Do not try to integrate notes into an existing document or write notes in the margin of a document. You should have 30 sets of notes representing 30 different Contracts classes, for instance. Then you should have one outline that you eventually integrate the notes into.

2. Do not try to organize or do anything with your notes in class. Don't bold, underline, format, etc. You don't have time for that. Just get the content down. Worry about the rest later.

3. Write down examples. All of them. You don't need to include them all in your outline, but examples will help you if you're having trouble processing the information later.

4. Write down different formulations of the same test or doctrine. In other words, if your professor is saying the same thing different ways, write them all down. Why? First, you can figure out later which version makes the most sense to you. And second, you might discover by looking at all the different iterations that you're not really understanding what's going on.

5. Write down relevant student questions and answers. A lot of valuable information comes out in response to student questions.

6. Write down wrong answers and why they are wrong. I don't mean every single wrong answer. But if a professor says, "That's a very common mistake," or, "I'm glad you said that," write it down. And don't make that mistake yourself.

7. Write down professor hints. Professors often give you clues as to what might be on the exam, what common errors they see, and what potholes to avoid. You need to lap that stuff up.

8. If you miss something, put some sort of placeholder in your notes and a keyword (e.g., something about a giant rock) and then immediately after class, ask a classmate about it.

You might be wondering at this point how you can listen *and* take verbatim notes *and* potentially be ready to answer a cold-call question. I know it's tough, but you're just going to have to find a way. I realize this is a totally unsatisfactory answer. But it's the truth.

Finally, you might be resistant to my advice. You might be thinking, *Well, that's not how I learn.* And that might be the case. I can tell you, however, that in my 15 years of teaching,[11] I only had two students who took minimal notes and were extremely successful—José and Stephen. They both just sat there and very occasionally jotted something down. It gave me anxiety *for them.* But, for whatever reason, it worked for them. Both were A students. But I think José and Stephen are the exception and not the rule.

By and large, my system works for students. If you think of class as "collecting information" time and after class as the "real work" time, then the approach makes sense. Of course, all of this is for naught if you don't do something meaningful with the notes, which is where outlining comes in. Brace yourself…Chapter 4 is coming.

6. Do Not Blow Off Your Legal Writing Class

Your legal writing class, LRW, gets a bad rap. At most schools, it is downgraded to a sort of secondary class that you have to do on top of your "real" classes. One Canadian blog refers to LRW as the "black sheep" of the 1L curriculum. I'm not here to say that LRW is the most important class you will take in law school. I don't think there's such a thing as "the" most important class in law school. But I will say that it is important, and you should absolutely not view it as a secondary priority.[12]

One of the greatest ironies of law school is that LRW is the most experiential of courses you can take—it tells you how to prepare the legal documents that you're going to be preparing for the rest of your life (memos, motions, letters, etc.). And yet, students don't seem to relish this experiential opportunity. They'd rather sit in a courtroom and just watch what other people are doing. Go figure.

---

11. Trump card, again.

12. Also, a special shout out to legal writing professors, who are blessed with almost infinite patience. They have what might be the most difficult job in the law school.

LRW is hard. It feels mechanical. It feels like there's a whole bunch of stupid rules you have to follow and if you don't, you're going to lose points. Yes, and... such is the practice of law. Law is a rules-oriented profession. No time like the present to get on board with that.

I think part of the reason that students do not like their LRW class is because it makes them feel insecure about their writing. Many students thought they were good writers until they got to LRW. Being told you are not a good legal writer (indirectly, through a low grade) takes its toll on your self-esteem and sense of identity. And we all know that self-esteem is everything.[13]

I get it. I thought I was a good writer until I got to law school. Until I got a B on my first legal writing assignment. *How dare she?!* I blamed the professor, of course... because that is what one does when one does not do well. But, on a more fundamental level, I began to doubt myself. I struggled to get my footing after that B and never liked my legal writing class after that. In retrospect, it was a wasted opportunity. I let my pride get in the way of a valuable learning experience. I also never got to the point where I was really *learning* about good legal writing. I was just trying to do things "the right way" and to give the professor "what she wanted." I was just ticking the boxes.

I would suggest that you not approach LRW as just ticking the boxes and then get frustrated when you don't tick them correctly. Really try to focus on themes and messaging about what you are doing and why. Do not make LRW about the minutiae. If you approach LRW as being about the minutiae, you will never be able to extrapolate what you've learned to other contexts, which is what you need to be able to do as a lawyer. This skill, unsurprisingly, is called *transference*, i.e., the ability of students to apply knowledge and skills from one context to another.

Example time. I sometimes teach an upper-level seminar on Conflict of Laws. As part of this course, students need to write a final 25-page paper. I noticed something strange the first time I taught the seminar: the rough drafts were bad. Even those written by really good students. I tried to get to the bottom of what was happening. I had taught many of these students before and knew that they were highly intelligent and good writers. What was going on?

I eventually figured it out. Students were trying to write an academic paper like they would a legal memo. They were trying *transference* but failing miser-

---

13. See my section on "snowflakes."

ably. That is because they were looking at LRW as having taught them a bunch of mechanical skills and rules, and they were then trying to write a paper based on those mechanics. Specifically, students were trying to use IRAC (Issue, Rule, Application, Conclusion) to write an academic paper. They were wedded to a very strict way of IRAC writing, which translated into unduly formal and stilted papers.

Instead of transferring the mechanics that they learned in LRW, I told them that they needed to transfer the general concepts. If you are going to argue that states should adopt a reciprocity requirement for the recognition of foreign judgments, which was the paper topic, it does not lend itself to being written in a strict IRAC format. Instead, I got them to loosen up and see IRAC not as a stricture but as a guidepost. Students insisted that they weren't taught to write this way "in legal writing" class. But they were. They just couldn't adapt what they were taught in LRW to a different context.

All of this to say that your LRW class is important. But less for the mechanics it teaches you and more for the frameworks it provides you with for thinking about legal writing.

7. Learn to Love Writing

Ok, "love" might be a strong word. Maybe I'll downgrade that to "like." Or even "tolerate." It always surprises me how many students say that they hate writing. They say that LRW is their least favorite class. They say that writing is stressful and hard and tedious. That might all be true, but I've got a message for you: *Writing is pretty much the bulk of what you do as a lawyer.* You might not be drafting appellate briefs every day of the week, but you will be drafting memos, letters, emails, motions, etc. If you think you're going to be the trial attorney who does little to no writing, you are sorely mistaken. Because that attorney does not exist.

So, my first piece of advice is to make peace with your future reality: You will have to write. A lot. You might as well learn how to do it now.

My second piece of advice is to get the basics down first. A number of students come to law school with less-than-exemplary writing skills. I don't mean that they are not good brief writers. I mean they can't distinguish between "their," "there," and "they're," and they don't know where a comma goes, much less what an "Oxford comma" is. If you are in this camp, own it. I had a former student who was told by a professor that his writing was bad, and that he needed to go back to basics. The student accepted this challenge and doubled down on the rules of syntax and grammar. His writing improved tremendously between his first and third year. But he was the first to acknowledge that he came to law school not knowing things he should have known.

My third piece of advice is to let go of the fear of writing. Students are often terrified of writing ("I'm going to do it wrong!"). Fear is an inhibitor to progress. *Let it go, let it go*...to be sung in the Elsa voice, of course.

My fourth piece of advice is to not approach writing as a set of rules that you need to memorize. I know that legal writing classes tend to be a bit formulaic because they are teaching general principles of good writing. But do not feel beholden to this structure for time immemorial. As I mentioned above, I've had students work on research papers who were so worried about IRAC-ing every paragraph that their point was completely lost by the end of it. Writing needs to be organic. It should also be clear and organized. At the end of the day, there is no plug-and-play formula for good legal writing.

My fifth piece of advice is to practice. Practice makes perfect. The more you write, the more comfortable you will feel writing. It is a skill that will develop in time. You will start off clunky and awkward. But it will get better. Seek out opportunities in law school that involve writing, such as seminar classes, law review, and advanced legal writing classes.

My sixth piece of advice is to pay very close attention to the corrections and suggestions your professors make. Do not make the same mistake twice. I had one student who had a habit of using lots of filler words (however, therefore, thus, consequently, nevertheless, etc.). After I pointed it out to him, he cut back on the filler by about 60%. His writing was much cleaner and more readable.

My final piece of advice is a little bit more substantive. And for those of you who know me, you know exactly how I would pronounce that—sub-*stan*-tive, not *sub*-stuntive. Do not try to make your writing sound fancy. Do not use the computer's thesaurus function to find a longer word. Aim for clarity and brevity. The goal of writing is not for you to sound smart.[14] It is for you to get your point across to a reader. I know this is going to feel strange and is probably the absolute opposite of the approach you've been taking so far, but trust me on this one.

---

14. A high school teacher once called my writing "highfalutin." At the time, I sort of took it as a compliment. By the time I got to law school, I realized it wasn't.

One quick story. When I was clerking, I was good friends with one of my co-clerks who was wicked smart and had a PhD. Her writing was very refined, and she used words that I hadn't heard of until I met her, such as "cathartic," "rarefied," "performative" and "comparator." I wished I could write like her. In comparison, my writing seemed kindergarten-ish. She assured me that my writing was great. *It is so clear!* That felt like a euphemism for dumb. And it felt that way for a long time. Sometimes even now. But I have learned to embrace my writing style. My writing tends to be direct, clear, and to the point. And, ultimately, I think that's what good writing should be.

FOUR

A Play-by-Play on How to Outline

The key is not the will to win. Everybody has that.
It is the will to prepare to win that is important.

BOBBY KNIGHT

1. Garbage In = Garbage Out

There are three pieces to success on exams in law school: (1) Inputs; (2) Studying; and (3) Exam Taking. If you are missing one of the pieces, you will not be successful. For example, if you have the wrong "inputs" (i.e., you are studying incorrect law, you have misunderstood the rules, you are missing pieces of the rule, etc.), you simply cannot do well in law school.

There is an expression in the field of computer science that you may be familiar with: GIGO (Garbage In, Garbage Out). It's pronounced *Guy*-go. I dated a computer guy at Cambridge who is a big deal in the field of machine learning, in case you're wondering why I know that. If your inputs are "garbage," then your outputs will be "garbage."

The outline component of law school success goes into the "input" category. If your outline is no good, your studying and exam taking will be no good. It makes sense. Think about this outside of the academic context. You are asked to build a birdhouse. Silly, I know, but I can't always be super creative. You have a hammer, nails, wood, and a saw. These are some of the tools you need to build a birdhouse, but not all of them. Because you are missing certain inputs, your output (the birdhouse) will be crap.

Outlining and notetaking are very closely related. If you don't take good notes, you don't have the raw materials to turn into a good outline.

2. There Is No Right Way to Outline (But There Sort of Is)

Students often ask, *Is this a good outline?* It's a bit of a trick question. There is no such thing as a good outline in absolute terms. A good outline is simply one that contains all the relevant information and is organized in a way that you understand it and can study from it when it comes time for the exam.

The outline is simply a means to an end. It has to facilitate your understanding of the material for the exam. Students get so hung up on creating outlines that they fail to see that the outline is only there to serve a function: to act as a study instrument. You can have the "best" outline in the world and still get a D on the exam.

You should not have anxiety about doing it right. Don't stress about whether you should use roman numerals, or letters or numbers. Don't stress about the heading system you choose or whether to put page numbers at the top or bottom. Do not get caught up in the fear that you're doing it wrong. There is no right and wrong here. Any outline that contains everything you need to know and is easy to study from is a good outline.

Even though there is no such thing as a good outline, there is such a thing as a bad outline. If the outline does not contain everything you covered in class, is disorganized, or has the law wrong, it is a bad outline.

3. You Should Outline Every Day (Hear Me Out)

Everyone knows that memory fades with time. Try to remember what you had for lunch yesterday.[1] Try to remember where you parked your car on Monday. Try to remember the plot from the movie you watched this past weekend.[2]

I'm sure you realize that you are not going to retain 100% of the information you learned on Day 1 on Day 30. What you probably don't realize is just *how much* you will forget. The science is shocking.

---

1. I remember quite readily what I had for lunch yesterday since I eat the same thing every day for lunch.

2. Maybe it's just me. Movie and TV plots tend not to stick around in my brain very long.

The "forgetting curve" shows how information is lost over time when you don't try to retain it. You lose about 50% of what you've learned in just *one hour*. Yes, you heard me right—*one hour*. By the end of the school day, you've lost about 70% of what you learned. *Holy schnikies!*

The following graphic illustrates this point:[3]

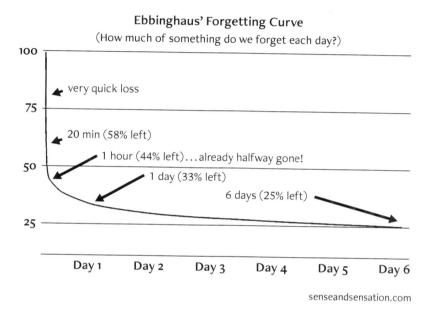

Ebbinghaus' Forgetting Curve
(How much of something do we forget each day?)

very quick loss

20 min (58% left)

1 hour (44% left)...already halfway gone!

1 day (33% left)

6 days (25% left)

Day 1   Day 2   Day 3   Day 4   Day 5   Day 6

senseandsensation.com

This should be horrifying to you. Basically, if you do nothing to retain the information you have just learned, it is lost. Pretty much forever. Subsequent attempts to retrieve the information barely counteract the forgetting curve.

Think about this for a moment. *Really think.* You do all this reading. You go to class. You take notes. Twenty-four hours later, all of this is effort is wasted. All your time and effort has gone down the drain. Sure, you can look at your notes and try to understand them two weeks later. Good luck with that.

If you do not outline on a regular basis, you are essentially sabotaging your own success. You are undoing all the good you've done. Which reminds me of a perfect story to illustrate this point.

---

3. *Reprinted from* https://commons.wikimedia.org/wiki/File:Ebbinghaus's_Forgetting _Curve_(Figure_1).jpg.

Last year, I went downstairs to grab some laundry. My husband, David, was running on the treadmill. I noticed that there was what looked like a small piece of paper on the plastic edge of the treadmill. I bent down to pick it up because I didn't want it to get accidentally sucked into the belt. I looked at it and said, "Is this a potato chip? Are you eating chips *while* running on the treadmill?" David looked at me guiltily. Indeed, it was a potato chip. He figured that because he was doing good (running) he could also do bad (eating chips). It doesn't work that way. Eating chips while on a treadmill negates all the progress you've made. Same thing with outlining. All the progress you make in reading and taking good notes is sabotaged if you don't outline right away. To sum this all up in a way you will remember: Don't eat potato chips while running on a treadmill.

Let's go back to the forgetting curve. As a law student, your goal is to counteract the forgetting curve. How do you do that? Easy. You outline the day of class when the material is fresh in your mind. Even a day or two lapse in revisiting the material will mean that things slip through the cracks. The two most common objections I hear to my suggestion to outline the day of class are *I don't have time* and *I prefer to wait until the end of the chapter when I can put everything together.* I'm going to shoot each of these down.

If you "don't have time," make time. Stop reading your cases three times, stop getting distracted by your phone, stop writing up useless case briefs. The "I prefer to wait" argument is slightly more compelling, but not much. The two are not mutually exclusive. You can outline after every class and then put it all together at the end of the chapter. Your outline is not set in stone. You can cut and paste and delete—it's called a computer. If you wait until the end of the chapter, you will invariably miss putting stuff in your outline that should be there.

I want to share my students' experience with conquering the forgetting curve. To understand some of these (and subsequent) passages, you need to understand the method of evaluation I adopted that semester.

It was January. Bar exam rates were abysmal. I decided that something had to be done. So, I introduced into my second semester Contracts class what I uncreatively called "Option 2." Option 2 involved students submitting weekly outlines to me, which I provided extensive feedback on. The focus was on macro-conceptualization and putting all the pieces together in an organized and systematic way. The outline was worth 15% of the grade. An additional

25% of the grade consisted of three separate quizzes. The final exam made up the remaining 60% of the grade.[4]

Here are some student reflections chronicling their experiences with Option 2 and the forgetting curve.

> My grade for the first semester of Contracts I was a B. Contracts was one of the more difficult subjects that I took in my first year. I initially thought the material would be easy and I did find offer and acceptance easy. The class became more difficult when we studied the Battle of the Forms and later doctrines in the semester. I think the problem I had was that I understood the material in class, but I never consolidated that knowledge after class. Instead, I waited until the end of the semester to recall the information, and my memory was not as reliable as I initially thought. I thought that I had done well when I took the exam, but there were issues that I had missed entirely and I think the reason for that is because there was material that I had not studied.... I was somewhat shocked about getting back my final exam in Contracts I. I thought that I had done decent on the final, but my raw score was a 34/100. I realized that there was a lot of information that I had just forgotten.

> This semester with Option 2, I outlined every day after class (for the most part).... There were approximately two times where I pushed off my outline until the Sunday submission, and the "forgetting curve" was very evidently in effect for those times.

> After the second week of Option 2, I got into the habit of updating my outline immediately after class. Now, Professor Monestier is going to show you the science behind the benefits of updating your outline immediately after class as opposed to waiting days later to do so. Taking the science into consideration is your decision but take it from me, it's very helpful to get straight into updating your outline immediately after class or at least before the day ends: the material is still fresh in your mind and you develop more of an understanding while updating your outline by doing so. Waiting until the last minute, like how I was doing initially, is not helpful and you tend to not remember what was discussed in class regardless if you have all of the notes.

---

4. You might be wondering what Option 1 was. Option 1 was the standard law school 100% final exam.

While I did well on my first semester of Contract Law, I knew my learning strategy had to significantly improve this semester. During my Fall semester, I made the rookie mistake almost all 1Ls make, which is to not outline soon enough. Professor Monestier had told us since last semester that the most efficient way to outline was right after class. After seeing the data on the Lost Learning Curve and on Spaced Repetition, I knew that I could not make the same mistakes again.

By the end of the semester, most students were sold on the "outline every day" approach. I would even get students who expressed feeling immense anxiety if they could not outline right after class. Once you get into the habit, you will not be able to imagine it any other way. Sort of like flossing.

Now I want to provide you with a post from a 1L that I found on Reddit:[5]

Stressed 1L: Am I screwed?

I'm in my first semester of law school and throughout the semester I've stayed completely devoted to my work and applied myself fully to the task of tackling 1L. I did little else besides going to class, reading, reviewing notes, and trying to understand concepts I was learning. Readings took (and still take) me quite a while to do. As such, I spent an enormous amount of time this semester reading concepts, briefing cases, and taking typed notes on my readings.

Around October, I attempted to start outlining because I was starting to see the bigger picture but by November I realized what I had outlined before was not workable and didn't really make sense to me. I started all of my outlines over again but, as I'm sure most you know, outlining is a very involved process that takes a while and should not be rushed.

Now, thanksgiving break is about to end for me and I'm only 50% done with my Civ Pro outline which is my first exam, 60ish% done with torts & 75% done with Contracts. My first exam is on Dec 7th and I'm constantly fighting off a mental breakdown Bc I just can't get over the feeling that I am royally screwed and will not be able to finish and properly study/do hypos before exam period starts (I have answered a few practice questions but I find that outlining helps me to issue spot more effectively). To top that off, I still have a week left of classes

---

5. I was told by my 1L class that Reddit is where students go for information about law school. Lord help us.

including 50+ pages for Civ pro reading. I feel so defeated because I have been working extremely hard and trying my ABSOLUTE best this semester to avoid this at the end - yet here I am.

Am I completely screwed? Can anyone who has been through 1L please give me advice on how to get through this period and tips on what I can do to be more efficient? On a mental health note, any tips on coping with extreme anxiety and avoiding a mental breakdown when time is so crucial? Thank you so much.

Stressed 1L: Yes, you are screwed. You'll probably get by with a low B or a C, but you will not get an A. This student learned the lesson too late. He or she was over-preparing for class and under-preparing for the exam. There's no recovering from that in November.

4. Your Outline Is One-Stop Shopping

OK, we keep on talking about this mythical "outline." What goes in it? The short answer is everything. This advice is contrary to the common wisdom. The common wisdom is that your outline should be fairly condensed, i.e., a short summary of all the legal principles you covered in a particular class.

I like to row against the tide. I do not think you should be aiming for short and condensed. You should be aiming to have *everything* that ever came up in the class down on paper. Most of my outlines in law school were over 100 pages. Don't stop reading, please. You can, and should, eventually take your monster 100-pager and cut it down to a "mini-outline." But you can't do the reverse. Here is what the outline should contain.

A. Full Legal Rules

The outline should contain fulsome, narrative descriptions of all the legal rules and doctrines. There should be no shorthand. This is because, ultimately, you are going to have to articulate the full rule on an exam, not an abridged version of the rule. For example, let's say you're defining impracticability. Impracticability is a doctrine that excuses performance of a contractual obligation where that obligation has become extremely difficult, expensive, or dangerous for the party who was to perform. Simply saying "Impracticability is when you get out of a contract because it's hard to perform" is not going to cut it.

B. Lots of Examples

The outline should contain examples from class and/or other examples. You should have examples for every concept covered and sometimes multiple examples. Isn't this overkill? No. The examples will help jog your memory on what things mean. It is sometimes really hard to revisit legal concepts after four or five months. Having an example that shows you what the rule means or how it plays out is invaluable. Bear in mind, you are not studying the examples. You are only putting them there as back-up in case your narrative description fails you.

C. Cases

You should put cases in your outline to illustrate how doctrines and rules play out. As I've said before, case briefs should be done *after* class, not before. Additionally, I would treat each case as a mini-hypo,[6] and apply the law to the facts of that case.

D. Statutory Sections

If you are dealing with a statute, then the relevant statutory sections should be in your notes, so you don't have to go look them up later. Ditto for Restatement sections.[7]

E. Everything Discussed in Class

You should assume that anything that comes up in class is fair game in terms of testing. Accordingly, you should write down policy arguments, hypotheticals, student questions and answers, and pretty much anything else that is discussed. Importantly, you should write down *wrong* answers so that you warn yourself to not make the same mistake.

F. Tips & Traps

Often professors will say in class "look out for X." This could be a tip (i.e., let me help you issue spot) or a trap (i.e., students tend to make this mistake). These tips and traps are gold. They need to be in your outline.

---

6. This doesn't work as well with Constitutional Law or Civil Procedure cases.

7. To be clear, the Restatement is not a statute even though it looks like one. The Restatement is like a wannabe statute.

The list for what the outline should not contain is much shorter and somewhat obvious. The outline should not contain things you did not cover, extra material from outside sources, and irrelevant material from the cases. Focus your outline only on what you learned in class or what the professor said you're responsible for.[8]

Now that I've told you to put everything under the sun in your outline, I want to explicitly state something that I think is implicit in what I've written so far. Your outline should be organized *around the legal rules and doctrines*. Not around the cases. Cases take on a secondary role in your outline.

I repeat: The focus is the law. The technical legal rules, the exceptions, the gray areas, the different approaches, the elements. Whatever. The law is the star of your outline. The cases, at best, have a supporting-actor role.

5. Conceptual Organization Is the Hardest Part

What an outline should enable you to do is to conceptually organize a large amount of information in a way that is understandable to an outside reader and easy to follow. This is *way* easier said than done. A lot of students do not understand what we professors mean by "conceptual organization."

Conceptual organization does *not* mean simply putting headings on things and numbering or bulleting them. Conceptual organization means that you have thought about the material and that you have put it together in a manner that is logical, comprehensive, and easy to understand. It is like taking all the puzzle pieces and putting them together in your own way.

I sometimes describe it this way: Your room can be tidy but disorganized. You are not aiming for *tidy* (i.e., looking pretty and neat), you are aiming for *organized*. Your goal is to put things in the right place. For example, a basic organizational principle is that you put "like" things together. So, if you are organizing your closet, you might do it in a variety of ways: by color; by item; by how often you wear stuff; by season; etc. You may even have organization within organization (e.g., organize by season and color). The same principles are true here. You need to figure out what is "like" and put it together. This will enable your brain to process all the relevant information for that topic, without having it be disjointed and popping up all over the outline.

---

8. I personally have never tested on something I haven't covered in class. I'm sure some professors do that, but it's a real "jerk move" (to quote from one of my student evaluations).

Let me give you an example. When we talk about misrepresentation in Contracts, I often lay out the elements first:

1. Misstatement of existing fact.
2. Misstatement was fraudulent or material.
3. Misstatement induced party to enter into the contract.
4. Reliance on the misstatement was reasonable.

Within each of these elements, we have a robust discussion as a class. For instance, under (1), we talk about opinions, predictions, and puffery. Under (2), we talk about the Restatement view of materiality and the expansive view of fraudulent misrepresentation. These discussions in class may happen out of order. For instance, we don't talk about opinions until much later in the class, since it comes up in our second case. If you just transcribed the notes into an outline in the order they were presented in class, it would not make much sense.

Your goal is to take *all the material* you have and put it together in a way that will enable you to eventually learn it. This will mean straying from the order it was presented in class, moving things around, elaborating and cross-referencing where necessary, adding context and examples, and all sorts of stuff like that. Students get nervous about putting things in a different order than it was covered in class. Don't be. How a professor teaches the material in class is different than how it should appear in an outline that you're going to study from.

It should be clear from the above that a lot of law will be thrown your way and that it is on you to repackage it in a way that makes sense. This skill will take some time to perfect, but it's probably a skill you use to some degree in your everyday life. Let me give you an analogy. Let's say that you've just finished watching the first season of *Game of Thrones*. I've never watched *Game of Thrones*,[9] but I've picked it because I hear it's really complicated. You're tasked with explaining the plot to someone who has never seen it before. Based solely on your summary, this other person must master the plotline and explain it to a third person.[10] If that were the case, you would give some serious thought as to

---

9. I will not watch anything with dragons, sorcerers, or any other mythical elements. One exception: *Outlander*. I went through a phase after watching the show where I wanted to join a Jamie Fraser fan club. I'm mainly over it now. But not entirely.

10. This is like you explaining it to your "exam-self" who will, in turn, explain it to the professor.

how you would go about explaining it. You couldn't just go episode by episode and jump around all the time. You'd have to think about how the characters and plots are related, and what makes sense to discuss first, second, third, and so on. You would have to engage in conceptual organization, the same thing that outlining requires you to do. If it helps, think of outlining as your *Game of Thrones* deconstruction exercise.

6. Follow Certain Easy Rules to Help Your Brain

In addition to being conceptually organized, your outline should be neat and tidy. It is much less daunting to study from an outline that is easy on the eyes than one that it looks like it was thrown together by a third grader who just discovered Microsoft Word.

In organizing your outline, you may find the following guideposts helpful:

1. Use attractive font. You have to look at this document a lot. Choose something that is aesthetically pleasing.

2. Use headings. Like A, B, C or 1, 2, 3. That way, you can readily separate and find different topics. Headings should be in larger font than surrounding text, or in some other way offset.

3. Align left. You should have 1-inch margins throughout. Do not start the document indented. I have seen outlines get so indented that pretty much all the words end up on the right side of the page. This is not easy to read.

4. Use Spacing Effectively. Have normal spacing (5 spaces) between a bullet or number and text. Do not squish them up against each other. This helps whatever you are writing stand out. Use single spacing (not 1.15) for the majority of the document, and double spacing to distinguish between things.

5. Number things where appropriate. For example, number elements or exceptions. This will clue your brain into the fact that you need to remember three of something or five of something. Don't number things or letter things that are not lists or elements. Use bullets in this case.

6. Choose two bulleting symbols and use them consistently. Don't use three or four or five different types of bullets.

7. Highlight and emphasize where appropriate. This should include underlining, bolding, and italicizing. Do not over-use this. When everything is underlined, bolded, or italicized, nothing is.

8. Be consistent. Be consistent with spacing, alignment, formatting. That will cue your brain into where you are in your outline.

9. Use indentation to your advantage. For instance:

    Rule: blah blah blah blah blah blah blah blah blah blah blah blah blah blah blah blah blah blah blah blah blah blah blah blah blah blah blah blah blah blah.

    Example: example example example example example example example example example example example example example example example example.

10. Do not squish things up. Use appropriate white space between things to visually offset different topics, approaches, etc. This makes things easier to find and separates them out in your mind.

11. New topic, new page. This helps your mind mentally move on to something new.

12. Do not over-bullet. You should only be going two (or maybe three) layers "into" the document. It is extremely difficult to memorize bullets with sub-bullets with sub-sub-bullets with sub-sub-sub-bullets.

13. Do not use acronyms unless you must. If you do, be sure to explain the acronym. You may remember that 3P meant "third party" when you drafted your outline, but you might not remember what it means when you go to study from it.

14. Say things once. Don't have five different statements of the test in five different places of the outline.

Yes, I realize that this is an overwhelming list, especially because I said that there is no right way to do this. These tips have been collected based on reviewing hundreds of student outlines. I want to be explicit about why I am recommending certain things in outlining. I am recommending them because they reflect basic organizational principles, take advantage of visual memory,[11] and prepare your "future self" for the exam. Not just so you have a pretty document for posterity.

---

11. For example, one rule which might look overly persnickety but is intended to help you when studying: Start new topics on new pages. This is so that you don't inadvertently blur doctrines together. You would be surprised but seeing a heading at the top of a page reorients your brain to the new topic and separates it from the prior one.

7. Do Not Worry About Length

One of the strangest things I hear from students is that they are worried that their outline is going to be too long. Presumably they are concerned that if they have a long outline, they will have more to memorize, and there is more work for them. *Madonna mia* ... I have trouble wrapping my mind around this.

When you take a law school course, you are expected to know everything the professor taught. If it takes you 100 pages to memorialize all the professor taught, then it takes you 100 pages. I don't quite understand how creating a 20-page outline is something to aim for. A 20-page outline is necessarily going to cut out material that the class covered. How it that a *good* thing? Sure, you have less to study. But you're only studying a portion of the course. This is a sure-fire way to get a bad grade.

Let me rephrase the above in case I wasn't clear. The length of your outline does not dictate what you need to know. What you need to know is dictated by the professor and the course. If you choose to cut corners to make it "easier" to study, you are only going to learn part of what you need to know. A 20-page outline does not mean you don't need to know 100% of the course.

For those students who are just too overwhelmed with a large outline, I would also suggest that they look at it this way: You can always take a mama outline and make it into a baby outline. You cannot do the reverse. You cannot magically create content to bolster and pad your baby outline.

I mentioned this already, but when I was in law school, every one of my outlines was over 100 pages. A couple of weeks before the exam, I would trim the fat (which I had already studied) and make a condensed version of the outline to study from. But that was only when I was sure that the fat was already in my mind, so I could just concentrate on the core stuff.

Here is a comment I received from a top student about the length of her outline:

In all of my other classes, I have followed the outlining method of Option 2 in terms of content being included and formatting. This has led to some very hefty outlines (for property in particular,) but I can see with the sheer volume of things we've learned how this will help in finals. ... I'd rather have a page [long] description of a topic vs some measly little list of elements that barely gets the analysis going.

I will add a disclaimer though...you are really the only professor who is really giving us the well-rounded picture we need to really succeed on the exam. In your class, it's just a matter of catching it all and making sure it's in my notes. In other classes, I am spending a lot of time in supplements trying to get the full picture or getting a better understanding of what is said in class.

I included the latter portion of the quote not just because the student compliments me, but because the message hits upon a reality you'll deal with in law school. Not all professors readily "give" you the law for you to include in your outline. In some classes, you need to work to find the law on your own, through the readings or through study aids. Those classes are definitely harder. But whatever style your professor has, they will ultimately be testing you on the law. As such, it's your job to figure out what the law is and get it into your outline.

8. What a Good Outline Looks Like

It's sort of hard in book form to show you what a good outline looks like versus what a bad outline looks like. Well, challenge accepted![12] Below, you'll find three different examples of an outline covering the topic of economic duress. Which one do you think is best? If you could only choose one to study from, which would it be?

DURESS: SAMPLE 1

A. Duress: Generally
  - ➤ Traditionally, duress was the "gun to the head" scenario—i.e., someone forced you to sign a contract under threat or fear of death or harm. In this case, the contract was void (because you had no choice but to sign). This obviously doesn't come up a lot anymore.

---

12. This expression brings back one of my favorite teaching memories. Marcus was a student in my Conflict of Laws class. One day in class, we were talking about an obscure section of the Restatement (Second) of the Conflict of Laws dealing with *renvoi*. Do not worry about what the means. It's hard and it will hurt your brain if I try to explain it to you. In any event, I said something like, "If anyone can figure this out, you'll get bonus points." I was 100% just kidding. The next day I got an email from Marcus with the subject line "Challenge Accepted" and a full-out interpretation of the section. I had to honor my promise to give bonus points and now make it a point to say out loud if I'm kidding.

➤ Now, we have the development of the doctrine of what has become known as "economic duress" (sometimes called "business compulsion"), which is a lot more likely to happen than traditional duress.

➤ With economic duress, you have a situation where the party with the greater bargaining power is basically trying to "blackmail" the other party and the other party has no reasonable alternative but to go along with it. If you can prove duress, the contract is <u>voidable</u> (i.e., subject to rescission).

➤ Competing Policy Interests: We want people to order their own affairs and we want to promote settlement and we want people to be secure in the knowledge that the law will back them up; but on the other hand, we don't want to enforce contracts that were made under economically coercive circumstances.

➤ Note: very hard to get out of a contract on the basis of duress.

B. Context: How Do Cases of Economic Duress Arise?

➤ Typically, those claiming economic duress are attempting to avoid the consequences of:

1. A modification of an original contract; or

   ➤ Parties agree to modify a contract (K1). The modified contract (K2) then takes the place of K1. A party alleging duress attempts to rescind K2 and go back to K1.

2. A settlement and release agreement

   ➤ Parties agree to settle all claims related to a contract (K1). They do this by entering into a settlement and release agreement (K2). A party alleging duress is looking to rescind K2 and go back to K1.

C. Elements of Duress

➤ **Basic Rule:** If a party's manifestation of assent is induced by an improper threat by the other party that leaves the victim no reasonable alternative, the contract is voidable by the victim. Accordingly, you need the following elements:

1. **Wrongful Threat:** The pressuring party wrongfully or improperly threatens the other party.

   ➤ A threat is improper in the following circumstances:

      a. What is threatened is a crime or a tort, or the threat itself would be a crime or a tort if it resulted in obtaining property,

      b. What is threatened is a criminal prosecution,

    c. What is threatened is the use of civil process and the threat is made in bad faith,

    d. The threat is a breach of the duty of good faith and fair dealing under a contract with the recipient.

    e. The threat is improper if the exchange is not fair and you're basically trying to take advantage of the other person (i.e., there's no legitimate reason for the "threat").

2. **No Reasonable Alternatives:** the party trying to get out of the contract had no reasonable alternative but to agree to the threat.

    ➤ A threat, even if improper, does not amount to duress if the victim has a reasonable alternative to succumbing and fails to take advantage of it.

    ➤ What are some reasonable alternatives? Availability of legal action (if viable—note that sometimes this won't be a real option because of timeliness concerns); alternative sources of goods, services, or funds; toleration of the threat if it's only a minor vexation. Will be fact-dependent.

3. **Causation:** Actual inducement of the contract by the threat (i.e., the threat must cause you to enter into the contract/modification).

    ➤ Usually, this is not an issue (because if you threaten someone, it stands to reason that it will cause them to enter into the contract).

    ➤ Note that the threat only needs to be a substantial cause (not the sole cause) of entering into the contract.

4. **Cause of Hardship:** Some (but not all!) courts impose a 4th requirement that the pressuring party must have caused the hardship.

D. Case Analysis: Totem Marine

Totem Marine Tug & Barge, Inc. v. Alyeska Pipeline Service Co.

Facts: Plaintiff Totem (towing company), entered into a contract with Defendant, Alyeska, to transport pipeline construction materials from Texas to Alaska. There were a series of complications (additional cargo, delays, etc.). Eventually, Alyeska terminated the contract. Totem contacted Alyeska about paying outstanding invoices of between $200,000-$300,000. Alyeska stated payment might take 6-8 months. Totem, facing creditors and bankruptcy, signed a settlement of $97,500 in exchange for a full release. It now wants to rescind the settlement and recover under the initial contract.

➢ **Elements**:

1. Wrongful or Improper Threat

   ➢ Alyeska was threatening to breach the contract unless Totem signed the release. This falls under d), above—failure to act in good faith in performance of contract.

   ➢ To show bad faith, Totem would need to convince the court that defendant Alyeska was refusing (or delaying) to pay an indisputable liability.

   ➢ If Alyeska had a plausible basis for claiming that it was not liable to Totem Marine at all or not liable for anywhere close to the amount claimed because Totem Marine committed a breach, then Alyeska would not be acting in bad faith.

2. No Reasonable Alternatives

   ➢ Did Totem have a reasonable alternative here? Probably not. Totem is facing (or claiming it is facing) impending bankruptcy; Totem was unable to meet its pressing debts unless it got immediate cash payment. Pursuing legal channels which would take years would not be an adequate remedy.

   ➢ If you were Alesyka, what would be some of the things you would want to find out about in discovery? Copies of financial statements; other sources of income; reasonableness of payment schedules (e.g., was it standard in the industry to have such short credit times); creditworthiness (could they get a loan); how many creditors did they have; did they consult a lawyer about bankruptcy (though this may be privileged). The goal for the party opposing rescission is to show that the alleged victim had other options.

3. Causation

   ➢ Did the threat not to pay cause Totem to take the money and sign the release? Court doesn't specifically comment on this. In most cases, if you show an improper threat and no other alternatives, it almost follows that the threat is why the victim entered into the contract.

4. Hardship

   ➢ Potentially an additional requirement is that the threatening party have caused the economic hardship.

> Did Aleskya cause the economic hardship? To a great extent, yes. To-tem wouldn't have incurred all those liabilities had they not been trying to fulfill their contract with Aleskya.

DURESS: SAMPLE #2

I. Duress

  a. Traditional Duress—somebody forced you to do something, usually by threat of physical violence.

  b. Economic duress (business compulsion)—forcing someone to agree through economic pressure

    i. If you can prove you are the victim of duress, you may be able to rescind the contract—there are two ways you can demonstrate duress in modifying contract—this is difficult to prove and the 3 elements are hard to satisfy

      1. Restatement Section 175: When Duress by Threat makes a contract voidable

        a. Improper Threat

        b. No reasonable alternative

        c. Causation—had it not been for the threat, the party would not have taken the contract

          i. **The pressuring Party has to have caused the hardship—sub req depends on court**

      2. "Wrongful Threat" Restatement 176

        a. threatened with crime or tort

        b. threatens criminal prosecution or civil process in bad faith

        c. the threat is a breach of the duty of good faith and fair dealing under a contract with the recipient

    ii. Release

      1. Totem v Alyeska

        a. Rule: Economic duress:

          i. One party involuntarily accepts the other's terms

          ii. Circumstances permitted no other recourse (no reasonable alternative)

          iii. Circumstances were the result of the acts of the other party

    b. Parties signed a release that stated that Alyeska may pay $97,000 (instead of the $300,000 owed)

    c. Totem wants a "release from the release" due to economic duress—alleged they had no choice but to sign release or go bankrupt and Alyeska knew this

    d. Alyeska threatens to withhold payment with the knowledge that Totem is on the verge of bankruptcy (improper threat)

    e. Was Plaintiff forced to accept the terms based on economic duress?

        ii. Court held that he had enough evidence to claim undue influence

    f. No reasonable alternative— (reasonable alternatives may include filing a lawsuit, toleration of the threat, getting a loan during litigation process, Etc.)

    g. Causation—There was an improper threat and there was no reasonable alternative (some courts hold that it need only be a substantial contributing cause)

        i. Alyeska would want to prove that they did not threaten and Totem had reasonable alternatives

        ii. Disagreement over the cause of hardship (not all courts care about this)

  iii. Modified Contract

    1. Going back and changing something about original contract, forming new contract

  iv. Policy—we don't want to let parties out of valid contracts because it undermines contract law, but if someone truly was coerced than we don't want to enforce these contracts

DURESS: SAMPLE #3

Traditional Duress

  a. You did something because someone forced you to

  b. Robbed the bank because there was a gun to your head

  c. This rarely happens

Economic Duress (Business Compulsion)

  a. Proverbial gun to your head

b. Only reason I entered into this contract was because I had no other choice

c. If you are able to prove you are the victim of duress, the remedy is to undo the contract

d. Rescind → undoing or voiding a contract (tear it up and throw it in the garbage)

e. Nobody breached if you are rescinding the contract... no consequences

Totem Marine Tug & Barge v. Alyeska Pipeline Serv.

Facts:

a. One party providing a service for the other, delivering cargo

b. Contract terminates, customer says I am going to pay you less money

c. Release agreement...

    i. Original contract

    ii. Release agreement

        1. A release is a separate agreement from the original contract

        2. The effect of the release is to rescind or undo the original contract

        3. This release was a product of duress...

        4. I only signed this release because I was under duress

d. You are going to deliver goods from here to there for $300k

e. Release → for $85k we are saying we are done with each other

f. This is in full satisfaction of the contract...

g. The party wants to be released from the release...

    i. They want to reinstate the original contract

h. Releases are one way to see duress cases...

    i. The other way is modification... basically identical

Modification

a. You have an original contract and at some point later, instead of a release, you have a modified contract

    i. There was 3x as much weight as they needed to transport... if they re-negotiated those terms, that would be a modification

    ii. There would be a new contract

b. Once you have a modified contract, this becomes the operative contract

    i. Often, the party will say they only agreed to pay more because of duress

c. Exact same scenario, but trying to get out of modified contract instead of release.

Judges

    a. Don't want to be too eager to let people out of their modifications

    b. If it is true someone signed one of these agreements because they are under duress, it seems unfair to hold them to this bargain

    c. If it truly is duress, maybe it shouldn't be enforceable

Section 175 of the Restatement

    a. If a party's manifestation of assent is adduced by an improper threat of a party that leaves the victim no other option

        i. Improper/Wrongful Threat

           1. Section 176 of Restatement

           2. You're threatening a crime or a tort

           3. You're threatening criminal prosecution

           4. Use of the civil process and acting in bad faith

           5. **MOST OFTEN THE CASE, THE THREAT IS A BREACH OF THE DUTY OF GOOD FAITH AND FAIR DEALING IN A CONTRACT**

               a. Usually people don't threaten a crime

               b. Usually the threat will be regarding something to the contract

                  i. Only going to give $10 instead of $100

                  ii. Where the exchange is not fair and you are trying to take advantage of another party

        ii. No reasonable alternative (but to give into the threat and sign the contract)

        iii. Causation (it is the threat that causes the party to enter into the contract)

        iv. In some courts but not all, the pressuring party has to have caused the hardship

    a. Alyeska is threatening to withhold payment

    b. The withholding of money is an improper threat

    c. The victim doesn't have any other reasonable alternative except to agree to the oppressor's terms

        i. Did you as the victim have any other choices?

           1. Filing of a lawsuit is a reasonable alternative

           2. Filing a lawsuit is going to take months or years, they would not see that money for a long time

d. **Depending on the facts**
   i. If you have a sale of goods and the supplier jacks up the price of bread
   ii. Instead of agreeing to their prices, you move on to someone else
   iii. Toleration of the threat is a minor vexation
   iv. Approach this from a commonsense point of view
      1. Could I have legitimately done something else instead of caving to the threat?
   v. No reasonable alternative because they had no way to pay their bills and were facing bankruptcy

e. **Causation**
   i. Not usually a big problem
   ii. If someone made an improper threat and you had nowhere to go, it follows that this is the cause

f. As long as the threat was a substantial contributing cause, then we are going to say the threat caused you to enter into the contract

Alyeska's Lawyer

a. They want to uphold the release
b. As the oppressing party you want to counteract:
   i. **The improper threat**
      1. It was the oppressive party making the improper threat that caused the weaker party to enter into this agreement
   ii. **The no reasonable alternatives**
      1. Am I the only deal in town? Do they have other accounts? Other sources of revenue? If you have other sources of revenue, you did have other choices, you could have paid off your debts and then sued us
      2. Is declaring bankruptcy a reasonable alternative? (probably not in this case)
         a. Maybe in a smaller business with lower stakes?
      3. Opening bid was $50k... negotiated it up to $85k... interesting
      4. Could they have done something beforehand? ... interesting
      5. Go to the bank and see if you can get a low interest loan
      6. If you as the oppressive party can show some break, the other party doesn't win

    iii. Causation

        1. One and three

    iv. Caused the hardship?

        1. *The oppressive party has to cause the hardship...*

Notes:

Duress is going to be a hard claim to make

Requirements are strict

Often you won't find an overt threat

Most parties have options other than agreeing to a modification or release

* * *

The correct answer is... 1!! Sample 1 is my version of a duress outline. Samples 2 and 3 are actual, verbatim, student outlines. Let me talk you through why samples 2 and 3 are not good outlines.

Sample 2 is very sparse; it barely contains any information. It is hyper-bulleted with very little meat. When a student picks this up after four months of not seeing the doctrine, they will have a hard time understanding the material based on the outline. Also (and you wouldn't know this), things are in the wrong place. The student fails to list several circumstances that constitute an improper threat and he/she makes hardship part of causation when it's a whole separate thing. It may look nice and bulleted, but it's like taking random notes and then automatically formatting them with bullets. It doesn't work.

Sample 3 has a lot of information, but it is all over the place. For instance, the student throws the Restatement section covering duress in the middle of the page, puts random notes down at the bottom and spends way too much time on the case brief. Also, you've gone way too deep into bullets when you have an (a), (i), (5), (b), (ii). Moreover, this student, like the other student, doesn't write in full sentences. When they go to study months later, the couple of words they've jotted down literally won't mean anything to them. For instance, the student writes "Nobody breached if you are rescinding the contract... no consequences." What does this mean? *I* know what it means, but I guarantee the student won't. It means that if the contract is rescinded because of duress, then, by definition, it is not a breach of contract. Therefore, you can't sue or be sued for breach ("no consequences"). But because the student failed to spell this out, this sentence will be gobbledygook when they read it prior to the exam.

9. Extreme Makeover: Outline Edition

I thought it would be helpful to show you how an outline could be improved to make it a more effective study tool. Below is an outline that one of my students, Makayla, submitted on the doctrine of mutual mistake. Without changing the substance, I reworked Makayla's outline to make it be more user friendly. I ensured consistency in formatting, cut down on the number of subheadings, and made the outline more narrative.

Makayla's Original Outline

I. **MUTUAL MISTAKE**

Mutual Mistake Generally
- Where both parties make a mistake.
- A mistake is defined as a belief that is not in accord with the facts.

Historical View of Mutual Mistake
- In the 1800's when the doctrine was first adopted, courts considered whether the misunderstanding was to substance or value.
- Where the mistake went to the substance or essence then the court would allow a recission
  - Ex: Cow case where the mistake was as to whether the cow was barren and that would affect the price and ability to use the cow. The seller wanted to get out of the K. The court viewed it as going to the substance. On the other hand if the cow was being used for milk then it would go to value because does not change the nature of the thing being sold.
- This old approach is no longer good because the two things are related. If something goes to the substance it has a direct impact on the value.

Current view of Mutual Mistake: Element Based
1. Has to be a mutual mistake as to a fact in existence at the time the K was made
- Fact in contrast with prediction.
- Here a fact is a provable statement not an opinion or though or prediction

2. Mistake relates to a basic assumption of the parties upon which the K was made and which materially affects the agreed performances of the parties.
   Restated
- A material fact that affects performance so the performance is no longer valuable to one of the parties

3. Assumption of Risk
- Did one of the parties bear the risk?
- is the party that is trying to get out of the K bear the risk? If so then you dont get to rescind if you assumed the risk on the basis of mistake

Three scenarios under the RST where the party bears a risk
1. When the risk is allocated to him by agreement

Restated

- K allocates the risk.

Example: "As is" clause example

2. Aware at the time the K is made that he has only limited knowledge as to the mistake but treats limited knowledge as sufficient

Restated

- Conscious ignorance standard- treating your limited knowledge as enough and moving forward with the transaction there is a due diligence requirement, can't allow people to say oops.

3. When the risk is allocated to him by the court in the instance that ,,,catchall

Restated

- Court allocates the risk

Case Application for Mutual Mistake

Lenawee County Board of Health v. Messerly

1. Has to be a mutual mistake as to a fact in existence at the time the K was made
   - In the Lenawee case, the mutual mistake was that the septic tank or system was working.
   - How would the septic not have been a problem?
     - If it was broken after the K was signed, then it does not engage mistake at all because the first element says that it has to be in existence at the time it was made.

2. Mistake relates to a basic assumption of the parties upon which the K was made and which materially affects the agreed performances of the parties.
   - The septic system functionality was a materially important fact because you can't live on a property where the septic tank doesn't work
   - It mattered here because the buyers thought the building was habitable and in turn could be used to for apartments so it affected their performance by preventing them from renting the property and they spent a ton of money on a property that needs to be condemned so they overpaid for the property

3. Assumption of Risk
   - Here there court reasoned that the P's assumed the risk because of the as is clause in the K.
   - The court allocated the risk to them because of what the K said

Question: There seems to be an overlap between this doctrine and those previously covered. Why is this case different?

Answer:

- This case not non disclosure because the septic tank malfunction was something that the seller did not know and under the doctrine of non disclosure, sellers do not have a duty to disclose something that you do not know.
- This is not misrepresentation because they never made the statement that this septic tank works perfectly or that there is no issue with it.

Makayla's Reworked Outline

MUTUAL MISTAKE

A. Mutual Mistake Generally

- Occurs where both parties make a mistake (a mistake is defined as a belief that is not in accord with the facts).
- In the 1800's when the doctrine was first adopted, courts considered whether the misunderstanding was to substance or value.
- Where the mistake went to the substance or essence then the court would allow a recission
    o Ex: Cow case where the mistake was as to whether the cow was barren and that would affect the price and ability to use the cow. The seller wanted to get out of the K. The court viewed it as going to the substance. On the other hand if the cow was being used for milk then it would go to value because does not change the nature of the thing being sold.
- This old approach is no longer good because the two things are related. If something goes to the substance it has a direct impact on the value.

B. Current View of Mutual Mistake: Element Based

1. Mistake of Fact: Has to be a mutual mistake as to a fact in existence at the time the K was made

   - Fact in contrast with prediction.
   - Here a fact is a provable statement not an opinion or though or prediction

2. Basic Assumption: Mistake relates to a basic assumption of the parties upon which the K was made and which materially affects the agreed performances of the parties.

   - A material fact that affects performance so the performance is no longer valuable to one of the parties

3. Assumption of Risk: Did one of the parties bear the risk?

   - Is the party that is trying to get out of the K bear the risk? If so then you dont get to rescind if you assumed the risk on the basis of mistake
   - Three scenarios under the RST where the party bears a risk

     1. When the risk is allocated to him by agreement

        o K allocates the risk, for example: "As is" clause

     2. Aware at the time the K is made that he has only limited knowledge as to the mistake but treats limited knowledge as sufficient

        o Conscious ignorance standard- treating your limited knowledge as enough and moving forward with the transaction there is a due diligence requirement, can't allow people to say oops.

     3. When the risk is allocated to him by the court in the instance (catchall)

        o Court allocates the risk based on fairness

B. Case Application

Lenawee County Board of Health v. Messerly
Facts: buyer and seller [insert a couple sentences]
Held: buyer could not rescind

Application:

1. Has to be a mutual mistake as to a fact in existence at the time the K was made

   - In the Lenawee case, the mutual mistake was that the septic tank or system was working.
   - How would the septic not have been a problem?
   - If it was broken after the K was signed, then it does not engage mistake at all because the first element says that it has to be in existence at the time it was made.

2. Mistake relates to a basic assumption of the parties upon which the K was made and which materially affects the agreed performances of the parties.

   - The septic system functionality was a materially important fact because you can't live on a property where the septic tank doesn't work
   - It mattered here because the buyers thought the building was habitable and in turn could be used to for apartments so it affected their performance by preventing them from renting the property and they spent a ton of money on a property that needs to be condemned so they overpaid for the property

3. Assumption of Risk
   - Here there court reasoned that the P's assumed the risk because of the as is clause in the K.
   - The court allocated the risk to them because of what the K said

Question: There seems to be an overlap between this doctrine and those previously covered. Why is this case different?
   - This case not non disclosure because the septic tank malfunction was something that the seller did not know and under the doctrine of non disclosure, sellers do not have a duty to disclose something that you do not know.
   - This is not misrepresentation because they never made the statement that this septic tank works perfectly or that there is no issue with it.

* * *

I picked a short and straightforward topic (topics do get more complicated than this!). The goal was to show you how much more organized the reworked version is. If you're thinking, *I could have learned the material based on Makayla's first outline,* I wouldn't necessarily disagree with you. But multiply this by about 100, in terms of length, and then by four (for your first semester classes). 400 pages of disorganized material is not easy to study from.

10. Student Reactions to My Method of Outlining

I would say that about 80% of students who have implemented my method of outlining have gotten fully on board. The other 20% either didn't see the method to my madness or decided to go at it their own way. Recall that I implemented what I called Option 2 in my Contracts class, which involved submitting outlines every week for credit and taking three quizzes throughout the semester.

Here are some student reflections on the outlining portion of Option 2:

[P]icking Option 2 was the best decision I could have made this semester. Option 2 helped me with developing my note-taking skills, my organization of information in my notes, focusing more on analysis, and my retention of information. I feel as though I already know the gist of everything that will be on the final because we have already had three tests on the material. I feel comfortable with the Contracts final coming up (and I never would have been able to say that last year) just because of Option 2 and it essentially forcing me to outline and retain that information. It got to the point where I would get excited in class because I was able to organize the information for my outline later; I got a strange satisfaction from filling out the outline, organizing it, and submitting it. I brought these skills from Option 2 into my other classes, especially in my outlines. I organize my outlines the way you suggested for Option 2 and I feel as though I can grasp the material better and have clearer analysis because of the way you guided us in our outlining. I also noticed an overall difference in my thinking due to the outline because, before, I was focusing too much on extra information in my case briefs that were not important. However, the outline format helped me condense that information and have a more effective outline and study-aid....Option 2 helped me become less complacent in my learning because law school is all about the long-game where the final is worth 100% of your grade so it is tempting to tune out mid-semester, but Option 2 doesn't let you do that! I truly am so glad that I picked Option 2 and really would recommend it to anyone that wants to do well in law school because it develops great habits. I can honestly say that I never had the motivation to outline every single week after classes, but Option 2 really showed me how effective and beneficial that is. It is one thing to be told you should constantly be outlining and going over information, but it is another to actually "have to do it" and see the results. When I picked Option 2, I prepared myself for a marathon and a lot of pain and stress. But now I can honestly say that Contracts is the exam I feel the best about and I never would have said that last semester.

Initially, I thought that this would be a breeze. I felt that my outline from last semester, considering that I was happy with my grade, was written well enough to allow me to do well on the outline submission and the quizzes. The reality was far from that. After submitting my first outline I was very disappointed with how I had performed and began to question the decision I made in choosing option 2. I began dismissing the process, fighting myself internally, and being stubborn in applying the feedback I was receiving and just continued performing in a way I believed was the way my brain naturally conceptualized the doctrines we were presented with in class. I didn't know that in being reluctant to apply the feedback, I was only hurting myself. I was stopping myself from really learning this organizational skill that has now helped me in so many ways. After constant struggle with myself, I caved in and decided to apply the feedback to see if this would actually help me learn better. This was truly the best decision because since taking this step, I have seen a great amount of improvement in the way I study for the quizzes and how much easier it is to fully know the elements of doctrines and apply them. Also, I found that this learning style allows me to retain the material a lot longer than the studying techniques I was used before [sic].... This option is honestly the way all law school classes should be run because I genuinely believe that this method of teaching would have an incredible effect on bar passage rates because the level of understanding is much more nuanced and the retention level is far more long lasting as compared to the crash studying methods many students including myself in certain classes partake in in preparing for exam. With this method, the material will stay with us longer and, if anything, we have a great outline to fall back on with tons of examples to refresh our memory. I am really glad I chose this option and hope to apply what I learn to every aspect of my law school career.

As I reflect on this semester, I realize that several things have changed about the way I approach law school. This semester, I believe, I have taken a more active role in my education and I believe Option 2 has been a reason for that change. I now spend more time reviewing class notes, being engaged in the conversations occurring in class, and organizing material as it's being presented to me. Option 2 has kept me on my toes in a way, ensuring I was actively learning and retaining material. This process has taught me how to properly outline and how to present material in the simplest yet most comprehensive way. I have created outlines for all of my courses using this format and I believe I am already better prepared for finals this semester than I was last. As I am studying for the final exam, I have realized that this process has helped me retain information from the beginning of the semester, and, instead of cramming it all into my brain now, I already have a solid base of knowledge.

As someone who was not "organized" prior, I did believe that my notetaking and outlining were at least decent. However, the experience with the outlining for this assignment was that my notes and outlining were all over the place.

I began realizing that I was under the illusion that my outlining was organized just because I was putting a lot [of] bullet points without there being any real reason for them until it was pointed out. The same goes with my spacing and the overall format of my notes. At the beginning of the outlining assignment, it did feel as though the process was time consuming and hyper-technical on formatting instead of the overall substance. As the weeks progressed, however, I stopped thinking about how the outlining was just an assignment to be done and came to realize that as I was focusing on formatting the outline, I was at the same time focused on the substance of the material and trying to make certain parts of my notes "fit." This made my notes easier to read not only substance wise but format wise. The addition of the white spacing and the eliminating bullets that were not necessary made my notes easier to follow.... Outlining the material helped studying for the test. The outline helped me as I was not going all over the place looking in my notes and my outline for the right concepts as everything was formatted in way that was easier to read and find. The material was easier to retain and the outlining definitely made studying for the test a lot easier. Hopefully this trend continues for the final. I do feel that my confidence and my overall understanding of the material has improved.

When I first began option 2, I struggled immensely with the outlining process. My outlines were unorganized and missing large chunks of important informa-tion. After the first week, what I needed to improve on was obvious but around week 3, I became frustrated because I was still struggling with the outlining process and wasn't too sure where to go from there. Although the way I had outlined first semester seemed to have worked for me then, the requirement for the outlining process for option 2 was a lot more organized than what I was used to. However, after multiple meetings and helpful feedback, when I finally conquered the outlining process, I felt a huge sense of accomplishment. I feel that with the organization of my outline, I am much more comfortable with the material. I have now transferred my outlining techniques from option 2 to my other doctrinal courses which has made the outlining process faster and more organized.... Overall, option 2 has made me work harder, prepare better for the final exam and learn contracts more efficiently.

Personally, I feel it helped to refine my outlining skills. I had a way of doing things last semester that I felt was great. However, after doing Option #2, I re-alized that organization is key and way more important than I thought. Having a succinct way of doing things makes the learning easier because your brain does less work, it just has to learn. Also, I felt that outlining throughout the semester helped me learn and retain information long-term, rather than just memorize. Last semester I would outline in chunks, maybe two or three times throughout the semester for weekends at a time, then I memorized the entire outline before the exam. Don't get me wrong I did very well on the exam, but as soon as I was done with the exam the information left my brain. While doing Option #2, I can see a huge difference in my ability to retain information, which is better for the bar exam. After each week of outlining and then going back to revise it, I was able to actually learn the information rather than just regurgitate it. Moreover, I am not as stressed out about the upcoming exam either because I don't have to memorize 80 pages worth of information, mostly I just have to review what I already know.

Through Option 2, I learnt how to outline, prioritize my time, note taking skills and general organization skills. The skills I learnt during Option 2 helped me in my other doctrinal classes especially when it came to outlining, which made studying easier. These skills transferred to outlining my other classes to the extent that I sent my Property outline to a friend who made a comment saying, "Your outline looks great and easy to understand like it was being graded by Professor Monestier." This is one of the many testimonies I have received about my outlines for different classes. This is the first semester that I can confidently say that I understood what was going on in contracts. Last year, I disliked contracts because I did not understand the concepts, but this semester has been different and it is because of Option 2. Option 2 forced me [to] re-teach myself the concepts after class through outlining, studying and Cali Lessons. I realized the helpfulness of Option 2 when I was studying for the exam. It was more like a review for me because I had studied for the quizzes beforehand. It made the revision easier and for the first time in my 1L year, I felt confident in contracts because I understood the doctrines and knew how to apply them. Even after the exam, I realize some mistakes I had made or some doctrines I could have argued but because of time constraints I was not able to make them. All in all, it made me see contracts in a different light and has been very helpful.

I'd like to add my voice to the chorus singing praises to [Self-Regulated Learning]….I can already sense the difference this pedagogical method will make. It's forcing me to slow down and evaluate my knowns and unknowns, and I've even rooted out some unknown unknowns in the process. I think the class has reached a consensus that this is the best method by which to learn any material, not just contracts or even law. It's refreshing that you care enough to put us (and yourself) through the process of continuous self-evaluation. In case there were any doubts, I think you're definitely doing the right thing here and that it is a worthy academic experiment.

FIVE

A Game Plan for Studying

I've missed more than 9,000 shots in my career.
I've lost almost 300 games.
26 times, I've been trusted to take the game-winning shot and missed.
I've failed over and over again in my life. And that is why I succeed.

MICHAEL JORDAN

1. Studying Does Not Mean the Same Thing to You as It Does to Me

Professors and books use the term "study" as though its meaning were self-evident. What it means to study is not self-evident. And I just want to prepare you now for the reality that my version of studying is probably *very different* than your version of studying.

My version of studying is also different than other professors' version of studying. I came across the following sample study schedule in a popular law school academic support book:

1. Read case briefs once.
2. Read outline twice.
3. Review Contracts flashcards with study group.
4. Work through one practice offer and acceptance question and one consideration question.[1]

---

1. I've adjusted it slightly to reflect the subject area I teach in, Contracts.

I about had a heart attack when I read this.[2] Not because I was insecure about my method of studying, but because it alarms me that students are getting what I think is bad advice. It is literally the opposite of what I'm going to tell you to do.

I am going to tell you not to read and re-read your outlines, but to *memorize* them. Totally different thing.

I am going to tell you that flashcards are a waste of your time.

I am going to tell you that study groups are a waste of your time.

I am going to tell you that practice questions have limited utility.

WT*? Actually, WT**? How is it possible that two different professors have diametrically opposed views on what it means to study? I don't know. But I'm fairly sure I'm right. And I've got the gold medal to prove it. And that's, what, the third reference to my gold medal? But, whose counting?

2. Start Studying for Exams at Least a Month Beforehand

I can't emphasize this enough: Exams are *everything* in law school. In most classes, exams and exams alone will determine your entire grade. All the reading, briefing, note-taking, and participation you've done is virtually meaningless, except as a lead-up to the exam.

You need a game plan. You need to understand what study techniques are effective and what study techniques are ineffective. You need to be open to new ways of studying. Being wedded to the refrain "But, this is how *I* learn" is not the way to go into this.

Many students balk at the idea of studying for exams anything more than a few days to a week ahead of time. I can almost guarantee that these students will not do well on the exam. Or, if they happen to do well on one exam, they will not have sustained success in law school. To do well on an exam, you must really learn and understand the material. The only way to do this is by giving yourself enough time to study.

The common objection, of course, is "I don't have time." You have to make time. If that means cutting back on the amount of time you are reading and

---

2. Much of the advice out there is, in my opinion, f**king terrible. Either that, or I'm f**king out to lunch.

preparing for class, then so be it. If it means you forego your daily 75-minute workout, then such is life. If it means you don't get to watch television for a month, then oh well. You absolutely need to find the time to do this.

At the beginning, it does not need to be a lot of time. It can be an hour a day during the week and more time on the weekend. As you get closer to the exam, you'll have to devote more of your waking hours to studying.

You will need a written study schedule. You should probably devise one on a weekly basis with your study goals for that week. You will need to simultaneously be studying for all your upcoming exams, so it will be important to figure out what to study when.

Let me give you an example of what I mean by a weekly study schedule. Let's say that you're taking four first-year doctrinal courses: Contracts, Torts, Criminal Law, and Civil Procedure. For the sake of simplicity, let's assume you covered six chapters in each of these courses. Your study schedule might look something like this.

Monday: Study Chapter 1 of Contracts and Chapter 1 of Torts.

Tuesday: Review Chapter 1 of Contracts and Torts; Study Chapter 1 of Criminal Law.

Wednesday: Review Chapter 1 of Criminal Law; Study Chapter 1 of Civil Procedure.

Thursday: Review Chapter 1 of Civil Procedure; Study Chapter 2 of Contracts.

Friday: Review Day (Review all previously studied material).

Saturday: Study Chapter 2 of Criminal Law; Study Chapter 2 of Torts.

Sunday: Study Chapter 2 of Civil Procedure; Review Chapter 2 for all subjects.

You might also keep a separate visual chart of your progress where you tick off all that you've accomplished that week and notate what you have left to go. That will give you a sense of achievement. It's the same feeling you get when you cross things off a to-do list.

3. Study Bite-Sized Chunks and
Keep Revisiting Material

What most students do in undergrad is cram. They devote a few days before the exam to "studying" and then spend hours upon hours re-reading the material, writing and reciting flashcards, and talking through the material in study groups. I am going to suggest a very different approach. The approach starts with the premise that you absolutely should not cram. I think this is probably apparent, given that I've just told you to start studying a month beforehand.

The way you should study is by taking the material in bite-sized chunks. You will study these chunks until you've learned them. By "learn them" I mean you can recite them off the top of your head. Then—and only then—do you move on to the next chunk. But (and here's the important part!) you have to periodically go back to the chunks you've already learned to make sure they are still in your head. And you'll be doing this in all your subjects. I know, it sounds overwhelming, right? I promise, it's not so bad. And it's way more effective than cramming.

The method I've just described to you has a name: It's called "spaced repetition," and it has a strong backing in the science of learning. The technique is exactly what it sounds like. You learn something. You wait a short period of time and then revisit it. Then, you wait a longer period of time and revisit it again.

Focusing on just one subject (e.g., Contracts), spaced repetition for the topic of "offer and acceptance" might look like this:

But, of course, you're not just learning offer and acceptance. At a certain point, you're going to have to throw the next topic into the mix—let's say "consideration" (top arrow).

And every time you add a new topic (e.g., "promissory estoppel"—top arrow), you keep doing the same thing.

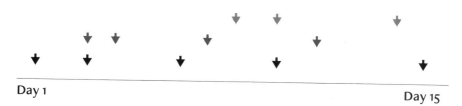

Day 1   **Day 15**

Essentially, your goal is to have "eyes on" the material on a regular basis. While this may look daunting, it's not that bad.

First, there are no hard-and-fast rules about spaced repetition. The general principle you should try to follow is that you revisit the material more frequently at the beginning and then less frequently as time goes on.

Second, describing it to you in written form makes it look complicated, but it's really not. If you were teaching a two-year-old how to count, this is the method you would use. One day, you would teach them the numbers up to five. The next day, you would get them to recite the numbers up to five and maybe add six and seven. A couple of days later, you might ask them to count to seven. A few days after that, you might add eight through ten.

Spaced repetition is what I use to work on my four-year-old niece, Emilia's, memory skills. I am the best and worst Zia of all time. The best because I am always in teacher mode. And the worst because I am always in teacher mode. I try to trick Emilia into thinking learning is a game. We have the word association game, the math game, and all sorts of other "games." For instance, my mother has a bunch of Royal Doulton dolls in a curio cabinet. Emilia recently asked what their names were. *Game time!!!* We picked seven dolls and gave them names (Ruby, Blueberry, Little Red Riding Hood, Noelle, Other Blueberry, Belle, and Flower Girl). The names were all given based on physical characteristics or memory associations. For instance, Belle is like Belle from Beauty and the Beast because she's in a yellow dress. Noelle is from the French word for Christmas because she's wearing a Christmas outfit.[3] After a day, I had Emilia recite all the dolls' names. She forgot two (Ruby and Belle). That

---

3. This is a different memory technique, and one that you probably use organically: making associations.

day, we also named two more dolls (Daffodil and Ms. Brittany). As you might guess, Daffodil has a yellow dress. Ms. Brittany is Emilia's teacher's name; she picked that name because the doll looked like a teacher. The following day, she recited all the dolls' names, but confused little Red Riding Hood with Ruby. We did this over the span of a week, gradually adding more and more names (Ms. Pauline,[4] Frida, Rapunzel, Cloudie,[5] Angel, Mama, Papa, Zia, and Dumbo). During this time, she forgot Frida three times (named after Frida Pinto),[6] called Daffodil Daisy, and was still a little shaky on which one was Little Red Riding Hood and which one was Ruby. But she can now recite all 18 doll names, no problem. She could probably recite the names without even looking at the dolls.[7] If these techniques can work on a child who needs help wiping her bum, they can work for you.

I will warn you, though, that spaced repetition is going to *feel* harder than cramming. This is because your brain will naturally forget stuff in time. It will feel like you've exerted all this effort to learn something, only to forget it and have to re-learn it again. But learning that is effortful and involves cognitive retrieval is what the whole goal of this is. That means it's working. It's like giving your brain a workout. No pain, no gain.

By studying in this way, you engrain the material in your brain so that it is *permanently* stored there, versus cramming where the material is lost a couple of days later. I feel like I read somewhere[8] that by revisiting the material over and over you are re-wiring your brain circuitry so that you have a straight path to the information.

Two analogies might be helpful.

---

4. Her other teacher.

5. My niece takes after me in that she comes up with the most unoriginal names for things. As you might guess, Cloudie is a doll that is sitting on a cloud. I'm totally this way too. If I had a dog, I would name it "Dog."

6. Her mom has a master's degree in Art History.

7. Note to self: Try this. Call it the "eyes closed" game.

8. I fear I'm turning into my dad, claiming knowledge I don't actually have. My dad throws out a lot of data, but I'm pretty sure he's making most of it up. How do I know this? Because of the 90% rule. Every statistic out of his mouth is 90%. "90% of students graduate from college." "90% of people vote for the same political party that they voted for last time." "Bill Gates is planning on giving away 90% of his net worth." But he says it so compellingly, you can't help but believe him. What's most interesting is that those times when I have tried to verify his 90% statistic, he has ended up being mainly correct.

Computer Analogy: If there are certain websites you visit often, the computer has a short-cut to these websites. I don't know how this works in the slightest—maybe something to do with cache or cookies. Who knows, who cares? My point is that the magicians who created the internet or the computer, or both, figured out a way to get you to Poshmark[9] or ESPN faster.

Lawn Analogy: Picture a house situated on the corner of a street. Instead of walking on the sidewalk all the way around the house, pedestrians cut across the lawn as a shortcut. The first time this happens, the grass is matted but springs back up. Second and third time, same thing. Eventually, though, if enough people take the shortcut, what happens? You will have a nice little bald patch running diagonally across the lawn. The lawn is your brain. Walking across the lawn is you revisiting the material over and over again. Eventually, you will have a straight path (devoid of grass) to the material in your brain. Moreover, that path will be permanent. It will still be there come time to study for the bar exam or when you are in practice.

Okay, now that I've given you the (let's call it) dumbed-down version of spaced repetition, let's look at how a couple of professors describe it. By the way, they call "cramming" by the fancier-sounding term "massing study":

As soon as we learn something new, we start to forget it. By periodically retrieving learned information, we slow the forgetting process. During periodic review or spacing study, the opposite of cramming or massing study, learners retrieve material after a period of time—days or weeks—has elapsed between study sessions to allow for forgetting before the next retrieval attempt. Spacing multiple study sessions over time is far superior to massing study in any single session because retrieval practice spaced over time stops the forgetting process.

But, spacing study feels less effective as students have to work harder to retrieve information from days or even weeks ago. When students learn a topic and wait a week or two to review the same material, the information is hard to recall and students feel like they are relearning material they already learned.

Like rereading, massing study creates illusions of competence when material that is easier to recall is judged better learned than material that is harder to recall. This is counter-intuitive because massing study works, only as long as a test is immediately after the massed study. But, what if the test is given a

---

9. This is the equivalent of Depop for anyone over the age of 30.

week or more later? Spacing study requires time between study sessions where information is forgotten, requiring students to retrieve or recall the previously studied material. The less accessible the memory, the more learning occurs when it is recalled and restudied.

One of the criticisms of retrieval is that it is only beneficial for memorization and other lower-order thinking and learning tasks. However, successive retrieval-based learning spaced over periods of time helps learners develop complex knowledge structures, connect and integrate new information to prior knowledge structures, and build depth and complexity with each successful retrieval and consolidation cycle. This process differentiates novices from experts in a field. When experts retrieve information, experts retrieve an entire integrated network of existing, interconnected information built over multiple retrieval and consolidation cycles spaced over years.[10]

I can't tell you how many students had no clue about this method of studying. I had a conversation with one student, Tiana, whose law school world was revolutionized by spaced repetition. Okay, "revolutionized" might be too strong a word. Tiana couldn't fathom not sitting down and studying everything at once. She just thought that was how you studied. When I suggested she try spaced repetition, she was hesitant. But she eventually tried it and it worked for her. At the end of the semester, Tiana wrote me this:

The greatest tool I have taken out of this experience is the spaced repetition method of studying. From the first quiz to the second, my score doubled (although still significant room for improvement) and my confidence by the third quiz increased as well. For the first time in law school I felt like I was on top of all the material and did not feel overwhelmed....

I am excited that I embraced [this method] and really put my best foot forward because it gave me a new perspective on studying. By the end, I found myself excited to outline and stay on top of the material.... I believe all students should try this method because I was adamant that this would not work for me, but it did.... I am excited and proud of my ability to begin studying several weeks out and not feel overwhelmed by the amount of material.

---

10. Jennifer M. Cooper & Regan Gurung, *Smarter Law Study Habits: An Empirical Analysis of Law Learning Strategies and Relationship with Law GPA*, 62 St. Louis U. L.J. 361, 372–73 (2018).

Spaced repetition is how I studied for every one of my exams. Not because I knew about the science of learning or anything, but because that was the only way that made sense to me. I have never, ever crammed in my life. And when November 1st comes around every year, I start urging my students to begin studying. They look at me like I just sprouted antlers. But *believe me*[11] . . . this is the way to go.

4. Flash Cards Are for Undergrads

This is going to be a controversial topic. Stop reading here if you are not going to keep an open mind. I say, "Ditch the flash cards." For most students this simply Does. Not. Compute.

Students are very wedded to their flash cards. I'm not sure when this trend started. Or maybe I just missed the boat on this trend entirely. But almost all students are comfortable with flash cards, used them in undergrad, and want to use them in law school. When I say to ditch them, it's like suggesting that I throw away their favorite childhood toy. Like I said, stick with me on this one.

Flash cards are not bad *per se*. But the light is just not worth the candle. I read that in a legal judgment once (*Beals v. Saldanha*, in case you're wondering) and it has stuck with me ever since.

Let me explain why. Three years ago, I had a meeting with 15 or so students who did not perform well on their first Contracts quiz. I started off with troubleshooting questions. I asked how many of them used flashcards. Fifteen people raised their hands. I asked how long it took them to prepare the flashcards; most said two to three days. I asked them how long they studied from the flashcards. They said, "about a day." They went over the cards four or five times.

I found this conversation illuminating. From my perspective, it is hard to imagine why a student would spend two-thirds or more of their available study time on what is simply a ministerial[12] task—i.e., writing out flashcards. And, if you think you are learning by writing them out, when you are simultaneously watching TV and occasionally texting, you are kidding yourself.

What is it about this little sheet of paper that is so special? No one could really answer me except to say that this is how they've always done it. Just

---

11. "Believe me" is a Grazian-ism.
12. Another law word!

because this is how you've always done it does not mean that this is how you should continue to do it.

Law school requires you to learn a lot of information. This is necessarily going to involve memorization. Then you need to go deeper and prepare for exam questions. When you are wasting so much time writing out by hand information that you've *already memorialized in your outline*, you are simply not going to have the time you need to adequately prepare. As I've said before, time is your most precious commodity.

I asked the students if they were just copying verbatim what was in their outline onto their flashcards. They said yes. I was still baffled. But why would you do this when you already have the information on paper? (albeit bigger sheets of paper). Cue the "but this is how *I learn*" chorus.

Reality to 1L Student: The size of your piece of paper does not determine how you learn. Even you have to (perhaps, grudgingly) admit that is somewhat ridiculous.

I was gobsmacked[13] by the widespread resistance to simply learning from the outline, which is, after all, the document you worked on all semester to help you prepare for the exam. I suggested a compromise. For two reasons: (1) to illustrate the absurdity of the "I only learn with small paper" approach and (2) to save students from themselves.

I suggested that students format their outline to include space between the different topics and then take scissors to the outline. You heard me. Cut up your damned outline into flashcards with a pair of scissors. It's a hell of a lot faster than spending three days writing out flashcards with a Bic pen.

The suggestion seemed to jolt this group into reality. I think they began to imagine a universe that did not involve flash cards. Though they weren't really sold yet, just *slightly* open to the idea. At least I had an in!

I then explained that if they didn't want to do the scissor method (which was intended as a joke, but theoretically could work), I would suggest the "cover and write" method. I suggested that they study a page of their outline, cover it up, and then write it all out in shorthand on a different sheet of paper.

I actually think the "cover and talk" method is far more efficient. It doesn't take a PhD to figure out what that is. After studying your outline, you cover

---

13. I've never been able to use that word before. So, yay!

it up and try to recite it out loud. Then you double check and see what you missed. Then you do it again. And again. And...well, you get my drift.

There is also another reason that I am not a fan of flash cards: because they present the law in an overly simplified and disembodied way. Oftentimes, students mix their flash cards up. And while this is actually a good way of learning some subjects, it's probably not a great way of learning law. To go from the definition of an offer, to the elements of promissory estoppel, to the measure of damages for an aggrieved buyer in a sales contract, feels random and nonsensical. In law school, you need to understand doctrines *as a whole* and how they fit with other doctrines. To jump from one topic to another to another really means that you're not adequately getting the full picture. You are memorizing, perhaps, but not learning.

You should get to the point where you are able to recite everything you know about a given topic. No hesitating. No thinking. No faltering. It should be a part of you. When you get to that point, then you are ready to move on to working through problems and preparing for how to tackle the exam.

I may not have sold you. That's okay. I know I faced an uphill battle. I'm fairly sure that it's a little early to be writing a eulogy for the trusty flash card.

5. You Must Memorize Material

Many law professors look with disdain upon memorization. They will say things like, *I don't want you to memorize. I want you to think, apply, and analyze.* Yeah, well, that stuff can't happen unless you memorize.

I don't love the word "memorize" because it has somewhat of a pejorative connotation. It seems to imply that you have learned the rule, definition, or doctrine and can recite it, but that you don't necessarily understand it. I prefer the word "internalize" to signal a sort of memorization *plus*. Regardless, it's all just semantics.

Memorization is important because some portion of the exam will involve you explaining the law. You don't want to be fumbling around for the right words for how to phrase something on an exam. You do not have time for that. You need to have the material locked and loaded in your brain and ready to spit out on paper.

I frequently encounter the law student in class who I can tell understands the material but is simply not able to articulate it. Of course, some of this is nerves, but not usually. Many students just can't say what is in their brain out loud. Which probably also means they wouldn't be able to put it on paper.

This is the difference between familiarity and knowledge. A student who is familiar with the information "gets it" on some level but will have trouble articulating it. A student who has memorized the material will be able to easily recite that information and then engage with the harder parts of the question.

The study techniques that most undergraduates and law students use breed familiarity, not knowledge. Things like re-reading material over and over, listening to an audio-recording of a class multiple times, watching YouTube videos,[14] and reading about a doctrine in a study aid are not effective study techniques. This is because they are entirely passive. The material will just not stick in your brain if you use these techniques. But the worst thing about these techniques is not even that they are ineffective—it is that they create the *illusion* of mastery. A student feels like they understand the material because they have seen it a number of times. This leads to a false sense of security as students go into exams.

Studying is like upside-down land. If it's hard, you are learning. If it's easy, you are not learning. Re-reading and re-watching are easy. Reciting the Article 2 version of the statute of frauds, along with the exceptions, is not.

Here is how a class valedictorian described his approach to studying for law school:

> I don't know that I have any other suggestions except to reiterate the importance of outlining early and often. I think that doing well is just about putting in the time and hard work, there's no short cut and trying to find it is just going to waste time 1Ls don't have. Other than that, just keeping it simple and using one word document for an outline is key. P.S. I spent countless hours in a cubicle in the library writing down everything I could remember about each topic over and over and that really helped to internalize the concepts (I'm sure I still have the notebooks to prove it!).

A different student of mine, who graduated second in his class, can still recite from memory almost everything he learned in Contracts three years later. When you have the material memorized, it will stay with you in some way, shape, or form for a long time. And that's a good thing.

---

14. Why, oh why?

6. You Don't Know the Material Well Enough Unless You Can Explain It to a Child

I don't want you to misconstrue the "memorization" section above. I am not saying that you should memorize a whole bunch of random rules until you know them by heart. Okay, I am saying that...but you need to do more than that. You need to truly *understand* what you're memorizing.

The way you know if you truly understand what you're learning is to break down the material as simply as possible and then try to explain it as though you were talking to a child. If you can do this, you understand the material at the level you need to understand it. If not, you are not ready for an exam.

Let me give you an example. I'm going to use the parol[15] evidence rule because I use it in the "Pre-Write Your Answer" section (coming up!). In that section, there's a whole bunch of legal talk. But to be able to engage with the material at that higher level, you need to understand what the heck the parol evidence rule is about.

The rule provides that where parties have agreed to integrate a final version of a written agreement, then neither party will be permitted to supplement or contradict the terms of that agreement with extrinsic evidence of prior or contemporaneous agreements, understandings, representations, or the like. *What the...?* Now, you could just memorize the definition, but that is completely meaningless. You need to understand what this means. Explain it to a five-year-old.

Here's how you would do it. You'd say something like the following: Sometimes parties sign really detailed written contracts. They want those contracts to be the be-all and end-all of everything. If you have one of those written contracts, then neither side can say, "But you promised [blank] before we signed the contract." In other words, you cannot try to bring in something the other person said that would go against what is in the written contract. For example, let's say you buy a car. You sign a really detailed written contract with the car dealership. Before signing, the car dealer had told you that he'd throw in free mats if you bought the car. But the promise of free mats is not in the final written contract. The parol evidence rule is going to block the car dealer's statement from being considered. You're SOL. Be prepared to buy mats. Unless an exception applies. Okay, a five-year-old would probably not understand this. But you get my point.

---

15. No "e"! That's one of my pet peeves.

The approach of deconstructing the material into it simplest terms and explaining it to a beginner is referred to as the "Feynman Technique." I'm not sure why I'm giving him credit for this since it's how I studied for all my exams—and I had never heard of the Feynman Technique. But, whatevs.

Here's a quote I'll leave you with that is sometimes attributed to Albert Einstein, but may have been said by Richard Feynman instead: *If you can't explain it simply, you don't know it well enough.*

7. Study Groups Are Stupid

Study groups are a big thing in law school. Students feel like they have to get into the "right" study group in order to succeed in law school. Or, they feel like if they don't have a study group, they are doomed for failure. Professors and academic support push study groups, which ups the pressure even more.

Like much of the advice I give, I'm going to diverge from the majority view. Study groups are, in my opinion, not all that helpful. Maybe that is because I never had a study group in law school (yes, I was "that" girl). I literally studied for every single one of my exams in law school by myself in my bedroom. One of my classmates, Arthur, would occasionally call me to test his knowledge, usually the night before the exam. Incidentally, Arthur is now super-successful and married to one of my best friends.

Studying by myself worked for me. And I do believe that it is really the only way that students can adequately internalize the material. You need to grapple with the material by yourself to really be on top of it.

I am not opposed to having a study group that gets together on a few occasions *after* all the members have studied individually. At that point, students can go through hypotheticals and identify areas of confusion. Then, individual members can regroup on their own and get back to real studying.

What I do not think is advisable is trying to learn through study groups. There is a lot of bad information tossed out, and a lot of time gets wasted.[16] I have a rule about studying—if it's fun, you're not doing it right.

If you have a study group, use the group wisely. And if you don't have a study group, don't worry about it. *You* will be taking your final exam. On your own.

---

16. I once had a large study group that got the entire parol evidence rule wrong because they were all following each other's lead.

8. Hypotheticals Are Like Drugs

I have noticed a trend in the past three or four years. Students are *obsessed* with hypotheticals. They are addicted to them. They beg for them. They expect professors to dole out more and more of them.[17] The addiction must stop.

Don't get me wrong. Hypotheticals are great, in the right context. Professors should be going over hypotheticals in class so that you can see how the law applies to a given fact pattern. Hypotheticals are also a very helpful tool to use after you have studied.

The problem, at least as I have observed it, is that students are using hypotheticals to learn the material, rather than using hypotheticals to apply what they have learned and explore the boundaries of their knowledge. In other words, students are not studying their outlines and *then* turning to hypotheticals. They are largely ignoring their outlines, or perhaps passively reading them over a couple of times, and then trying to learn the material through hypotheticals.

It is certainly possible to learn through hypotheticals. But it is *highly* inefficient. And with the vast amounts of law school material you need to learn, what's the wisdom in doing it this way? Given that you have created an outline already, why would you pretty much ignore it and focus instead on hypotheticals? Several reasons present themselves.

First, studying the old-fashioned way—by memorizing material—is boring. Doing hypotheticals is way more engaging. Second, because hypotheticals are proactive (i.e., you have to work through the material), there is more of a sense of purpose associated with working through a hypothetical. Third, getting a hypothetical correct provides reinforcement that you are getting the material right (the high!).[18] Fourth, hypotheticals lend themselves to studying in groups and we know that students love to study in groups. Fifth, academic support personnel and "how to" books heavily push hypotheticals.

---

17. For example, my Sales class this semester involved pre-recorded classes and a 75-minute Zoom session. During that session, we exclusively did review and hypos (usually half a dozen or more problems per class). Apparently, a semester's worth of hypos was not enough. Here is a comment from a student: "I think spending more time giving hypos and handing them out in advance would be helpful.... The more examples and hypos the better. Or maybe having us try a hypo on our own first in advance of class." Dear Student: Get yourself to a Hypoholics Anonymous meeting.

18. This may lead to a false sense of security. Just because you got one hypothetical right does not necessarily speak to your ability to do well on the exam.

These are just my personal impressions on what might explain this hypothetical craze lately. And again, I want to repeat that hypotheticals are a valuable tool and *should* be used by law students. But perhaps not in the way that they are currently being used.

Here is how I think you should use hypotheticals. First and foremost, you need to study your outline (or a least a chunk of it) in the way I described earlier. When you feel like you know the material inside out, then turn to some hypotheticals. What you learn through the hypothetical then needs to make its way back into your outline.

For instance, let's say that you've studied offer and acceptance in bilateral contracts and feel like you understand everything about it. You then do a hypothetical and, after looking at the answer, realize you were making a major mistake: you thought the mailbox rule applied to all forms of communication, not just the acceptance of an offer.[19] Once you've realized your mistake, you must update your outline and re-study the material. Accordingly, studying and doing hypotheticals should be an iterative process.

One quick clarification: I am using hypotheticals as a generic term to refer both to shorter problems (say, from a book) as well as practice exams. Practice exams are just one big hypothetical. So usually, students want to do a gazillion hypotheticals during the semester and then a gazillion practice exams as part of the studying process.

Let me talk specifically about practice exams. I don't think I mentioned this yet, but I recently joined Twitter. I know, *welcome to 2012*. I joined not because I tweet, but because I want to spy on what's going on. Perfectly valid use of social media. In any event, there was a thread (that's what it's called, right?) where professors were chiming in on the most important "tip" they would give law students about preparing for exams.

I don't think professors should be giving "tips" about how to study. A tip to me just sounds like a shortcut—a fast and easy way of doing something. It took me over 100 pages to explain to you how I believe you should study (from reading to notetaking to outlining to memorizing to doing hypotheticals). If it took me 100 pages to do this, do you really think the advice is amenable to being encapsulated in a 280-character Twitter "tip"? Okay, now that I've got that off my chest...

---

19. This is a pretty major mistake. If you have made a mistake like this, you also need to get to the bottom of how this happened, so it does not happen again.

Almost all of the Twitter professors advised that students "do practice exams." I thought the advice was weird, or at least, missing something. How about, *learn the material extremely well* and then test your knowledge through practice exams? Maybe that was implicit in what they were saying, but I don't think so. And I don't think that students are doing the first part ("learn the material extremely well"). They are just skipping to the second part.

In fact, I came across advice from a leading academic support authority which makes it explicit that you should skip to the second part.[20] They suggest you do as many practice exams as possible. They suggest that you look high and low for practice exams—ask your professor, ask academic support, consult supplements, scour the internet. They suggest that you don't worry about having everything memorized or organized before practicing. Just PRACTICE! Here's a poem I made up to summarize this advice:

If you want to do your best in school,

Be sure you know the golden rule:

Do practice problems every day

And that will keep bad grades at bay.

Do practice problems on a train.

Do practice problems on a plane.

Do practice problems at the school.

Do practice problems by the pool.

Do practice problems in a Jeep.

Do practice problems in your sleep.

Do practice problems on your run.

Do practice problems just for fun.

Find practice problems everywhere.

Do practice problems anywhere.

Sorry, I couldn't resist! Clearly, we can cross creative writing off the list of things I'm good at.

---

20. This is an example of the conflicting advice I told you about earlier in the book. *Oh no, what to do?! Who to believe?* You figure it out.

I really don't think this is good advice. I said this before, and I'll say it again. You just spent all semester reading, going to class, taking notes, and preparing an outline. Why aren't you using all that to your advantage? Why are you glossing over what you did for four months and going straight to practice problems/practice exams?

More importantly, *what the f**k are you going to "practice" if you don't know the relevant law?* To use a sports analogy: it's like you're going to be playing a football game, but you don't know the rules. Isn't it better to learn the rules first, *then* try to play, rather than trying to learn the rules *by* playing? There's just too much to know to try to assimilate the law through practice exams. Think about it. You're going to learn four or five doctrinal courses *through* practice exams? Yup, that makes a lot of sense.

One other thing. Practice exams that are not drafted by your professor are virtually useless. Every professor will have a certain exam style and certain issues that they like to test. If you can get your hands on your professor's old exams, great. Use them. Practice. Whatever. But if you're going to some random exam bank to pull exams from another professor, that's just a waste of time. What some professor at Florida State conjured up on a Contracts exam ten years ago is not going to be the same thing I'm going to conjure up for you.

I will end on a final point. If you are insistent on doing every hypothetical or practice exam you can get your hands on and you don't agree with my advice, fine. You are the captain of your ship. All I would say is not to expect that your professors give you dozens of hypotheticals and a bunch of practice exams and then go through them with you. More on that coming up.

9. Pre-Write Your Answers

Many of the exams you will have in law school are open book. The theory behind open book exams is that the practice of law is, in effect, open book. Professors are not testing your ability to regurgitate the law, but to apply the law.

Beware of the open book exam trap. If it seems too good to be true, it is. Many students think that an open book exam will be easier than a closed book exam. They spend time perfecting their outline so that on the exam, they can just "look up" the right answer. Umm...it does not work that way. An open book exam is basically the professor telling you, "I don't care what you have in front of you. This exam is going to be so hard it won't even matter."

You need to prepare for an open book exam in the exact same way as a closed book exam. You should never have to open your textbook or turn to your outline during the exam. I say this from experience. Every single one of my exams in law school was open book. I did not consult my outline in any of my exams. In fact, my outline was under my chair during exams. If you subscribe to this mentality, then you will be a step ahead of everyone else who has been lulled into a false sense of security by an open book exam.

Open book exams present an excellent opportunity to pre-package your exam answers. There are only so many topics that a professor can test. You should write up sample answers (along with blanks for the facts) for every testable topic. Some topics lend themselves to this better than others. For instance, let's assume that you are pre-packaging a parol evidence rule answer. Your template might look something like this:

> The parol evidence rule is a rule that provides that where parties have agreed to a fully final and complete contract (an "integrated" contract) then neither party will be permitted to introduce extrinsic evidence of prior or contemporaneous statements, promises, or representations that contradict or supplement the terms of that agreement. The parol evidence rule is designed to give primacy to the written contract. These facts present a parol evidence rule problem because [**blank**] is trying to admit evidence of [**blank**] to [**supplement/contradict**] the terms of the parties' written agreement.
>
> To determine whether the evidence of [**blank**] is admissible, we must first determine whether we are dealing with an integrated contract. An integrated contract, as noted above, is a final and complete written memorialization of the parties' agreement. To determine whether the contract is integrated, there are two approaches:
>
> 1. The four corners approach: This approach determines integration by looking only to the four corners of the document itself. Here, [**application & conclusion**]
>
> 2. The contextual approach: This approach determines integration by examining the contract in light of the extrinsic evidence that the party is seeking to admit. The evidence is not yet admissible but is simply looked at to ascertain whether it bears on the finality and completeness of the contract. Here, [**application & conclusion**]

It is clear that under [**blank**] approach, the contract is likely integrated. Presumptively, if the extrinsic evidence supplements or contradicts the agreement, it is barred by the parol evidence rule.

Here, [**blank**] evidence [**supplements/contradicts**] the written agreement because [**blank**]. Accordingly, absent an exception, evidence of [**blank**] will be barred.[21]

Obviously, not everything is going to fit cleanly into your pre-packaged answers. But it is a good starting point, and it puts you ahead of the curve compared to your classmates who are just winging it.

Importantly, you should prepare a template for your answers even if you have a closed book exam. It need not be as detailed a template as for an open book exam. But you should know that if you are given a question on X, here are the five steps you're going to use to answer the question.

Here is an email I received from a student who took much of my outlining and exam advice, including the suggestion to pre-plan answers:

I just wanted to touch base on the exam preparation...

I did something very different and felt like a big girl when I took your advice. After reviewing my outline, memorizing material, and recalling it, I sat down and preplanned my answer. IT WAS AMAZING! The light bulb finally went off yesterday. I know, but better late than never, right?

It felt so good to preplan my answer. I can't describe the feeling, but I can tell you it felt like I was really discussing the doctrine with a client...

I know you said that preplanning is essential, but I never did it the way I did last night. I just wish I started this from the beginning. But it is okay! I'm taking summer classes so I'm going to use Option 2 Skills for them. I don't even know how else to say this, but I think you actually found the formula to academic success in law school.

Again, not sure if you know this, but this option changed my life. I'm not perfect and jeez did I miss stuff today, but I am getting better, and I have you to thank for that. I am very serious. Without Option 2 and support this semester, I do

---

21. The actual template would also contain all the exceptions as well as a discussion of merger clauses, but this was just to give you a rough idea of what I mean.

not think I would have survived with the pressure. I will not know my fate until grades are released in the summer and I know my GPA. But guess what? No matter what happens, I have the tools I need and will keep at it.

10. Practice Like You Play

I had never heard this expression before my husband used it at some point a couple of years ago. Since then, I've adopted it as my own. To be clear, I've been espousing the concept for years—I just didn't have a catchy phrase to give it.

When I was in law school, I would time myself writing out my sample answers from memory or taking a practice exam. Back in those days, we took exams *by hand*. I know, most of you can't even fathom that.[22] I would literally handwrite answer after answer until my hand hurt, as it invariably would the day of the exam. I was what you might call...hardcore.

This step is critical for two reasons. First, it will show you how well you are doing translating what is in your brain into black and white. It's one thing to "cover and write" or "cover and talk," and it's a whole different thing to write full sentences and paragraphs in a timed setting. Oftentimes, students realize during this stage that the process of putting what is in their minds onto paper is not as easy as they thought. You'd rather know that well in advance of the exam so that you can get better at it.

Second, even though you are starting a timer in the comfort of your own home and the timer literally means nothing at this stage, there will be an adrenaline boost associated with self-timing. This better approximates how you'll be feeling the day of the exam. Take that feeling and multiply it by ten. On exam day, your heart will be racing, your palms will be sweaty, your throat will feel tight, and you'll have butterflies in your stomach. Okay, maybe not all of these will happen to you—but some of them definitely will. It will be important to be able to perform under these real-world conditions.

---

22. My husband took his law school exams on a typewriter. Now, that's hard for even me to wrap my mind around.

SIX

Demystifying Exams

You get the job done or you don't.

BILL BELICHICK

1. Don't Count on an Exam Review Session

At the end of the semester, many professors have exam review sessions. These sessions are important because they can give you some clues into the professor's mindset in terms of grading (e.g., "Make sure to discuss policy arguments," or, "I will not read anything over x number of words."). They can also flag for you some bigger picture issues that the professor wants to bring to your attention. For instance, my exams are always tightly timed. This is deliberate. I'm not saying it's the best approach to drafting exams. I am saying it's my approach. This has consequences on your end. First, it means that you need to know the law cold, which I've already told you. Second, it means you need to be vigilant about time on the exam. You cannot go five minutes over here and ten minutes over there. If you do that, you will not get through the exam. I always warn students in the exam review session to force themselves to move on if they are at the time limit laid out on the exam. These sorts of things are invaluable nuggets that you will get from an exam review session.

But wait a sec…isn't the title of this section "Don't Count on an Exam Review Session?" I'm confused. Fair enough. Exam review sessions are important for the reasons I described above. But do not count on them to signal which areas of law will be tested or to re-teach the law.

I had a conversation with a student last semester who based his studying on his perception of the amount of focus I put on something in class. Really bad idea. Like I've said before, everything is fair game. Do not try to read the tea leaves. If anything, what you cover in an exam review session (e.g., through a hypothetical or sample exam) probably won't be on the real exam. But that would be reading the tea leaves, which I've told you not to do.

I think students regard exam review sessions as a condensed and digestible summary of the entire course. This makes no sense. I just spent 40 or 50 hours teaching you all the material you need to know. Do you think I can somehow capture all that material again in a one-hour review session? It's foolish for students to believe that a review session will provide a detailed and meaningful substantive recap of the material. And frankly, it's maybe a little unwise for professors to even have these sessions.[1]

2. Common Misconceptions About Exams

Law school exams are all pretty similar. They usually involve "fact patterns," and you are expected to apply the law you have learned to the facts. It's really not that hard, if you know the law. Many misconceptions prevail around law school exams. Here are the big ones.

A. Issue Spotting

First up, issue spotting. I kind of hate the term "issue spotting" because it suggests that it is *a thing*. I know I'm alone in the wilderness on this one, but I believe issue spotting is not really an independent skill. Instead, it's a function of knowing the law. In other words, if you understand the law as well as you should, you *will see* what legal issues are relevant. In this respect, it is a backward-looking relationship, not a forward-looking one. People make it seem like there's some magical "issue spotting" step in the exam process. There's not. Issue spotting is just what comes of knowing and understanding the law.

For example, let's assume that I've learned everything there is to know about Contracts. When I read the fact pattern, things will jump out at me. When I see an acceptance by mail, I will think "mailbox rule." When I see someone say, "I'll have my lawyer draft that up," I will think "formal contract contemplated."

---

1. I am excluding professors who use these sessions to go over a sample exam and/or to provide general guidance to students.

When I see someone paying $5 for a car, I will think "consideration." What I'm saying is that issue spotting comes from knowing the law. Accordingly, your focus should be on that, not on some esoteric notion of "issue spotting." I have trouble convincing students of this, so here are a couple of messages I got from 1Ls after their first semester Contracts exams that back me up:

> I personally felt that time was okay, I did not feel too rushed. Also, just as you said, the more you know the information, the better you will be able to spot issues. I felt that I was able to spot most of the issues and hopefully articulated and argued them well.

> First off, I am happy that one more exam is out of the way! The exam is what I expected, it was tough but fair. There were no surprises in my opinion. Like you said, after studying, the issues seemed to jump out at me.

Quick summary of this section: Issue spotting is not a thing.

B. The "Right" Answer

Second up. Getting the "right" answer. There is usually not a right answer on a law school exam. We professors made this exam up out of thin air. It's not a real case. These are not real people. There is no real answer. Your job is not to get the right answer, but to address the legal issues presented in a logical and comprehensive way. There is certainly an element of judgment involved. But we are far more interested in the back and forth of your argument than your legal conclusion. Unless, of course, your legal conclusion is a stupid one that does not flow from the analysis you just did. For instance, if you just spent forever arguing that Max is unlikely to have a restitution claim and then conclude that "there's a good chance" he'll succeed in restitution, that's a problem.

C. Organization

Third, organization. Students have this crazy idea that if they just "organized" their answer better, their grade would have gone from a C to an A. No. Organization is not what distinguishes good from bad answers. Unfortunately, some academic support materials overemphasize "organization" as an independent value and get students to focus on the wrong thing.

Here's an email that my husband, who is an adjunct professor of law, received recently from a student in his Evidence class:

As the final exam approaches, I find myself concerned about the essay portion of the final. My primary concern is how formal the essay is supposed to be. Are we required to include headers, subheadings, and an introduction?

This email is like a gut-punch for professors. Your "primary" concern is whether to use headers, subheadings, and an introduction? This does not bode well.

Certainly, it would be ideal if all your exam answers were clearly organized. But organization does not make or break an exam. Professors understand that exams are stressful and done under significant time constraints. If you forget to discuss the most relevant issue until the end because you somehow missed it initially, you will likely still get full credit for it. Do not cling to the "organization" myth.

D. IRAC

Fourth, IRAC (Issue, Rule, Application, Conclusion). When I was in school, it was called IRAC. Now, it's morphed into different things at different schools.[2] Whatever your school calls it, it's the same thing. It is the skill that you're taught in your legal writing class that informs your approach to legal problems. You are told to apply IRAC on your exams. And you should. But not in an overly formal and mechanistic way. I've seen some students literally write out:

Issue: The issue here is [insert].

Rule: The rule here is [insert].

Application: The way this applies is [insert].

Conclusion: In conclusion, [insert] should win.

What started as a helpful guidepost for writing an exam answer has turned into a strait jacket that completely stymies legal analysis. When professors say "use IRAC," they don't mean to use it in a literal sense. They mean to use it as an approach. They mean that what they are looking for in an answer is your ability to flag the relevant legal issue, explain the guiding legal principles, and then apply those principles to the facts—all while identifying nuances and areas where the answer is not so clear-cut. Legal thinking should follow this process

---

2. *See* https://writingdejure.web.unc.edu/resources/legal-methodology/.

organically. Like issue spotting, IRAC is not a *thing* to aim for on an exam. It captures the very essence of what the exam is designed to test.

Students are hearing more and more (from who, I don't know) that the key to exams is IRAC. I've been getting so many questions on IRAC lately. One student set up a meeting with me to specifically ask whether I "wanted IRAC" on the exam. What does this even mean? I answered "yes and no." I mean, I want you to talk about the rule and apply it. But I don't want some IRAC template answer. She seemed confused.

I asked her about the assignments she had been doing for my class all semester (we had done eight).[3] I asked whether she used IRAC for the assignments. She said no. I asked her whether she talked about the issue presented in the assignment, the legal rule, and whether she did an analysis. She said yes. So, she *did do* IRAC. She did it naturally and without being told to do it. It was like a lightbulb went off. She finally appreciated that IRAC is just how one approaches legal problems—and, frankly, is what you would do if you had never even heard the term before. There is a section later in the book where I talk about several terms I want to abolish from our lexicon (spoiler alert: one of them is "financial aid"). Here's another term I want to abolish: IRAC. *I know, heresy!* The problem is that the term has caused more confusion than necessary. And the overfocus on IRAC as a master template for all things legal has not served students well. Okay, let me get off my soapbox.

* * *

You should know that these are not just my idiosyncratic views on "misconceptions." Other professors have flagged many of the same issues. For instance, Professor Keating talks about ten myths of law school grading. His Myth #3 is "My Grades Would Be Higher, If Only I Could Learn 'Exam Technique.'" This essentially encapsulates much of what I am saying above. Here is how he describes it:

> This very prevalent student myth is probably heard most frequently early in the second semester of law school, after the students have received their very first set of law school grades. This belief is not entirely myth; there are, indeed, some students whose initial exam grades in law school are artificially low

---

3. I think I mentioned I'm hardcore.

because of some problem in exam-taking technique rather than because of deficiencies in their substantive knowledge. Furthermore, students as a group probably become more adept at taking exams as they take more of them. However, how many students can legitimately expect that their exam technique will significantly improve over time relative to their peers, whose exam techniques are also presumably improving with experience?

I am convinced that such "technique-deficient" students are the exception rather than the rule. When students come to me after receiving their exam grade to ask how they can write a better exam, I first re-read their exam closely to see if I can discern any problems of style or approach. Typically, however, my response to the student after re-reading the exam is the same: Know the subject matter better and be able to apply the law to the facts of the exam. This, of course, is not the answer that students want to hear. Instead, they want to be told some secret about exam "technique" that somehow they have been missing. After all, these students are positive that they knew the material much better than some classmates who somehow (presumably because they knew the secret) got better scores on the final exam. It is the prevalence of this myth that keeps alive a whole industry of nationwide "exam technique" seminars that offer the dubious guarantee that if the student's grades do not increase, the student can take the course again "for free"!

This myth is perhaps the most understandable of all the student grading myths, because it is so directly a function of the student's need to "sleep through the night" (Myth No. 2). As human beings, we all have a need to explain away our failure to perform at the level where we thought we should be.[4]

Why did I include this lengthy excerpt? (Other than I promised the publisher over 300 pages.) Basically, so I could show you that this is not just a "me" opinion.

3. Law Students All Make the Same Mistakes

I've been grading exams for 15 years. I've literally graded thousands of exams across more than half a dozen subjects: Commercial Law (Canada), Civil

---

4. Daniel L. Keating, *Ten Myths About Law School Grading*, 76 WASH. U. L. Q. 171, 174-75 (1998).

Procedure (Canada), Conflict of Laws (Canada), Contracts I (U.S.), Contracts II (U.S.), Sales (U.S.), and Conflict of Laws (U.S.). My observations below are based on a pretty large sample set.

Here are the biggest mistakes I see students make on exams.

A. Issue Spotting

I know, I just said it's not a thing. It's not. But I needed a title. Students often miss "live" issues on the exam—i.e., issues that they were supposed to discuss. There are two reasons for this. First, the obvious one. They didn't know the law well enough to see the legal issue presented. I keep on harping on this, but if you know the law, you will see the issue.

The second one is a little different. Students often have blinders on and see the legal issue as only one thing, instead of recognizing that there are sometimes different ways to skin a cat.[5] For instance, oftentimes a Contracts exam will test consideration in conjunction with promissory estoppel (don't worry about what either of those things mean). Students will either see it just as a "consideration" problem or just as a "promissory estoppel" problem, but not both. Students who do this will leave half the points for the question on the table. It's not that they didn't know the law, it's just that they get so caught up in chasing down an answer that they forget there might be another issue involved. It's almost as if they are like, "Got it, done," which prevents them from seeing the problem in a more holistic way.

B. Getting Bogged Down in Non-Issues

Non-issues are the biggest exam time suck. Many students get bogged down in non-issues because they approach exams with the wrong mindset. They think that writing an exam involves going through a checklist of every single topic they learned that semester. Some professors tell students that this is actually how they should approach the exam. Maybe it is for that class, but not for most exams. And most importantly, not for the practice of law. I do not need a student to tell me what is readily apparent from the facts.

---

5. For those who are offended by this common expression, I hear that I should substitute "There are many ways to eat a kiwi." Pretend I wrote that instead. Though, seriously, that's the best we can come up with?

For instance, if the "call of the question"[6] involves breach of contract, I do not need to you start at ground zero and start talking to me about contract formation. *The offer was when Mary said, "I offer to buy your business for $500,000." And the acceptance was when Bob said, "I accept."* So, you're telling me there's offer and acceptance. No duh? And the fact that I asked you about breach *of contract* should probably have signaled that there was a contract to breach. I don't need you to start at Adam and Eve. You do not get points for telling professors about non-issues. All you do is waste time and predispose a professor to thinking that you don't know how to distinguish between live and non-live issues.

Students tend to feel insecure about *not* mentioning everything under the sun. But wouldn't it be logical to start at whether there *is* a contract before moving on to breach? No. Look at it this way. In Contracts, you're probably going to cover at least the following topics (all of which have multiple subtopics):

- ➤ Mutual Assent
- ➤ Offer and Acceptance
- ➤ Consideration
- ➤ Certainty of Terms
- ➤ Promissory Estoppel
- ➤ Restitution
- ➤ The Statute of Frauds
- ➤ The Parol Evidence Rule
- ➤ Interpretation
- ➤ Implied Terms
- ➤ Excuses for Non-Performance (e.g., Misrepresentation, Duress, Unconscionability, Frustration, Impracticability, etc.)
- ➤ Modification
- ➤ Express Conditions
- ➤ Substantial Performance and Breach
- ➤ Anticipatory Repudiation
- ➤ Damages
- ➤ Rights of Third Parties

---

6. What you're supposed to be talking about.

Are you telling me that your plan is to go through this list *for every question* on your Contracts exam? It's completely nonsensical.

Let's assume your question is about damages. Here it is:

> Joe says to Ernie, "Would you like to buy my car for $15,000?" and Ernie says, "Yes." They sign a written contract to that effect, where they spell out all the details of the transaction. Joe breaches and sells the car to someone else for $17,000. Discuss the measure of damages Ernie is entitled to.

How stupid would it be to start the answer to the question like this:

> Here, there is an offer because Joe said, "Would you like to buy my car for $15,000?" and Ernie said, "Yes." Thus, you have offer and acceptance, and con-comitantly, mutual assent.

> Then they drafted up a contract in writing so there was no statute of frauds problem. The statute of frauds requires a contract for the sale of goods of $500 or more to be in writing. Here, there is a sufficient writing, so we don't have a statute of frauds issue.

> And there clearly is consideration. The consideration on Joe's part is the prom-ise to sell the car for $15,000 and the consideration on Ernie's part is to buy the car for $15,000.

> And we don't have a certainty of terms issue because the problem tells us that the writing spells out all the details of the transaction.

> There are no issues presented on the facts that deal with promissory estoppel or restitution. Also, we don't have an interpretation issue because the parties are not disputing any of the terms of the contract. Further, we don't have a parol evidence rule issue because no one is trying to introduce evidence to contradict or supplement the terms of a fully integrated agreement.

Can you see what I mean? This is all *stupid*. If the question is about breach of contract or damages, go to that issue right away. Otherwise, you'll waste all this time where you get zero points. As a professor, when I see this on an exam, I literally skip over it—i.e., I do not read it.

I recently graded a final exam where only 111 out of 934 words were relevant to what the question was asking (about 12%). The student got a very low score even though they wrote a novella. They got something like a 2 or 2.5 out of 10. The student barely engaged with what the question was asking, and instead took me on a trip through Article 2 of the Uniform Commercial Code. Nice try, but no points for you.

Now, I'm going to give you a caveat. If one of your professors says that they want you to talk about non-issues, *then f**king have at it.*[7] It's stupid, but they are grading your exam.

C. Not Using Facts You Are Given

You should assume that every fact on the exam is there for a reason. The vast majority of professors do not throw random sh*t into exams just because. When there's a date, a number, a quote from a character in the exam, a strange factual nugget, all these things are usually important. Your job as a student is to figure out where the fact goes (i.e., what legal issue does it speak to).

So many students fail to use the facts they are given. Let me give you an example. In one of my practice exams, there's a mom who ostensibly enters into a contract with her daughter. After the daughter accepts the mom's offer, the mom says, "That kid sure is gullible. Always believing pie in the sky promises."[8] I did not just put that quote in there for fun. I did not put that in there to make the story interesting for you (cause, it's all about you, right?). These sorts of things need to raise alarm bells for you.

D. Not Explaining Enough

Students often appear to be racing through their answer to get to the end. There is barely any explanation of the law or application of the law to the facts. There is no elaboration. There are conclusory answers. These exams will always be in the C or lower range. The point of an exam is to prove to the professor that you know the law. It's your time to show off. More is more.

Last year, one of my Contracts students informed me that my favorite expression was, "But, why?" The entire class agreed wholeheartedly. I never noticed that I ask this question *all the time.* The class emphatically insisted that

---

7. My 1L Contracts class tells me that one of their professors wants them to go through a checklist of issues and talk about them even if they are not applicable. I have trouble believing that's what he said. But I'm not about to get involved in that.

8. I didn't draft the exam. I don't use the expression "pie in the sky," but that's neither here nor there.

I did. For example, a student might say, "The buyer's reliance on the seller's representation was reasonable." And I would respond, "But, why?"

On some level, I didn't like that this had become a bit of a (good-humored) joke with the class.[9] But on another level, I wore it as a badge of honor. There is nothing wrong with being the "But, why?" professor. Law is about the "But, why?" And, importantly, exams are about the "But, why?" Your most used word on an exam should be the word "because." It should be everywhere. The student who informed me that I was the "But, why?" professor got an A on the Contracts exam. Here's the email she sent me after I shared the good news with her:

> I hate that I gave you a complex about it, but I have to say that asking myself "but why?" a million times a day while studying is the only thing that helped me truly understand the statute of frauds. And the cover and write method is how I can recite it from memory!

Back to your exam. Take the full amount of time and write as much as you possibly can. Explain the "but, why" for everything. A general rule of thumb is that you should never finish an exam early. Exams are never meant to be finished early.[10] If you see a student leaving an exam early, you should not feel anxious about your own performance—you should feel bad for them because they are walking out of there with a B, tops.

E. Getting the Law Flat-Out Wrong

This one pains me. There is no excuse for this. Unfortunately, a number of students just have the law wrong. There's no recovering from this. If your law is wrong, your analysis is wrong. You're lucky if the professor throws you a bone and gives you a few points. This is solely on you. You have the textbook; you have over 40 hours of classes; you have a gazillion study aids at

---

9. The "But, why?" appeared in one of my students' exam answers this year. The student wrote, "Courts frown on this much like Professor Coombs frowns when people call TB12 the best QB ever, or when students frown when Professor Monestier says, 'but, why?'" Most professors advise not to use humor on an exam. That's probably good advice. But, for me, a funny sentence here and there gives me a reprieve from the endless hours of drudgery that is grading.

10. Unless you have one of those new age-y professors who believes in giving you all the time in the world. *We wouldn't want to stress you out with time limits!* Cause that'll really help you on the bar exam.

your disposal; you have a professor and sometimes teaching assistants who are willing to meet with you to help with areas of confusion. If, after all this, you still don't know what substantial performance is, there's not much I can do about that.

F. Rewriting the Facts

I have seen this happen every year for 15 years. I don't really get it. I wrote the exam. I know what it says. Don't re-tell me what *I said*. All the time you spend doing this is time completely wasted. If you ever find yourself doing this—Stop. Regroup. And write the answer, not the question.

4. Law School Exams: *Like It's Hard?*

I'm pretty sure you're thoroughly freaked out by now. But don't be. It's not that hard. I've got in mind the scene from *Legally Blonde* where Warner says to Elle, "You got into Harvard Law School?" and she responds breezily, "Like it's hard?!" Same thing with law school exams. I'm going to replicate a short assignment I've given my students to show you that it's not that bad. Exams are just this, but longer and with more facts.

Assignment

Al just graduated from law school and is having a party at his house on June 20th. Al contracts with Bill, who owns a window cleaning company, to clean all 30 windows of his house on June 19th. Al specifically tells Bill that he is throwing a party on June 20th and that he needs all 30 windows cleaned before then. Bill arrives at Al's house the afternoon of the 19th. After cleaning 16 windows, Bill realizes that he still has three other cleaning jobs to do that day for very important clients. Bill tells Al that he has finished cleaning the front windows, which are the ones most visible to guests, but that he could not clean the remaining 14 windows that day. He then leaves to go to the next job. Has Bill breached the contract with Al? If so, is this a material breach? A total or partial breach? Please discuss the rights and remedies of the parties.

* * *

Here are two student answers. Not a word in the answers was changed.

Student #1

To begin, Bill most likely has committed a breach of this contract. Any non-performance of a promise, however small, is a breach and entitles the non-breaching party to damages. Bill's promise under the contract was to have **all 30** windows cleaned before June 20th. Anything short of cleaning all 30, including only cleaning 16, Bill has breached his promise and the contract. The only argument that he did not would be if he made some arrangement to come back the next day and clean the windows before the party that Al is having. This depends on if "before then" refers to before the date of June 20th or before the party. I am going to assume that "before then" means before the date of June 20th and since the windows aren't cleaned and Bill has left for the day he has breached the contract.

If this is a **material** breach, Al's duty to perform has not yet arisen and he is not yet required to pay Bill. He may still need to pay Bill something in the end depending on what type of material breach Bill has committed. A breach is **material** if the breaching party <u>has not</u> rendered "substantial performance." What constitutes substantial performance is not determined according to any specific percentage or bright-line rules. What may not be substantial performance under one contract may constitute substantial performance in another. The decision will always be a fact-based inquiry according to a variety of factors. One thing to consider is that Bill hasn't committed what most would consider substantial performance in a colloquial sense. 16/30 windows are roughly 53% of the windows cleaned. In more realistic cases that substantial performance is upheld the debate was around performance of 75-85%. It would be difficult as a threshold matter to convince a judge that 53% performance is "substantial" but as this is a fact-based inquiry the other factors warrant consideration.

The <u>purpose of the contract</u> with Bill was to have Al's windows cleaned in preparation for his party. Bill may have cleaned the windows "most visible" to the partygoers but has not completed Al's objective. Not only are almost half of Al's windows not cleaned, but the ones that weren't cleaned are also going to look *even worse* in comparison to the clean ones than if the others hadn't been cleaned in the first place. This objective would be <u>difficult to satisfy in a suit for damages</u> as well. Maybe Al could get another cleaner to come in the next morning to clean the windows for a higher price than Al could then recoup through damages, but it will take months for that case to clear the court system and the cost of window washing is probably not enough to litigate over from Al's perspective. Bill's breach is also a <u>willful breach</u> that is borderline bad faith. He decided that his contract will Al was less important than not meeting his other obligations and decided to have Al pay that price. This is going to cut against Bill having completed substantial performance. Although the <u>injury to Al</u> is not huge as dirty windows are not the end of the world, Bill barely completed half of the performance required and walked away willfully. All in all, this is most likely a **material breach** meaning that Al does not yet have to pay Bill and may not have to pay him at all.

Once a material breach has been determined, it must be determined if the material breach was partial or total. If the breach was only a partial material breach, then Al cannot walk away. He must give Bill time to "cure" his partial breach. At this point, Al is entitled to damages for the breach of a contract as a "breach is a breach is a breach." However, whether or not Al's duty to perform has been discharged will depend on the distinction between total and partial breach.

There are arguments to be made that he is a total breach by Bill. Al <u>communicated</u> to Bill's company the reason for needing the window cleaning and set a specific date the cleaning needed to be done. Delaying finding a replacement to give Bill time to cure his breach <u>would reasonably appear to hinder Al's ability to get a replacement</u>. Realistically Al could treat this as a partial breach and call Bill and have him come back to the house and cure the breach by cleaning the rest of the windows. However, Bill had two other cleaning jobs to do and will not be available to cure the breach before Al's party. That means if Al tries to give Bill the rest of the day/evening to cure the breach, he very likely will be trying to find a replacement the morning of the party to come and rush clean the windows before the start of the party. (Most likely paying a premium for the rushed service.) The other factors mentioned above including extent of the performance (53%), the willful nature of Al's breach, and the difficulty in adequately compensating Al through damages all cut towards this being a **total breach of contract.**

I would argue that this is a **total material breach** by Bill. This means that Al's duty to perform (pay Bill) has been discharged and Bill is allowed to walk away from the contract and enter another contract with someone else to clean his windows. However, just because Al *can* walk away does not mean that he *should* walk away. Because the line between total/partial breach is so blurred in all cases, and especially in this one where it is a borderline total breach, the safest thing to do is give the other party the time to cure the breach and then sue for damages once the date of performance has passed without a cure. As explained above, Al is not likely to get all his windows cleaned in time for his party. Even under a partial material breach, his duty to pay does not arise until the breach is cured. So while he has an argument to walk away from this contract *now* as it is a total breach, he is already entitled to damages, and repudiating the contract now, no matter how justified, is not going to gain Al anything. Al has the right to walk away as the total breach has discharged his duty of performance. He will put himself on the best **legal** grounds for an eventual suit for damages by waiting until after the party, withholding payment because the breach will most likely not be cured, and then sue for damages. The court will take into consideration in any eventual litigation that Al gave Bill time to cure the breach but did not do so.

Student #2

1. Whether Bill breached the contract.

The first issue here is whether Bill breached the contract with Al to clean 30 windows by June 20. Here, Bill breached the contract with Al. Al needed the windows cleaned by June 20, but on June 19 Bill told Al that he could not clean the remaining 14 windows that day and left. Assuming Bill did not come back and finish the job this is a breach because Bill did not complete his promise to clean 30 windows by June 20. A breach is a breach, no matter how minor. However, just because there was a breach, this is not fully determinative of the rights and remedies of the parties. If there is only a breach, but the breach was not material, Al would still be entitled to recover damages.

2. Whether Bill's breach was material.

To determine the extent of the remedies of the parties, the issue now becomes whether this was a material breach. To determine whether Al materially breached the contract, we must determine whether Bill substantially performed. If Bill substantially performed, then the breach is not material, and Al must still perform his end of the bargain, subject to an offset for damages. However, if Bill did not substantially perform then he materially breached, and Al may not have to render counter performance, depending on whether it is a total or partial breach. There is no bright line rule for when a party has substantially performed, however the court will look to a number of factors to determine whether a party substantially performed. These factors include the purpose of contract, whether the breach was willful or inadvertent, the extent of performance rendered, the extent of benefits receive by the injured party, type of contract involved, whether the injured party be adequately compensated in damages, what is the cost of remedying the defect, the harm to the breaching party, whether timing was important, and whether the aesthetic look of something important.

Factors that weigh in favor of this not being substantial performance and therefore a material breach include the following. The purpose of the contract was for all of Al's windows to be washed prior to his party so his house would look nice for his guests. That purpose is now not fully met because of Bill's breach. Regarding whether the breach was willful, Al could argue the breach was willful, no matter what, Bill would not be able to wash at least one customer's windows that day, and he chose to not wash Al's windows instead of someone else's. Bill can try to argue that it was not willful because he was overbooked that day and he at least needed to show up to all of the jobs, so he had no choice but to leave. Al has the stronger argument because Bill could have finished the job but chose not to. Regarding the extent of performance, Bill cleaned over 50% of the windows, 16 out of 30, and Bill also washed the most important ones, those in front of the house. While there is not bright line rule for how much performance is substantial performance, performing just above 50% of the performance does not weigh in Bill's favor. Regarding the cost to remedy the defect, here it is unclear as to what this would be or if Al could even find someone to wash the remaining windows on such a short notice. Regarding timing, here timing was very important, Al needed the windows washed by the next day, that was one of the main purposes of the contract. Regarding the aesthetic look, here this was very important, Al wanted his house to look nice before his party. Regarding whether the injured party could be adequately compensated in damages, here to the extent this could be done, Al could have the cost of the windows that were not cleaned offset from what would be paid to Bill, but it would be hard to put a number on any harm done beyond that, so Al may not be able to adequately compensated in damages for the harm.

The following two factors weigh in favor of Bill substantially performing and therefore not materially breaching the contract. Regarding the extent of the benefits received by the injured party, Al, here Al received the most important part of the service, that being the cleaning of the windows that are most visible to his guests. Regarding the harm to the breaching party, Al is harmed in that all of his windows will not be washed before his guests arrive and his house will not look as nice, which is not particularly severe.

In looking at the totality of the factors, they weigh heavily in favor of Bill not substantially performing such that he materially breached the contract.

3. Whether the breach was total or partial.

The question now turns to whether this was a total or partial breach. If this is not a total breach, meaning it is partial, then Al's duty to perform is not discharged, it is simply suspended and he does not need to perform at this point in time. If it is a partial breach Al must give Bill time to cure the breach. However, if it is a total breach then Al's obligation to perform is discharged and he does not have to perform at all. To determine whether a material breach is total, the court looks to the factors noted above for substantial performance, but also considers whether the injured party is hindered in making substitute arrangements due to the breach, as well as the importance that timing played in making the contract.

Here, Al needs the rest of his windows washed before the start of his party the next day. It is unclear as to what the market for window washer are, but it is highly unlikely he can find someone to wash his remaining windows in this short amount of time. Timing was also a very important issue in the contract, time was of the essence as Al needed his windows washed the next day. This all weighs heavily in favor of this being a total material breach.

4. Rights and remedies of the parties.

Because Bill did not substantially perform and this breach was a total breach, Al may simply walk away from the contract, although he does not have to. He does not have to render his counter performance of paying Bill.

* * *

Hopefully I didn't make you more nervous about law school by providing you with these answers. What I was aiming to show you is that exam answers involve weaving law and facts together. Both of these students write clearly and in plain English. And while you may not have exactly understood the concepts tested (total/partial breach, substantial performance), you probably got a good flavor for what they were saying.

Like I said, an exam is just this, but only longer and with more details thrown in. If you think you would be able to do the above problem (after being taught the material), then you will be able to tackle a law school exam.

5. Watch the Clock Like a Hawk

Students run out of time on exams all the time. *How the f**k does that happen?* Because they aren't paying attention to the time. They are approaching the exam as a leisurely stroll in the park when, in reality, it's a 100-meter sprint. It is bad to run out of time on an exam. A professor can't give you points for something you did not write. No matter how well you did on the first four (of six) questions, your grade is going to be capped at a B-...if you're lucky. It'll actually probably be lower than that.

Think of it this way. There is a ceiling on how well you can perform on a given question. A professor is not going to give you a 12/10 on an answer. If writing three good pages would have gotten you a 10/10, writing six pages is just a waste of time. Students often don't know where to stop in their answer. Let me give you an example based on an exam I just graded. The exam had six questions. The student wrote 14 pages. He or she devoted six full pages to Question 1. Almost half the page count for one question! How does that make any sense?

What I would suggest is this. Professors often give suggested time allocations. Follow them almost to the minute if you can. If you go over time on one question, you must make it up on another question. If a professor does not provide time allocations, then they should designate how much a question is worth (e.g., 20% of the grade; 35% of the grade). If you can find out this information ahead of time, then do the math and translate for yourself how many minutes this is. If you don't know how much each question is worth until the day of the exam, then do some quick math before you start. Bring a calculator if you have to (180 minutes x 20% = 36 minutes). If your professor does not tell you how much the question is worth, then they probably shouldn't be teaching. Harsh, but true. It is unfair to students not to tell them what the value of each question is.[11]

One very practical suggestion for you. Bring a watch to the exam that easily allows you to calculate time.[12] If you have an analog watch (one with hands), set

---

11. I've seen it happen though. You have my full support in going to the Dean to complain about this.

12. All exam software has built-in timers as well.

the hands to 12:00 and then start the watch when the proctor says "go." Having your watch set to 12:00 more readily enables you to keep track of time.

For the actual exam, you need to be working as fast as you can. This is why it is important to have everything memorized, answers pre-planned, and everything ready to go. You do not have time to read the fact pattern three times. Read it once, carefully, the first time. Use a pencil to underline or circle things and take marginal notes. You do not have time to do detailed outlines on your scrap paper. You do not have time to write out acronyms for everything you've studied or a checklist of all the issues that might present themselves on an exam. I have seen students have more ink on their scrap paper than on their actual exam. That does not bode well for the grade.

6. Don't Make Dumb Mistakes

Do not make dumb mistakes on exams. By dumb mistakes, I don't mean getting something of substance wrong.[13] Let me give you a couple of examples of dumb mistakes.

On my first year Civil Procedure exam, things were going swimmingly. I had pre-written my answers for the open book exam, I spotted all the issues, I was writing as fast as my hand would let me. I just finished writing an answer on standing but I felt like it had not flowed well. *Hmmmm.* I went back and read the question again. I then noticed that the question was not about standing, but about *intervention*, which is a whole different thing. I felt the blood leave my head. Time for massive panic. My first instinct was to go back and substitute the word "intervention" for "standing." I did that for about half the answer. Remember, I'm doing this with liquid paper and a pen because we didn't take exams on computers when I went to law school. I realized this wasn't going to work because, well, they were different legal tests. I crossed out the whole answer and started over again. I did the best I could but ended up wasting about 20-30 minutes out of a three-hour exam because of this stupid mistake.[14]

---

13. Though it is a dumb mistake if the professor repeated something a million times or put it up in black and white on the chalkboard or Power Point and you copied it down wrong.

14. I know you're all wondering, *How did you do on the exam?* I ultimately did fine on the exam; I got an A. And, irony of ironies, I ended up teaching Civil Procedure my first two years in academia. But I never really forgave myself for such an egregious error. *Why didn't*

Here's another dumb mistake that students make (a lot). When students read through the question, they usually underline, highlight, circle and make marginal notes. This is all good; it's stuff they should be doing. But then when they go to write their answer, they fail to look back at what they wrote. I had one student, Xavier, who was disappointed in his grade, a B-. After talking about the exam, he said, "I guess I just didn't see these issues." I pulled out the exam question sheet and showed Xavier where he had indeed flagged the issues. But for some reason, he hadn't written about them on the exam.

You can't make these kinds of mistakes. I am aware that there's a lot of adrenaline pumping through your veins but forgetting to write about issues that you actively spotted[15] is just careless.

7. Stuff the Burrito

I'm sure you're confused by title of this section. Bear with me. One of the things I see all the time is students writing short, measly answers to exam questions. Like I've said, it's almost like students are trying to write the least amount possible to be done with it and move onto other, more interesting, things.

I was driving to school one day thinking about this. I knew I wanted to have a conversation with my students about this issue, which I had been seeing in their quizzes. But I also knew that simply saying "write more" would not resonate. So, I came up with an analogy: the burrito.

What students were giving me was a sad burrito. It was a gluten-free burrito that had a few vegetables and brown rice tossed into it. Nobody wants to eat that burrito. Instead, what you should be aiming for is a big-a** Chipotle burrito. One that that is stuffed to the gills with *carne asada*, white rice, salsa, sour cream, cheese, and guacamole. One that is so big you can barely fit it in your mouth. A new expression was born: *Stuff the burrito*.

Stuffing the burrito is what you should be aiming to do on the exam. Write as much as you can. Then write more. Longer answers are almost always better.[16]

---

you read more carefully? How did you not notice that the facts weren't working with the standing test? Why would you waste even more time trying to liquid paper over the wrong answer?

15. I know, not a thing.

16. Unless you are dealing with a professor who imposes word limits. Which is just mean on an exam, and possibly lazy on their part. Yes, I know, there are pedagogical reasons why professors have word limits. But I still think they shouldn't.

8. Learn from Your Exams (But Don't Expect Your Professors to "Go Over" Them with You)

Students are encouraged by academic support professionals and in books like this to seek out their professors to "go over" their exams.[17] I have concerns about this push to have students "go over" exams because I think there is confusion as to what this process should look like.

I think it is a very valuable exercise for a student to look over his or her exam, along with a sample answer or a rubric. Students should spend a while trying to figure out where they went wrong and why. I have often facilitated this process by distributing exams, walking through a sample answer, and then letting students sit with their exams. The point is for the *student themself* to do the learning.

Instead, I think what students have in mind when they want professors to "go over" an exam is a very different thing. I think they want the professor to flag for the student every misstatement of law, every *non-sequitur*, every area where they did not elaborate enough, etc. In short, they want the professor to *tell them* where they went wrong. This top-down "learning" is not my jam, as you'll see in the chapter on self-regulated learning.

The professor cannot be expected to sit down with 100 students and "go over" every exam individually. I have done this in the past, and it is a dreadful process. I would spend the better part of a month meeting with students, just to have the same conversation over and over. It was exhausting. And more importantly, I don't think any student took away anything valuable from the conversations.

In my experience, these meetings invariably involve the following questions, "Where did I go wrong?" and "How can I do better?" Students ask these questions as though there were a three-sentence answer. There is not. If you did not get the grade you expected on the exam, the exam was not the problem. It is what happened *way before* the exam that was the problem. The note taking, the outlining, the studying, the practice exams, etc. I can't know where in the process things broke down—it is on you as the student to figure it out.

---

17. I read one academic support article that encouraged students to ask their professors to *read through* the exam with students to model careful reading and flag all the issues. *Honestly, I can't even....*

I often find myself saying, as gently as possible, "Well, the fact that you got a C+ shows me that you weren't super-solid on the law." The student will swear up and down that they knew the law inside out. Then I point out that they wrote, "The revocation was effective as soon as it was put in the mailbox (mailbox rule)" and that this is incorrect. Though they feel like they knew the law down pat, they didn't.

Students do not like hearing "You just didn't know the law well enough." That seems like too vague an answer—and a problem that is hard to fix. Instead, they want to hear something like, "Well, you could have used more headings." They want something easy and readily fixable. Incidentally, whether you use headings has no bearing on whether you're going to get a good grade.

We live in an age where if we have a problem, we want a quick solution. We are all guilty of that. But succeeding in law school is simply not a quick fix thing. Succeeding in law school requires sustained and purposeful effort throughout the semester.

Back to "going over" an exam. There is truly limited utility to going over an exam as a means of improving your exam performance. What I mean by this is that, in almost all cases, students don't have an "exam" problem. They have a "something way prior to the exam" problem. If you use the exam review as a diagnostic, as a way to figure out what you didn't know and why, then it is a very helpful process.

For instance, take the erroneous application of the mailbox rule. How did that happen? Were you not paying attention in class? Did you have it down in your notes correctly, but you somehow committed it to memory differently? Was there just a big gap in your notes? The point is to figure out where in your study process things went awry. You are never going to get a question about the mailbox rule again (until maybe the bar exam). So simply revisiting the rule after the professor tells you that you got it wrong is not particularly helpful.

9. The Proof Is in the Pudding: Karen's Story

I just finished up grading for the semester. I reached out to some of my students who received top grades to let them know the good news.[18] After I told

---

18. This is one of the best parts of my job. I love delivering good news. I have had fun with it in recent years with students I know can take a joke. For instance, I got Ryan on the phone and told him that I had something serious to talk to him about. I told him to

Karen that she received an A in Contracts, she sent me an email expressing how happy she was with the news. She also said, "This semester I used all of your studying tips and they made the world of a difference in how I studied and learned the material for this final and all my other exams." *Tell me more….*

I asked Karen if we could speak on the phone (yes, I'm obnoxious like that). So, Karen, tell me *how helpful* my guidance was to you. Be specific. I need the ego boost. Karen relayed specifics about her approach to law school her 1L year and how it gradually changed, in large part, based on my advice.

I asked Karen whether she would be willing to share her story with you all—and she said she'd be happy to! I mean, she probably didn't have much of a choice since what's she going to say, "No, Prof. Monestier, I have better things to do than help you with your book." But, still, I appreciate the completely non-coerced narrative that she has provided.

Here is Karen's story:

I want to start off by saying to take all of Professor Monestier's advice. I can tell you from experience that doing everything she says will give you the grades that you want in law school. I had Professor Monestier for Contracts I, and throughout the semester she gave us the advice that she is giving to all of you throughout this book. I thought her methods sounded like an incredible way to learn the material and study. But I thought that I didn't have the time to start studying over a month before the exam and knew that I needed flash cards to memorize all the material that she wanted us to know for the exam.

Throughout the semester, I read every case and spent *a lot* of time briefing them before class. I was normally too scared to say the wrong thing, so I didn't ever volunteer to speak in class. Also, I didn't start studying a month before the exam (like she told us) and instead memorized the material in a few days using flash cards. I felt confident for the exam because I had memorized every single thing we had learned that semester. However, while I was taking the Contracts I exam, I felt like I was scrambling. I didn't have enough time to finish, and I wasn't applying the correct doctrine to each question. My grade reflected how I felt during the exam. And I was extremely frustrated because I felt like I understood the material throughout the semester and had memorized everything we

---

remember that grades weren't everything and that one bad grade doesn't define you. I did this whole build-up and then told him he got the CALI in the class. Sort of mean, I know. But fun for me.

learned. Contracts is a course I really enjoyed and felt like I was always on top of the material. So, I made it my personal mission to get an A in Contracts II.

During Contracts II, I did things differently. I still read all the cases before class. However, I stopped spending all of my time briefing the cases and only took quick notes on the case to jog my memory during class. During class, I actively participated by raising my hand as much as I could. I would also think of an answer in my head to every single question Professor Monestier asked. I left every class feeling like I really understood the material we had just learned.

Importantly, I also wrote down everything Professor Monestier said and took those notes, organized them, and put them into my outline. I didn't leave anything out of my outline, and it ended up being close to 100 pages long. But it was one stop shopping because, once it was complete, I only used my outline to study for the exam. Yes, you heard me, I said goodbye to my flash cards!

I started studying for the exam about a month ahead of time (I was much busier during this semester, so that goes to show that you always have time to use this method to study). I started by focusing on one topic and would read it over a few times and then cover it up and try to speak everything I just read. I then would check to see how much I remembered. I did this over and over again and would add other topics in once I felt confident that I completely understood a topic. I kept building up until I could basically speak my entire outline without looking at it.

To be clear, I wasn't just memorizing the material, I was working with the material. I knew the elements of a specific doctrine because I understood the purpose of the doctrine and had worked through all of the examples we covered in class. Because of this, when I went to apply the doctrine, knowing the elements came naturally.

When I took the Contracts II exam, I *finally* realized that law school exams are not about issue spotting. Because if you have worked to learn the material well, you won't have to issue spot because it is clear what doctrine you should apply to the question. Throughout the exam, I felt calm and confident. I knew the doctrine that applied in every situation and was no longer scrambling for a list of seven elements that I memorized in my head.

All of this hard work paid off because I got the A! And more importantly, I feel like I will know Contracts II forever because I didn't just quickly memorize it in a few days; I worked with the material for months. I used Professor Monestier's advice in all of my classes and saw the same results.

My advice to you is to not be like me and wait until your 2L year. Do everything she says because it will change your law school experience and will give you the results you want!

Thank you, Karen, for the ringing endorsement of my study methods. Your check is in the mail. Karen is not a one-off. Here are a few other messages I received from students about my study methods (these ones were completely unsolicited):

Oliver: When I first got to law school, I was middle of the pack, trying to figure it out. But your studying approach has significantly changed my performance not just in Contracts but every other class. Hopefully people can start realizing that this approach works. It was a pleasure learning from you these past two semesters.

Christopher: When our paths crossed last spring, I was a mediocre law student coming off a mediocre fall semester. Your approach to law school, which I call 'The Monestier Method' changed everything for me. I graded into the Honors Program and was selected for Law Review after a strong spring. You gave me the framework and confidence to do that. I am forever indebted to you for instilling . . . in me [what I needed] to become a successful law student. I really think you have a gift for teaching and inspiring your students.

Anastasia: I want to thank you for everything you have taught me, not just in contracts, but to become a better student and lawyer after I graduate. No other professor has had such a positive impact like you have had on me. I have seen my grades rise, and my thought process expand since following your learning approach and I truly thank you.

Carlos: In all seriousness, I truly can't study any other way because of how effective your process was for me. It does work, and anybody who thinks it doesn't is just crazy!

SEVEN

Learning How to Learn

I never lose. I either win or learn.

NELSON MANDELA

1. Law School Is Not Undergrad

I am sure you've heard this before: Law school is not undergrad. The sooner you take that to heart, the better. I honestly don't know much about what undergrad is like nowadays. Plus, I went to undergrad in Canada, and maybe things are different there. What I can tell you is what I hear students say time and again: *I didn't have to try in undergrad. I barely did any work in undergrad and got A's. Undergrad was a joke.* Everyone's undergraduate experience will be different, but there certainly is a common refrain to what I'm hearing.

If this is what undergrad is, or has become, then law school is not undergrad. To do well in law school, you need to work hard. Even then, success is not guaranteed. There is a big difference between working hard and working smart. Law school does not reward effort. It rewards results.

Students who are used to getting A's in undergrad may need to brace themselves for B's and maybe lower. Not everyone can get an A. For many students, this will be a huge blow to their sense of identity and self-worth. They won't know how to cope. And will likely immediately resort to "Something's wrong with the professor. I am an A student, not a B student." Newsflash: You might have been an A student at Cotton Candy College, but you are a B (or a C) student in law school.

The good news is that anyone can *become* an A student. It's not easy, but it is possible. One of my former students, Ryan, was a terrible student in high school and skated by in undergrad. When he got to law school, he decided to take a different approach. Ryan worked incredibly hard, did not cut corners, and was very deliberate about what advice he took. He wanted to prove to himself that he could do it. Ryan graduated *summa cum laude*, is currently clerking, and has a full-time position lined up at a big law firm. With effort, dedication, and hard work, anyone can be like Ryan.

2. Become a Self-Regulated Learner

One of the most important predictors of law school success is whether a student is a self-regulated learner. *A what?* Let's break down the academic talk.

At a very basic level, self-regulated learning is the idea that the student takes responsibility for their own learning. Learning is something students *do* for themselves, not something that is *done to* them. Self-regulated learning involves a student controlling their own learning experiences through things like goal setting, progress monitoring, and self-testing. Barry Zimmerman, one of pioneers of self-regulated learning theory, says that self-regulated learning is "not a mental ability or an academic performance skill; rather, it is the self-directive process by which learners transform their mental abilities into academic skills."[1]

I'm not going to tell you exactly how to be a self-regulated learner, since part of the process involves *you* figuring that out. Google it; there's a ton of literature on self-regulated learning generally and in the law school context specifically.

The concept might still be a little elusive to you at this point. You might not even know whether you are a self-regulated learner. A helpful question to ask yourself is how involved you are in your own learning. Are you a passive recipient of information? Or do you work to synthesize information, figure out what you know and don't know, and look for ways to put the puzzle pieces together? If the former, you are not a self-regulated learner; if the latter, you might be a self-regulated learner.

Most students have no experience with self-regulated learning. Learning is not about learning, but about results. Students are consumers of education rather than active participants in learning. Students are the product of the iPhone generation, which has shortened attention spans and created expectations of instantaneous gratification in the form of good grades.

---

1. Barry J. Zimmerman, *Becoming a Self-Regulated Learner*, Theory Into Practice, Vol. 41, No. 2, Spring 2002, at 64–70.

One professor describes the state of affairs this way:

Legal educators do not need empirical research to tell them what they already know: many students coming to law school are ill-prepared for the academic rigors of law study. Undergraduate institutions are failing to teach greater numbers of students how to study and learn, how to self-regulate their learning, and how to think critically. ... Many students entering law school lack strong critical thinking skills for legal educators to build on. Moreover, compared to previous student populations, these students often have poor and ineffective study habits, weak critical thinking and writing skills, and are thus less academically prepared for the case method and Socratic method.[2]

Here's a perfect illustration of what I mean. I received the following comment in a student evaluation from someone who was not satisfied with having individual feedback and multiple sample student answers to practice problems. Instead, he or she wanted me write out verbatim exactly how questions "should" be answered:

After the assessments, you provide the class with [ ] student responses.... This in my opinion is not helpful, I would want to see how *you* would respond to these questions word for word, so I have a template, a guide in the least, to base my future responses from. I think that you are a good teacher, who knows the material extremely well but the critique I have is that you do not teach us properly how to construct our answers. You tell us what you want, and have us work through problems verbally but personally I need to see the words written and formed to know what you expect. ... I hope that you at least provide us with more constructive responses in your own words and at least a rubric to follow from maybe even a past exam that helps us in some capacity. Often, I feel like a baby thrown into the pool and forced to learn how to stay afloat in your class.... I just hope that you can alter your teaching style more to adapt to how we learn not have the class adapt to how you teach.

Dear Lord. Whenever I re-read this email, I become so agitated it makes my eye twitch.[3]

---

2. Jennifer M. Cooper, *Smarter Law Learning: Using Cognitive Science to Maximize Law Learning*, 44 Cap. U. L. Rev. 551, 552–53 (2016).

3. Teaching students like this makes me just want to say *no mas* to teaching (is the fancy law firm job still on the table?). Thankfully, these students are still the minority.

When I try to nudge students, even ever so slightly, in the direction of self-regulated learning, many become standoffish. *Just tell me the answer! I need *you* to give me feedback. Can't you just tell me how to do better?*

Let me give you an example. In my Contracts classes, I sometimes give a series of short assignments over the course of the semester. I provide written feedback on these assignments where I flag things the student did wrong. I also provide students with several sample answers.[4] One student, let's call him Brandon, did very average on the assignment. He wanted to set up a meeting to "go over" it with me. I said no. I told him that the assignment was only worth three points and that he had already received plenty of feedback. He was not happy. I offered him the opportunity, instead, to try to integrate the feedback he received and re-write the assignment, which I would hypothetically grade. He did not take me up on the offer.

Two months later, I received an email from Brandon that said:

> Honestly, initially, I was hesitant about not having [more] feedback or you not "holding our hand" in helping us learn. Then, even more, to hear we should not use the flashcards. However, once I got over it and took your advice, I have stated this to multiple students, and I genuinely believe it; this has been the most beneficial class I have taken thus far in my law school career to prepare me for the Bar exam fully. I appreciate your teaching style a lot more after I had time to sit down and study the material. Your method not only helped me to learn study habits for your class but to look for self-evaluation and learning [opportunities] in other classes as well. Your training wheels can seem stuck in the mud, but once you let them off, you feel like you're flying.

What Brandon did not say explicitly, but I think he meant, is that he has taken ownership of his learning. Instead of me providing a detailed road map, he created his own road map. Unfortunately, not every student is Brandon. Many students have no conception of what self-regulated learning is and put it on the professor to somehow magically ensure that they learn.

Professors unintentionally reinforce the message that learning is something that is done to students, not something that students do for themselves. They provide students with flowcharts, handouts, checklists, rubrics, dozens of practice questions, on-demand office hours, and everything else under the sun to

---

4. Frankly, this is way too much handholding to be consistent with self-regulated learning, but you've got to start somewhere.

make sure the student "gets it." I admit—I am guilty of doing many of these things. I genuinely want to help students learn and there is a fine line between being a good professor and being a helicopter professor. Here's an excerpt from a great article on the topic:

> [T]he negative consequences of helicopter professoring are vast. Over involvement in students' learning processes prevents them from developing autonomy in their learning experience and encourages them instead to rely on others to an unhealthy degree. In school, they may become dependent on professors for some basic habits of successful, self-directed learners, including efficient time-management, a willingness to struggle with challenging material, and resourcefulness. "[I]f we walk students through every step [of an assignment,] we send a strong message about [the assignment] and about learning in general: namely that it is a direction-following game, that the answers reside with the teacher, who will walk you through the steps to the puzzle until you arrive at the right answer." This level of helicoptering encourages students to merely "'do school,' to go through the motions without really learning."
>
> Some level of difficulty and struggle is necessary and even desirable as part of the learning process. Helicopter professors inadvertently deprive students of the joy of learning that comes in the discovery process. Instead, they convert helpful scaffolds into "new forms of crutches" that hinder students' learning.
>
> Students who are helicoptered in the classroom may complete a particular course of study "without much of a sense of how to work on their own or think for themselves." They develop an unrealistic idea of what it means to learn something, to work at a particular task for themselves, or to find a way out of a particular educational morass. Helicopter professors give students little room to develop or take responsibility for their learning and their lives.
>
> The stunted cognitive growth that helicopter professoring may cause leads to future problems when students enter the workplace. Employers will likely have very different expectations of students and may be far less likely to helicopter them on the job. Arguably, this is uniquely problematic in the legal field where the primary value a lawyer, even a new lawyer, brings to a task is independent problem solving and creative thinking.[5]

---

5. Emily Grant, *Helicopter Professors*, 53 Gonz. L. Rev. 1, 6–7 (2018).

I hope I've convinced you that self-regulated learning is the learning you should be engaged in. I implore you, read up on it. And start law school from Day 1 as a self-regulated learner. Also (and this is not self-serving at all), if a professor tells you to "figure it out yourself," don't be mad at them. Be thankful for them.

3. Create Your Own Roadmaps

This is an offshoot of the above, but I think it deserves its own section. Part of being a self-regulated learner is developing your own roadmaps. You will only learn by doing, not by passively receiving.

Let me give you a concrete illustration on what I mean. One of the most complicated things that you're going to tackle in your first year is a topic referred to as "Battle of the Forms." Sounds exciting, right? It's not. This a really tricky section of Article 2 of the Uniform Commercial Code that involves lots of twists and turns and is sort of like a choose-your-own-adventure.[6] If you google "Battle of the Forms," you'll find a ton of flow charts.

Here's a small sampling of these flow charts. By the way, if you can't read them, good. That's intentional. My point is to show you what I mean by these flowcharts, not to have you use them (that's the opposite of my point).

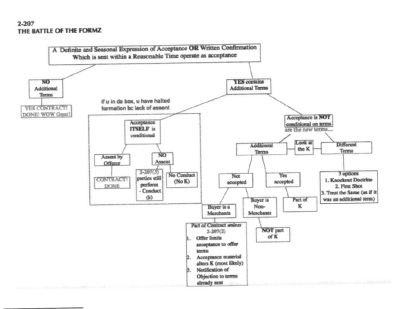

----

6. You probably don't know what those books are. But they were awesome.

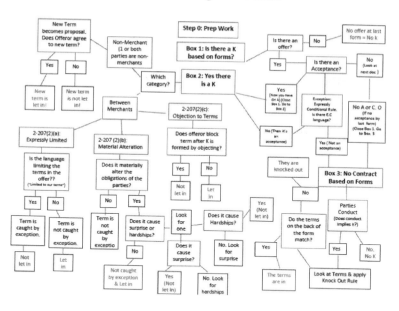

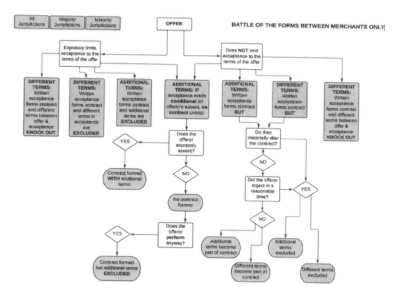

It's not a good idea to use other peoples' flowcharts, just like it's not a good idea to use other peoples' outlines. You need to work hard to conceptualize battle of the forms in your own way. By creating the flowchart, you are learning the material on your own terms. And just to be clear, you do not need a flowchart to understand battle of the forms. Many students simply understand it conceptually without all the arrows and "if this, then that." The point I'm making here is the same point I make throughout the book: Take control of your own learning. Do not expect a book or a professor to give you shortcuts. Because it is through *doing* the work that you will learn.

4. Develop a Growth Mindset

There are two types of academic mindsets: a fixed mindset and a growth mindset. They are what they sound like. A fixed mindset is premised on the idea that intelligence is innate and immutable. A growth mindset rejects that premise. It is based on the belief that "if at first you don't succeed, try and try again."

Maybe you're not sure which of these two universes you inhabit. Here's a quick litmus test. You hand in an assignment worth 10% of the total grade. You get a 4%. What is your reaction (after you stop crying)? Do you feel depressed and hopeless, like you're just not cut out for law school? Or do you put on your big boy/girl britches and say, "How can I do better next time?" If the former, you probably have a fixed mindset. If the latter, you probably have a growth mindset.

The author[7] of the leading book on the topic of academic mindset writes that "research has shown that the view you adopt for yourself profoundly influences the way you lead your life."[8] I have witnessed the difference between fixed mindset students and growth mindset students for many years. Invariably, the latter have more success in law school and in life.

Although difficult, it is possible to shift your mindset. You need to let go of your predetermined beliefs about intelligence and success. You need to embrace challenge and struggle. You need to be prepared to be kicked and then kicked again.

I had one student, Frank, who started off as your fairly average student. He was very set in his ways and circumspect about any advice I gave him. He was also *pissed* when he got a not-so-good grade on the first quiz he took, despite

---

7. Total overachiever. Professor at Stanford. PhD from Yale. *See* https://profiles.stanford.edu/carol-dweck.

8. *See* Carol S. Dweck, Mindset: The New Psychology of Success 6 (2006).

studying for days. Frank is a former football player. He looks like he could be a bouncer. He's also Italian (so he's a paesano of mine) and has a very Italian vibe. I sort of mean a classed-up Jersey shore vibe.[9] Frank went from "I'm not buying what you're selling" in his first semester to "I'm all about the growth mentality" in his second semester. He really is one of my success stories. You too can be Frank—even if you didn't start out that way.

5. Learn from Feedback

Today's law students *crave* feedback. When I went to law school and when I started teaching, there was very little in the way of feedback. You went to class, took notes, studied for the exam, and got your grade. Your grade was your feedback.

As I mentioned before, in recent years, there has been a push for formative assessments to provide students with feedback earlier than the final exam. Formative assessments can certainly be helpful learning tools. But I fear that in some ways, they are becoming counter-productive. Here are some of the unexpected problems I've encountered in recent years with formative assessments and feedback.

First, it seems like no amount of feedback is ever enough. Students want more, more, more. Every semester, I grade three exercises or quizzes, provide individual redline comments, and distribute sample answers. This amounts to grading 180 assignments, plus 60 exams. Every year, this is not enough. Students want me to grade more of their work. They want one-on-one meetings. They want even more feedback. Here's a typical reaction lamenting the "lack" of feedback:

> I was really hopeful at the start of this semester because she had assigned weekly essays that forced us to spell out the material. This was helpful in itself. However, I did expect more feedback on the assignments she did grade. Instead, I received general comments and student samples of the answer which doesn't really help me to understand what I am missing in the course....I am still hopeful to have more feedback in the upcoming classes. As a [sic] said, I was hopeful for this semester that there would be more substantive feedback and more chances to work with THE PROFESSOR on discussing the material. I

---

9. I ran that reference by Frank, and he thought it was hysterical.

know student aids are a great resource. However, it is always better to "hear it from the horse's mouth" so to speak.

So let me get this straight. I marked up your individual assignment with feedback that was specific to you. And, in addition to that, I gave you five or six examples of answers that got a perfect score. And you need more? *What the f**k are you looking for?* Under this standard, no professor could possibly give students their desired amount of feedback.

Second, even though students claim to want feedback, they really don't. They get very defensive when professors do provide feedback. For instance, if I make a comment that a student did not provide the full definition of something, they will resist the feedback and argue that they did. One student wrote on an evaluation once that I should only provide "positive" feedback.

Third, so many students who ask for feedback fail to implement it. They do not actually go through the feedback in meaningful detail and adjust the next time around. It seems like much of the feedback falls on deaf ears.

Fourth, I'm coming to realize that feedback frequently means "shortcut." Often, when a student wants feedback, they want a quick and easy way of fixing the problem. They want the feedback to be concrete and easy things they should do in the future—e.g., break up paragraphs, use subheadings, make sure your last line is the conclusion. Things that don't require a lot of work. Or they want the professor to provide them with a paint-by-numbers approach to legal problems. They want to be told, "If you see X problem, then the first thing you do is A, the second thing you do is B, etc." They essentially want *you* to do all the work for them. Now, I do believe in assisting students with frameworks and scaffolds, but not in providing them with a foolproof template for every possible answer out there. Because that template doesn't exist. And even if it did, I wouldn't give it to you.

Fifth, feedback from the professor is taking the place of self-directed learning. This is the worst thing of all. Students seem to be looking to the professor for a thumbs up or thumbs down on everything they do, instead of trying to figure things out themselves and developing the ability to self-regulate.

Just to be clear: I think feedback is valuable, provided it is used by students correctly and does not make them reliant on external sources of validation. And, of course, the above are generalizations and do not apply to all students. There are many students I have encountered over the years that have been very receptive to feedback and have benefited greatly from it.

Where does this leave us? I suggest the following guideposts for students with respect to feedback:

> ➤ Do not have unrealistic expectations for your professor. Your professor likely teaches dozens of students per semester and simply cannot provide the in-depth feedback you want.

> ➤ Focus closely on the feedback you do get. Spend time with it. Make sure you understand it. Never make the same mistake twice.

> ➤ Do not be defensive about feedback. I know this is hard, but you need to accept that your professor knows more than you. Learn from them. That's what they are there for.

Think of feedback as a "bonus" that you may get from time to time. Ultimately, though, you need to be the source of your own feedback. If you have doubts about some area of law, *you are responsible* for self-diagnosing the problem and fixing it.

Feedback on this section (or on the book, for that matter) is not welcome.

6. Seek Criticism, Not Praise

My first year teaching in the United States, a student said to me, "Most professors give criticism in a compliment sandwich. You give criticism in a criticism sandwich." The statement stuck with me—partly because it was so catchy, and partly because it was true. I am not the professor who praises students for every little thing they do. Not every answer is "excellent." Not every attempt is worth "an A+ for effort." There are professors out there who are very complimentary to all students. All the time. I think these professors do students a disservice.

Don't get me wrong: Everyone loves being praised. Me included. We even like being praised when we know we don't really deserve it. Let me give you an example. I have an amazing dental hygienist, Denise. Every time I go to the dentist, she compliments me on what "a great job" I've been doing flossing. She always says, "It really shows how well you've been taking care of your teeth." Even though I didn't do anything special, I bask in the compliment. It makes me happy all day. *Yes, I've been doing an amazing job flossing!*

You can see why the very complimentary professors are well-liked. And despite the Denise situation, I don't believe in praising students if what they did is not truly worthy of praise. If what they did was simply read and understand the case. Or articulate the legal rule correctly. These are my *basic expectations*. These are not things that, in my mind, are worthy of compliments. Why? Several reasons.

First, I grew up in a household where compliments were rarely doled out. There was an assumption that you were going to do well in school. You didn't get extra pats on the back for doing your job. I once got an A on an assignment, and my dad's reaction was, "Why didn't you get an A+?" I knew some kids who got gifts and money for doing well in school. Not in my household. That isn't entirely true. I do remember getting a gift in 6th grade for doing well. It was an electric typewriter.

Second, if everything is excellent, nothing is excellent. I reserve praise for those situations where a student performed in a way that was beyond my expectations. I don't want to dilute the meaningfulness of compliments by dishing them out all the time.

Third, giving praise for things that don't merit praise is disingenuous. I refuse to be disingenuous. If I say you did a "good job," it means you did a good job.

Fourth, praising students for non-praiseworthy accomplishments builds a false sense of self-esteem and leads to decreased resilience. I have seen students who have been told they are A students throughout undergrad not be able to handle getting a B (or, God forbid, a C). Heaping unwarranted praise on students sets them up for disappointment—disappointment that they will have trouble coping with.

Fifth, students hear what they want to hear. For those professors who give criticism in a compliment sandwich, guess what the students will hear? The compliment and the compliment. They will relegate the criticism—the meat of the sandwich—to an ancillary afterthought. When, in fact, the criticism was intended to be the main thrust of the feedback.

Sixth, students learn from criticism, not from praise. When a student gets an answer wrong in my class, I will say, "No, that's not correct." Other professors might say, "Well, I see where you are going with that...." The student who was told "That is not correct" will, nine times out of ten, never get that question wrong again. The student who was told that they were on the right track will feel validated in their almost-right (but still wrong) answer.

Please allow me to digress for a moment. Usually, professors don't want to say "No, that's wrong" to a student. Accordingly, they have adopted a series of expressions that really mean "No, that's wrong" but sound better than "No, that's wrong." Expressions like "I see where you're going with that" or "By that, are you saying…?" or "Not exactly" or "That's close." After all, we don't want to hurt students' feelings. There is no greater sin that a law professor can commit than hurting a student's feelings. Students who take offense to the "no" are looking at this the complete wrong way. They are looking at the "no" as the professor signaling some sort of personal failing on the student's part. Getting an answer wrong is not a personal failing—it is just getting an answer wrong. I'm not being mean. I'm not being harsh. I'm being accurate. And clear. For your sake and the sake of the rest of the class. If a professor says, "I see where you're going with that," the whole class is left wondering. *Was the student's answer wrong, or right? What do I write in my notes? What part of the student's answer was wrong and what part was right?* To make one student feel better about him or herself, the professor ends up confusing the whole class. When you step back and appreciate that the professor is teaching a class, *and that it's not all about you*, you should relish the "no." It provides a clear signal that you were on the wrong track and enables you to regroup.

Back to what I was talking about….

I want to be clear that when I talk about criticism, I am using the term in a very broad sense. I use the term to denote telling the student that their answer is not correct, explaining why, and redirecting them. I don't use the term in a pejorative or chastising sense (i.e., "You didn't read the case carefully enough!" or, "You clearly weren't paying attention.").

I want to share an experience I had at my first law job. I worked as an associate attorney at a large pharmaceutical company. At my first performance review, I sat down with my supervisor. He proceeded to say a whole bunch of really nice things about me. At this point, I was like, "I am amazing!" Then he said, "I was once told that you should never do a performance review without giving the employee some suggestions for improvement." *WT*? Where was this going?* Then he said, "One thing that I've noticed is that you are very reactive, but not necessarily proactive. You're good at doing things we tell you to do, but you don't take initiative. You don't speak up at meetings unless you're spoken to." And stuff like that. *Excuse me!?* I was not happy leaving that meeting.

This meeting was over 15 years ago. To this day, I have no idea what good things he said about me. But I remember that one bad thing. I went through the gamut of emotions that I see my students go through: denial, frustration, anger, self-doubt. And then I set out to prove him wrong. Because I was *pissed*. After that, guess who didn't shut up at meetings? And guess who was weighing in on every email chain? This girl (thumbs pointed at me!). I admit that I did this out of a sense of spite and not because I was truly grateful for my supervisor's advice. The gratitude came later. Much later.

Now, with the benefit of time, I can see that my supervisor's criticism is some of the best advice I ever received in my life. It forced me to get out of my shell and stop acting like a student and start acting as a lawyer. I did not see it that way at the time. I thought he was wrong, and mean, and didn't know what he was talking about. But he did. I was just too young and foolish to know that.

What does this have to do with you? I always love closing the loop. Your professors—at least the good ones—are like my supervisor. You will not like what they have to say. You will be angry at them. You will think they are out to lunch. You will think they are too hard on you. If these things are true, they are doing something right. A good professor should not be heaping unwarranted praise on you; a good professor should be pushing you to be better. You should try as best you can to be *grateful* for your professor's feedback instead of *resentful* of it. If you're in the latter camp, I understand. Clearly, I was that way too. But then, do something with that resentment. Prove to them that they were wrong. That's what I did. And here we are today: with me writing this book and being "proactive" about giving everyone my opinion.

7. Struggle Is Normal and Good

Struggle in law school is not only normal, it is desirable. It is only through effortful practice (and failure) that true, long-term learning happens. Unfortunately, law school makes you feel like struggling is a bad thing and that if you don't ace your cold call or get an A on your legal writing assignment, you are stupid and hopeless.

I confess to sometimes being in the cohort of professors who expects students to get it right—and right away. I have to remind myself that I've taught these courses for over a decade. And that students are new to all of this. My job is to teach students how to fish, not to expect them to become expert fishermen (fisherwomen?) right away.

I am writing this section from my parents' house in Toronto. My dad is...how can I say this...not adept at technology. He struggles with his cell phone. He can sort of navigate Facebook. Sort of. There end up being random likes everywhere that I'm not sure he intended. He also posts clip art every morning that says "*Buon giorno!*" (or something like that) with a picture of a

cartoon character. I don't know where this Italian clip art even comes from.[10]
One time he was looking on Kijiji (like Craigslist) for a treadmill. Kijiji has a list
of standard pre-written questions you can ask a seller. My dad clicked on "It is
still available?" The seller replied, "Yes, it is." My dad then wrote, "No, *grazie*."
I died of laughter and was embarrassed by proxy.

Every time I visit, I "practice" computer and phone stuff with my dad.
I show him how to do something and then get him to do it. And then I get him
to do it again the next day. And three days later. And think of tricks to help
him remember how to do it. He struggles at the beginning, but he eventually
gets better.[11]

This is how I try to approach teaching. When you enter law school, you are
all novices. You need to practice. You need to exercise your analytical and criti-
cal-thinking muscles. You need to fail the first time (and maybe the second and
third time). But failing leads to learning. Struggling leads to learning. Instead
of regarding struggling as a bad thing, look at struggling as a good thing. I truly
believe *if you are not struggling, you are not learning.*

There's a great article I came across recently that backs this up.[12] Here are
some brief excerpts:

> I frequently tell students, especially 1Ls, "You're not dumb, you're new. I under-
> stand the difference." I say that in an effort to reduce their reluctance to ask
> seemingly dumb questions. I tell them I expect them to struggle, and I tell them
> that if they're not struggling, they're probably not doing something right. In
> short, I'm trying to make them feel that struggling is normal.
>
> . . .
>
> What the research doesn't discuss is this: Law students should struggle in the
> classroom. The law is a complex specialty, and those just entering legal edu-
> cation are by and large unfamiliar with the demands being placed upon them.

---

10. Proof that Facebook is evil for making these available to my dad.

11. Incidentally, my dad is now taking a computer class at the local Italian club. He
informed me that it's not a computer class, it's a *tablet* class, "because a tablet is different
than a computer." He doesn't like the class very much because "they don't have a good way
of explaining." Unlike me...who is an expert explainer.

12. Catherine M. Christopher, *Normalizing Struggle*, 73 Ark. L. Rev. 27, 36, 40, 44
(2020).

Overall, "learning is deeper and more durable when it's effortful." Students who breezed through high school and college may be brought up short when law school proves challenging. It is important for law faculty to help students understand that effortful learning is quality learning. After all, if law school were easy, everyone would go.

. . .

Happily, scientific research demonstrates that the best learning happens while the learner is struggling. Law schools can capitalize on this fact to teach students that struggle is effective and beneficial. This in turn will create more resilient law students and happier, more effective lawyers.

To be clear, I'm not saying all this stuff about struggle because I've read a bunch of articles on the science of learning (though I have). I am saying this for two reasons. First, I have witnessed firsthand that the students who really grapple with the material (and struggle) tend to do the best in law school. Second, and probably more important for me, I was a student who struggled in law school.

I mentioned this before, but I was not great about processing what was going on in class. I would often leave class wondering, "What just happened? I have no idea what he was talking about." I distinctly remember my Contracts professor repeatedly referencing the *Pao On* "move"—and not having a clue what the hell he was talking about. Everyone else would be like, "That was a pretty easy class." This would cause extreme panic (unsurprisingly) and, of course, a great sense of insecurity.

I would go home, sit with the material, and try to put it all together until I understood it. Tears may sometimes have been involved. I would have to revisit the readings and then craft my outline in a way that I understood the material. This took a long time. And it required recognizing what I didn't know and what I needed to figure out. In short, I struggled. I was never one to leave class and think, "I got this." But the effortful struggle paid off. Because I worked with the material and had a hard time with it, I learned it at a deeper level than other students.

As a professor now, what worries me most are students who say, "Oh yeah, I understand"—not students who say, "I'm not sure I totally understand. I'm struggling a bit." If you're in the former camp, I would advise you to have a healthy dose of skepticism about what you know and don't know. And if you're in the latter camp, recognize that this struggle is completely normal and work through it.

8. You Are Not a "Visual" Learner

I hate to be the one to break it to you, but you are *not* a visual learner. You may have a preference for visual learning, but it's just that: a preference. It does not mean that you learn better though visualization than through any other method of instruction. *What? That's gotta be wrong.* Nope. It's not. Studies have shown time and again that there's no such thing as a visual learner or an auditory learner. Or whatever else you think you are.[13]

Why am I telling you this, other than to blow your mind? Because pigeonholing yourself, or having yourself pigeonholed, into a particular type of "learning style" works to your detriment. You will come to believe that you are not adept at processing verbal or written information as well as you are visual information. And believing that can become a self-fulfilling prophecy.

Moreover, believing that you have a learning style gets in the way of real learning because you become frustrated and angry that you're not being taught the way you'd prefer. And it also gives you a convenient scapegoat when you don't do well. Instead of taking responsibility for your shortcomings, you can blame it on the professor whose teaching did not mesh with your "learning style." I get this a lot, as I'm sure other professors do. Here are two recent comments from student evaluations to show you what I mean:

> I understand that we should know the material cold. I just feel that I did not learn much and the style of teaching simply does not work for my specific learning needs.

> …[T]here are many ways in which students learn. Professor Monestier should be a little more open to other methods in which students learn in order to accommodate more students than those who learn best through her method.

In short, some students bring with them an expectation that the professor will present the material according to each individual student's learning style. When professors fail to do this—because, um, well, it's *f**king impossible*—students lament that the professor's teaching was out of synch with the student's learning style. Give up the ghost on this learning style B.S. Please.

---

13. *See, e.g.,* https://www.theatlantic.com/science/archive/2018/04/the-myth-of-learning-styles/557687/; https://poorvucenter.yale.edu/LearningStylesMyth.

9. Do Not Be a Snowflake

Collins English Dictionary defines the term "snowflake generation" as "the young adults of the 2010s (born from 1980-1994), [who are] viewed as being less resilient and more prone to taking offence than previous generations." I would agree with this basic definition, but I don't think the snowflake generation ends at those born in 1994. Today's law students are snowflakes.[14] They are special, precious, and unique. And they melt at first contact with something hard. Go ahead, take offense. That will prove my point.

In the snowflakes' defense, it's not their fault. They grew up with helicopter parents and went to schools that prioritized self-esteem over learning. They were kept away from anything which might cause hurt, offense, or discomfort. They were kept away from peanuts. Today's snowflakes are being kept away from sugar and gluten.

I have to set the stage here for you, so you know where I'm coming from. I grew up in a different time. My parents were the antithesis of helicopter or snowplow parents, or whatever style of parenting is in vogue these days. They did not tell me I was "wonderful" and "special" at every opportunity. They did not care about my "self-esteem." They did not devote their lives to making me "safe" and "comfortable." Back in those days, parents let kids be kids. Parents would throw the kids in the backseat, *sans* seatbelts. Parents did not arrange playdates. They didn't give a rats a** if you were bored. Parents did not suit kids up like they were going to war just so they could ride their bikes. Parents smoked in the house and in the car. Parents did not give their kids time outs. They gave them a good swat on the rear. Parents were not worried about giving their kids organic and GMO-free food. They fed their kids Chef Boyardee[15] followed up with a big glass of Tang. I'm not saying that this was a better approach to growing up. But I am saying that it was a decidedly different one to that which you've probably experienced. And like it or not, this informs my view on life and on teaching.

---

14. I *know* it's totally overused. But that does not mean it's not true.

15. I only had Chef Boyardee once in my life. It was so impactful I remember it to this day. I was probably seven or eight. I saw all the commercials on TV and really wanted the ravioli. Now, I've told you that my family is Italian. My mother makes the best pasta, and she refused to buy pasta in a can. But every week at the grocery store, I would *beg* for Chef Boyardee. One week, she caved and bought it. She made it for me and my brother. We literally took one bite and spit it out. Chef Boyardee was never mentioned at our house again.

I want to give you a concrete example of what I mean about self-esteem not exactly being a priority in those days. My brother, Dennis, played hockey and soccer growing up. He was always the smallest kid on the team.[16] But he was a solid player in both sports, probably one of the top five kids on the team. Did my dad praise him after every game? Did my dad, after a loss, say, "You'll get 'em next time, champ?" That's hysterical. The highest praise out of my dad's mouth was "That was decent." If it was not decent, Dennis—and the rest of us—would know about it. There would be a play-by-play reconstruction of the game on the way home, with critiques of everything Dennis did wrong. So, yeah, not exactly a self-esteem builder.[17]

There is a great book you should read called *The Coddling of the American Mind: How Good Intentions and Bad Ideas Are Setting Up a Generation for Failure*.[18] The authors, Greg Lukianoff and Jonathan Haidt, argue that many of the problems we see on college campuses stem from what they call the three great untruths:

1. What doesn't kill you makes you weaker;

2. Always trust your feelings; and

3. Life is a battle between good people and evil people.

Essentially, they posit that the culture of safety-ism which has developed to protect students has interfered with students' social, emotional, and intel-

---

16. Note to self: Check with Dennis to make sure his feelings will not be hurt by this statement.

17. I find myself taking the dad approach with Emilia. She is growing up in a time where "great job" is uttered all the time. I was recently playing dolls with her. We decided to have a singing and dancing contest with five dolls. I crowned a "winner." Afterward, Emilia wanted to crown *another* winner. Nope. There can only be one winner. But she's clever (I like to think she takes after me). She said, "No, this is a different competition, with only the four dolls who didn't win. So, there can be a new winner." Nice try, Emilia. But I see through what you're doing. I think she's going to be a good lawyer. One more Emilia story to prove she's going to be a good lawyer. We were playing pretend in her bedroom, and we heard a car alarm go off outside. She gets very nervous with loud noises and started asking a million questions: *What is that? What happened? Where is it? Why?* I went into teacher mode. I said, "Emilia, are we inside or outside?" She said, "Inside." I said, "Where's the car alarm? Inside or outside?" She said, "Outside." I explained, "So if we are inside and the car alarm is outside, how am I supposed to know what's going on?" I thought the argument was compelling. She shut me down by saying, "Well, Zia, there's a window." Touché.

18. https://www.thecoddling.com/the-book.

lectual development. Lukianoff and Haidt argue that students are anti-fragile and require stressors to grow into fully formed adults. Speaking specifically of children, they say,

> Children, like many other complex adaptive systems, are antifragile. Their brains require a wide range of inputs from their environments in order to configure themselves for those environments. Like the immune system, children must be exposed to challenges and stressors (within limits, and in age-appropriate ways), or they will fail to mature into strong and capable adults, able to engage productively with people and ideas that challenge their beliefs and moral convictions.

They also emphasize parents' and teachers' obligation to help prepare students for the real world:

> Given that risks and stressors are natural, unavoidable parts of life, parents and teachers should be helping kids develop their innate abilities to grow and learn from such experiences. There's an old saying: "Prepare the child for the road, not the road for the child." But these days, we seem to be doing precisely the opposite: we're trying to clear away anything that might upset children, not realizing that in doing so, we're repeating the peanut-allergy mistake. If we protect children from various classes of potentially upsetting experiences, we make it far more likely that those children will be unable to cope with such events when they leave our protective umbrella.

I cannot do the book justice in a few short paragraphs. But I wholeheartedly agree with its basic premise. We have witnessed the rise of the least resilient, and most coddled, generation ever. Let me give you some examples of what I mean:

I had a student who asked not to be called on when discussing *Hamer v. Sidway,* a contracts case involving consideration, because she found it triggering.

I had a student bawl in my office when she did not get full points for an *extra-credit* assignment.

I have multiple students every semester who ask not to be called on because they are having a "hard day."[19]

---

19. I don't mean "death in the family" hard day. I mean "I just had a stressful meeting" hard day.

I have had students throw temper tantrums when I don't immediately cave to their demands.

I had a student who came to my office crying and asked not to be called on for a week because he was going through a breakup with his girlfriend.

I have students who have had self-admitted "breakdowns" because their final exam was going to be proctored remotely.[20]

This is just a small smattering of how coddling manifests itself in law school. Law school professors and administrators are complicit in the coddling. They prioritize "feelings" and "comfort" above all else. I actually received an email from a colleague of mine who felt it was her duty to pass along that she heard some students were feeling "upset" and "scared" in my class.[21]

Oh no, students are "scared" in my class! I'm so sorry for being *scary*. I guess I didn't get the memo that law school was a place that deals in feelings rather than truth or facts. My bad.

The anti-resilience is most acute when it comes to grades. Students are indignant when a professor dares give them anything other than a stellar grade. I had a student get a 1.5/3 on a quiz, which was an average score. Within five minutes of getting his grade, he sent me an angry email saying how ridiculous it was that he got the grade he did. He believed he deserved at least a 2/3 on the assignment.[22]

Leaving aside the wholly unprofessional nature of the email, which I did address with him, what struck me is that he was this angry over *half a point*. He could not process getting less than he thought he "deserved," and he turned his perceived failure into anger directed at me.

This is a very common reaction among today's law students who have become accustomed to A's and praise (yes, that was meant to rhyme!). Two pro-

---

20. Just like the bar exam during Covid. Here are examples of the types of emails I receive: "I feel like the mental health of students is in question at this point. The multiple assessment failures have caused myself and other students to feel like failures and to have breakdowns with each other."; "I am finding myself to be very depressed, concerned, and having multiple break downs when I think about this exam. This is nothing against you, however, I think there needs to be a change and I think considering changing the exam to open book is an important consideration to help with the mental health, fear, and overall anxiety surrounding this final."; "I am also one of those students who has had multiple breakdowns over the exam grades, because with all of the studying and preparation, the grades do not reflect it."

21. Thank you, colleague, for doing your civic duty.

22. Portions of the email were in ALL CAPS. NEVER use ALL CAPS.

fessors conducted an informal study on the use of formative assessments in the doctrinal curriculum. Much like I did, they gave small quizzes and graded them using raw points (not the curve). They explained some unanticipated consequences associated with giving these assessments:

> First, there was substantial student resistance; especially the first time we imposed this quiz schedule. Students disliked being required to write "exam answers" so often and were frustrated by the low scores they received on their initial quizzes. They also were resistant to making any changes in their approaches. These students were second- and third-year law students, who generally saw themselves as competent and were not inclined to accept any implication to the contrary. We had thought (a bit naively) that students would welcome the feedback, but because they had not seen raw scores as opposed to curved grades before, they were frequently dismayed by their scores, and this dismay turned to resentment.[23]

Yup, been there, done that. If you had just called me, I could have saved you the trouble. Any professor who willingly continues to give assessments like this despite the bullsh*t they have to deal with deserves a raise. Me included.

To be fair, not all students direct their anger at the professor, though some do. Some students will privately fall into a deep pit of despair over a bad grade. And I don't even mean a bad final grade. I mean a bad grade on a virtually meaningless assignment. I can't tell you the number of tears that have been spilled over one or two points. I have witnessed these tears firsthand and have also heard about them after the fact. If all it takes to blow you over is a slight breeze, you need to get some heavier shoes.

Part of me feels like I'm being a little harsh. And I *really* don't want to get nasty emails from students telling me how I'm "insensitive" to their "mental health issues." I am very empathetic to legitimate mental and physical health concerns, as I am to challenging personal circumstances. But what I'm seeing is not that—it's another thing altogether.

It's the total inability to cope when you are told your performance is something other than amazing. It's the expectation that education revolves around

---

23. Karen McDonald Henning & Julia Belian, *If You Give a Mouse a Cookie: Increasing Assessments and Individualized Feedback in Law School Classes*, 95 U. Det. Mercy L. Rev. 35, 58–59 (2017).

you and your "needs." It's the fact that many students have no perspective on how minor these concerns are in the context of *real* problems.

I have someone close to me who has been dealt a really sh*tty lot in life. Like *really* f**king sh*tty. But he deals with it. He doesn't sulk and complain—though he has every right to. He is the epitome of resilience. And I admire him more than words can express. So, when I see students lose their minds over half a point or start crying in my office over a break-up with somebody they've been dating for two months, I have very little patience. People have #realproblems. Get a grip.

10. Learn from Your First Semester

Most of this book is focused on your first semester, since you're probably reading this book either the summer before law school or at the beginning of your law school journey. But there is life after your first semester...it's called your second semester. And your second and third year.

Your first semester may not go as you planned. In fact, mathematically, there's a good chance you won't be super happy with your grades. What then? Then, pick yourself up by your bootstraps[24] and move forward more intelligently. *Wait, are you suggesting we aren't intelligent?!* God, do I need to explain everything to you? I am not suggesting you are not intelligent. I am suggesting that whatever you did first semester did not yield the results you wanted—so moving forward, be smart about what you do and how you do it.

First off, take responsibility for your grades. If you got a C, that is on you. Not on your professor. Not on the exam software. Not on anything else. Take whatever time you need to be depressed, angry, frustrated, or whatever about your grades. Then, move on. Do not carry those emotions over into your second semester. Those are unhelpful emotions that will only serve to bring you down.

Second, figure out why you didn't get the grade you wanted or expected. It is *not* because you didn't "organize" the exam answer well enough. It is *not* because you weren't "good" at issuing spotting. It is *not* because you didn't "use IRAC" on the exam. Figuring out why you got the grade you did takes work. You need to work backward and identify where in the studying process things went awry.

---

24. Another old person saying!

Third, adjust. If you did not do well first semester, don't approach your second semester the exact same way. What's the expression that fits here? Insanity is doing the same thing over and over again and expecting different results. Or something like that. And to be clear, it's on *you* and only you to figure this out and adjust. This is not something that your professor or academic support can or should do for you. Remember, learning is something that you do for yourself, not something that is done to you.

A quick note for those of you who do get very good grades first semester: Keep your nose to the grindstone[25] and keep working. Do not, under any circumstances, brag about your grades. Everyone *hates* that person. Also remember that second semester, everyone ups their game. It will be harder for you to get an A second semester than it was first semester.

11. Recommended Reading

I really cannot do justice to the literature on self-regulated learning and the science of learning in this section of the book. I highly recommend that you read (or at least look at) some of the following articles. Most of them will be available with your Westlaw or Lexis subscription. But many of them are posted and available for free on SSRN.[26]

Christine Bartholomew, *Time: An Empirical Analysis of Law School Time Management Deficiencies*, 81 U. Cin. L. Rev. 897 (2013).

Megan Bess, *Grit, Growth Mindset, and the Path to Successful Lawyering*, 89 UMKC L. Rev. 493 (2021).

Elizabeth M. Bloom, *Creating Desirable Difficulties: Strategies for Reshaping Teaching and Learning in the Law School Classroom*, 95 U. Det. Mercy L. Rev. 115 (2018).

Jennifer M. Cooper, *Smarter Law Learning: Using Cognitive Science to Maximize Law Learning*, 44 Cap. U. L. Rev. 551 (2016).

---

25. *Id.* You probably don't know what "Id." means. But look at the context. I have faith that you can figure it out without even looking it up.

26. https://www.ssrn.com/index.cfm/en/. SSRN is a repository where academics post published articles and works in progress. I get emails from them about once a month telling me I'm in the top 10% of authors. Thank you for stroking my ego, SSRN! But when I look on my profile page, I see that I'm ranked 21,558th. Not exactly that impressive, is it?

Rebecca Flanagan, *The Kids Aren't Alright: Rethinking the Law Student Skills Deficit*, 2015 BYU Educ. & L.J. 135 (2015).

Edwin S. Fruehwald, *How to Help Students from Disadvantaged Backgrounds Succeed in Law School*, 1 Texas A&M L. Rev. 83 (2013).

Shailini J. George, *Teaching the Smartphone Generation: How Cognitive Science Can Improve Learning in Law School*, 66 Maine L. Rev. 164 (2013).

Laura P. Graham, *Generation Z Goes to Law School: Teaching and Reaching Law Students in the Post-Millennial Generation*, 41 Ark. L. Rev. 29 (2018).

Karen McDonald Henning & Julia Belian, *If You Give a Mouse a Cookie: Increasing Assessments and Individualized Feedback in Law School Classes*, 95 U. Det. Mercy L. Rev. 35 (2017).

Louis N. Schulze, Jr., *Using Science to Build Better Learners: One School's Successful Efforts to Raise Its Passage Rates in an Era of Decline*, 68 J. Legal Educ. 230 (2019).

Ruth Vance & Susan Stuart, *Of Moby Dick and Tartar Sauce: The Academically Underprepared Law Student and the Curse of Overconfidence*, 53 Duq. L. Rev. 133 (2015).

Susan Stuart & Ruth Vance, *Bringing a Knife to the Gunfight: The Academically Underprepared Law Student & Legal Education Reform*, 48 Val. U. L. Rev. 1 (2013).

Carolyn V. Williams, *#criticalreading #wickedproblem*, 44 S. Ill. U. L.J. 179 (2020).

EIGHT

Learning How to Think

Too often we . . . enjoy the comfort of opinion
without the discomfort of thought.

JOHN F. KENNEDY

1. Embrace Uncertainty

One of the ways that law school is different than undergrad is that there are no right answers. Except that sometimes there are. Confused yet?

Students come to law school expecting the law to be a static set of rules that they just memorize. One of the questions I get asked a lot by students in class is, "So what's the law?" or, "What's the right answer?" *F**k if I know.* Students don't seem to like that answer (which I obviously don't say in class). Students who want a "right" answer to put in their notes and memorize for exam time tend not to fare well. They fail to appreciate that the law is full of uncertainty, which is a beautiful and a frustrating thing all at once.

Let me give you an example. One of the topics I cover in Contracts is liquidated damages. A liquidated damages clause is one that parties put in their contract specifying that if a party breaches, he will owe $x in damages. Simple enough. But not really. These clauses are not automatically enforceable. Instead, a court will need to decide whether these clauses are a penalty, in which case they are unenforceable. There is a multi-prong test for doing so. But parts of the test don't make much sense and are internally inconsistent. And with respect to the core part of the test—assessing whether the number chosen was a reasonable approximation of harm—there is the additional question of whether to assess this at the time the contract was made or at the time the contract was breached. We go through all this in class, and then I'll get a question, "So is the $10,000 liquidated damages clause in the case a penalty?" *F**k if I know.* And, who really cares? You just need to know how to argue that it is a penalty, and how to argue that it is not a penalty.

Trying to get students out of the fixed answer mindset is difficult. They really want definitive answers that the law just doesn't provide. If you wanted definitive answers, you should have gone to accounting school. But that's right, you hate math.

With all that said, there are some right and wrong answers in law school. It's not all up in the air. For instance, if you say that in contracts, silence generally equals acceptance, you would be wrong. If you say that expectancy damages put you in the position you would be in if the contract had not been entered into, that would also be wrong.

And sometimes you are given a very straightforward problem where there is only one legitimate argument to make. For instance, you might be given a fact pattern where a seller in an advertisement claims that this is the "best washing machine you've ever laid eyes on." The question might be asking you to determine whether this statement in actionable in contract. The answer is no.

So, the law is all about uncertainty. Except in cases where it's not.

2. Cases Are Not Gospel

Students tend to misunderstand the value of cases in law school pedagogy. They are led to believe that cases are the be-all and end-all of law school. In some courses, they are. In most courses, they are not. In most courses, cases are simply a *vehicle* for teaching you the law. They explain the law and they apply that law to the facts of that particular case. There is nothing magical about *Lucy v. Zehmer* or *Petterson v. Pattburg*.

This leads to my next observation. You can, and should, critique cases. Judges don't always properly articulate or apply the law. *What?!* Judges sometimes engage in results-oriented reasoning. That is, they decide what they want the outcome of the case to be and then find a way to get there. In doing so, they sometimes make a bit of a mess of the law.

I often work with students to critique cases in class. This is higher order thinking, which is a *good thing*. Sometimes a student will ask me why I assign cases that I think are wrongly decided. This view rests on an erroneous assumption that the law is clean and neat and precise. It is not. As a lawyer, you're going to have to make sense of the conflicting law in front of you. You're going to have to distinguish and critique cases to best represent your client. Law is not a static set of rules given to us by esteemed and infallible judges. Law is messy.

Students who think that a case is like a sacred message from on-high aren't looking at cases the right way. Certainly, the case was put in the textbook for a reason—usually to present a rule and show you how it plays out. But that does not mean everything in the case was perfectly expressed or that there weren't problems or inconsistencies with the court's reasoning. The very fact that many cases have dissents shows that a legal opinion is not sacrosanct. What I am essentially doing by asking students to critique the case is to "write" a dissent. It is designed to test how well you know the law and how well you can manipulate it.[1]

3. Make Responsive Counterarguments

You're probably like *what the f**k is a "responsive" counterargument?* Let me give you an example that I use with my class to illustrate what a non-responsive counterargument is. Growing up, my brother and I would fight. We would often have the "you're stupid, you're ugly" fight. I would tell Dennis he was stupid. And he would respond that I was ugly. Yes, super-healthy childhood behavior. As you can tell, my family is not dysfunctional in the slightest. Dennis's response ("You're ugly") is a non-responsive counterargument. It may have been true, but it didn't address the argument I put on the table: "You're stupid." A responsive argument would be "I'm not stupid. I got straight A's on my report card." I'm laughing out loud as I write that.

The non-responsive counterargument happens *all the time* in law school. For instance, I teach a class where we talk about whether a seller has a duty to disclose that a property is "stigmatized" when selling a house. Specifically, the case we cover involves whether the seller needs to disclose the occurrence of a murder-suicide in the house. Student #1 might argue, "No, a seller shouldn't have to disclose because that would open the floodgates to all sorts of dis-

---

1. I am not using the term in the way you might think. *See* https://www.merriam-web-ster.com/dictionary/manipulate.

closure obligations." I would then ask for the counterargument. Student #2 might respond, "Yes, a seller should have to disclose because not disclosing amounts to bad faith." Okay, that might be true. But…it doesn't address the floodgates argument. A responsive counterargument would be something like, "The floodgates argument is a red herring. We are *only* talking about disclosing the existence of a murder in the house. We can deal with other disclosure issues on a case-by-case basis." It's not that the bad faith argument was wrong or bad, it's that it wasn't responsive to the point Student #1 made.

There is always time to make the affirmative arguments you want to make. But you can't let the other side get in arguments, unchecked. I'm fast-forwarding a bit now. When you're in practice, you never know what argument is going to resonate with a judge. If your opponent makes an argument that sticks with the judge and you say *nothing about it*, you are going to lose. This is why you need to make responsive counterarguments. You need to shoot down your opponent's argument on the merits—not just get sidetracked with your own arguments.

4. Be Precise

Precision matters in law. Unfortunately, students tend not to be very precise. When a professor insists on precision (which, I would define as "accuracy"), students think the professor is being nit-picky or a stickler. I sometimes get comments on evaluations saying "She wants things phrased a certain way." Nope. I don't want things "phrased a certain way." I want things phrased the right way.

I was recently singing Christmas songs with my niece, Emilia. She sort of knows the lyrics. But she's not very precise. For instance, this is how she sings Rudolph the Red-Nosed Reindeer: "Rudolph the old red reindeer…". No amount of telling her the right words will get her to sing it any other way. I let it go—because, well, she's four. But I see this all the time from 23-year-olds. It's sort of in the neighborhood of right, but not quite.

Time for an example. I often have students say, "Article 2 applies to the sale of goods between merchants." This is right and wrong, all at the same time. Literally applied, it is true. Article 2 does apply to the sale of goods between merchants. But what the students mean by this sentence is that Article 2 *only* applies when you have a sale of goods between merchants, which is wrong. If you are articulating the scope of Article 2, the *correct* statement would be:

"Article 2 applies to the sale of goods." Even more accurate would be: "Article 2 applies to transactions in goods." Come on, does this really matter? *Hell yeah!* If what you have imprinted in your brain is that Article 2 applies to the sale of goods between merchants, then when you see a problem with me selling my TV to my neighbor, you're not going to think Article 2 applies. A lack of precision, in other words, will have spillover effects.

Law turns on minute details. It turns on words like "and" or "or." It turns on commas in statutes. It turns on the use of a word in one place and the lack of that word in another place. Which brings me full circle to my first sentence: Precision matters.

5. Consider Consequences

Students tend not to be great at understanding the implications of their legal arguments. When a student gives me an answer in class, I often ask something like, "Okay, if that's the position we're taking, what are the logical consequences?" The student looks at me blankly. They think they are "done" because they gave me the answer and fail to understand that the answer has consequences—for the law, for litigants, or for society generally.

In Sales, for instance, one of the first things we cover is "hybrid transactions." A hybrid transaction is one that involves both goods and services. Having carpet installed, for instance, is a hybrid transaction. It involves goods (the carpet) and services (the installation). Generally, with hybrid transactions, courts must categorize the transaction as one that is subject to the common law or one that is subject to Article 2. If the transaction is subject to Article 2, then the immediate seller warrants that the goods will be of merchantable—i.e., satisfactory—quality. If they are not, then the seller is liable. Way too many details, I know. Sorry. In any event, we get into this issue with all sorts of hybrid transactions: a dentist filling a cavity, a hospital providing blood to a patient, and an interior designer ordering furniture for a client. Students are able to appreciate how to apply the relevant test, the predominant purpose test, to determine whether the transaction is subject to the common law or to Article 2. But then, that's it. That's where it ends.

In the dentist scenario, for instance, if a student says that the transaction is subject to Article 2, they fail to consider the second and third order effects of that conclusion. When I ask them to walk me through the consequences, they falter.

What I'm looking for are the broader implications of what the student is saying. I don't want them to stop at the sentence, "The transaction is subject to Article 2." What would this mean? Would this mean that all dentists are liable to all patients if the filling material is defective? What if the dentist got the filling from a reputable third-party supplier? Would liability extend to personal injury (if, for instance, the patient swallowed the filling)? Would dentists absorb the cost of this increased liability, or would they pass it along to patients? Would categorizing the transaction as subject to Article 2 be a net positive or negative for consumer protection?

This sort of thinking takes some practice. But it's essential to being a lawyer. Seeing where your argument leads really helps you focus on whether it's an argument you should be making. It also helps you anticipate counterarguments. The best offense is a great defense.

6. Don't Have Tunnel Vision

Students tend to have tunnel vision and fail to appreciate the potential complexity posed by legal problems. They are often wedded to *their* view of the legal issue and are unable, or unwilling, to broaden their focus. Law involves understanding that things are not always cut and dried. I don't just mean on exams (though this is how it plays out concretely). I mean in general.

I see the tunnel vision a lot with element-based doctrines. An element-based doctrine is a rule of law that has different parts that need to be satisfied before the plaintiff can succeed. For instance, to recover based on promissory estoppel, the plaintiff must prove that: (1) There was a promise made by the defendant that was intended to be relied on; (2) The plaintiff detrimentally relied on the promise; (3) The reliance was reasonable; (4) Injustice can be avoided only by enforcement of the promise. When I give the class a hypothetical involving promissory estoppel, students make up their mind intuitively and then plug in facts that support their argument. Instead of letting the law guide the result, they let the result guide the legal analysis. This is what I mean by the results-oriented reasoning that I spoke about above. The process should be the reverse. You do not make any judgment calls until the end.

Let's use a case I teach, *Shoemaker v. Commonwealth Bank.* In that case, the plaintiff homeowners had a mortgage with the defendant bank. The bank sent a letter to the plaintiffs because they had not been purchasing homeowners' insurance as required by their mortgage. The letter indicated that it was the obligation of the homeowner to buy insurance and if they didn't, the bank might be forced to do so on their behalf and then add it to the mortgage payment. In *Shoemaker*, the bank did arrange for insurance for a period of time and then let it lapse. Lo and behold, the property burned down with no insurance on it. Most students reading this case will have sympathy for the homeowners and decide that yes, they can win on a promissory estoppel claim. After making that decision, they plug a couple of facts into the elements, and *voilà*, a (bad) answer is formed:

> There is a promise when the bank promised to buy insurance for the home-owners. Obviously, the bank intended for the plaintiffs to rely on the promise because otherwise, what was the point of the letter? The plaintiffs relied on the promise because after getting the letter, they didn't buy insurance. This reliance was reasonable because a bank has an interest in protecting its property and the homeowners know that. It would be an injustice not to enforce the promise because the plaintiff's house burned down, and the bank can easily absorb the loss.

Do you see from this answer how the student picked the result (yes, the plaintiff should recover) and then everything they said went to support that conclusion? That is not an *analysis*.[2] That is a plug and play.

Occasionally, a student might throw in a counterargument here or there, but they usually fail to engage with it at a deeper level. Here's what I mean:

> There is a promise when the bank promised to buy insurance for the home-owners. Obviously, the bank intended for the plaintiffs to rely on the promise because otherwise, what was the point of the letter? The plaintiffs relied on the promise because after getting the letter, they didn't buy insurance. This reliance

---

2. To give you an idea of a real analysis, consider just the first part of the test: Is there a promise by the bank to the homeowner? It sort of looks like there's a promise when the bank says in the letter that if the homeowners don't get insurance, the bank might be forced to purchase insurance on their behalf and add it to the mortgage payment. But let's think about that a bit more. Is that really a promise? It almost seems more like a threat. Plus, the bank didn't say they were *definitely* going to buy the insurance, just that they "might" be forced to do this. And the so-called "promise" doesn't have a duration. If this is a promise, is it a forever promise? That is, was the bank promising to do this for the duration of the mortgage? Is it possible that even if the bank made a promise, the promise was over and done with when the bank chose not to continue this practice? You see how much digging is involved for just *one* element of the doctrine.

was reasonable because a bank has an interest in protecting its property and the homeowners know that. <u>It is possible that the homeowners should have exercised some due diligence and checked on the status of the insurance, but this is a weak argument.</u> It would be an injustice not to enforce the promise because the plaintiff's house burned down, and the bank can easily absorb the loss. <u>On the other hand, the plaintiffs were in breach of the original mortgage. But still, overall, I think they would succeed in their claim.</u>

The counterarguments here were just throwaways. The student added them in to pad the answer but did not meaningfully address them.

Obviously, we all have instincts about justice, fairness, and what the right result should be. But be careful about taking those instincts and just running with them instead of stepping back and looking at the issue from a 180-degree vantage point (or is it 360 degrees?). Whatever. You get what I'm saying.

7. Exercise Good Judgment

One of the hardest things about the law is that it involves exercising good judgment. And I don't mean just good legal judgment. I mean good judgment—period. Sometimes when you get to law school, you end up being encouraged to think *too much* like a lawyer. It's like you throw common sense out the window because you're knee-deep in the complexities of choice of law, battle of the forms, or defamation law. I have recently found myself saying, "Pretend you are not in law school. How would a person on the street answer this question?"

One Contracts professor, Jeffrey Lipshaw, even wrote a book called *Beyond Legal Reasoning: A Critique of Pure Lawyering*.[3] The author essentially argues that students should sometimes *stop* thinking like a lawyer. Professor Lipshaw provides an illustration of the problems associated with thinking too much like a lawyer. He relays a situation involving United Airlines dragging a passenger off a plane. United's lawyers took the position that this was permissible under the airline's contract of carriage.[4] What United chose to do then flowed from that legal conclusion. No one apparently told United that the right *legal* interpretation of the contract of carriage might not dictate the best course of action.

---

3. Jeffrey Lipshaw, Beyond Legal Reasoning: A Critique of Pure Lawyering (2017).
4. https://boston.suffolk.edu/lawmagazine/stub-feature-article-4.php#.YcS9iVlOnIU

Just because you have a winning legal argument does not mean you need to deploy it. Here, the best course of action would have been to forget the contract of carriage and apologize for dragging a passenger off a plane. A person without a law degree would have figured that out no problem.

Here is what Professor Lipshaw says is wrong with thinking too much like a lawyer:

> You lose sight of the fact that the pure logic of legal reasoning is essentially indifferent as to moral outcomes. Once a lawyer sets a particular problem into a particular legal theory, the logic of the law takes over and dictates the anticipated result. Understanding how to translate stories into legal theories is the fundamental skill we teach in the first year. It's like learning to draw if you are going to be an artist. But when your client needs good advice, you may need to call on business acumen, good sense, or morality.
>
> So this "unlearning" is something students need to do later, after they've mastered the basic legal reasoning skills, because following purely legal logic can lead lawyers and clients astray.

If I may, let me sum up this section for you: Think like a lawyer, but not too much like a lawyer.[5]

---

5. This reminds me of something that one of my friends said to me when I first started dating my husband. She said, "Just be yourself. Well, not your *self* self. You know what I mean." Indeed, I did know what she meant. I hid the crazy until we were married. And you know that my dad laid down a "no return policy," so we're all good.

NINE

Your Professors

Treat people the way you want to be treated. Talk to people the way you want to be talked to. Respect is earned, not given.

NUSSEIN NISHAH

1. Figure Out Your Professor's Style and Adjust Accordingly

I often tell my students, "You aren't taking Contracts. You're taking Contracts *with me.*" Another professor's Contracts class might look very different from mine. One size does not fit all.

Navigating personality and style differences among professors is one of the biggest challenges of being a 1L. The challenges also exist as a 2L and 3L, but by then, you are better at it. In your first semester, you might have five different professors who have five unique styles. You will come to understand and appreciate these styles more as the semester wears on. For instance, you might have "the nurturing" professor, the "storyteller" professor, the "pure Socratic" professor, the "high expectations" professor, the "scatterbrained" professor, etc. You might feel a bit of intellectual whiplash going from one class to another.

Such is the nature of law school. Your teachers did not go to school to learn how to teach—so they all bring their own personalities, styles, and idiosyncrasies into their teaching. And you must learn to adapt to each of these professors to thrive in their classes. As much as you wish Professor A could be like Professor B, she is not going to be. If wishes were fishes....[1]

One of your goals must be to find a way to make these different styles work for you. You will likely have clear preferences for one style over another. Students who are very linear and logical tend to like me; those who are more abstract thinkers, not so much. I would suggest looking at these differences as a real opportunity to learn from lots of different types of people. While you might mesh better with one than another, that doesn't mean you can't learn from someone who uses a style that is not your preference. And—reality check—the real world is going to be full of people who don't think the way you do. The earlier you learn to adapt and thrive in settings that aren't your immediate comfort zone, the better.

More concretely, getting to know your professor's style might also mean tailoring your experience in a particular class to the professor. If you know that one professor is big on the details of every single case, you might focus more on the cases. If you know another professor is more interested in policy, you might focus more on understanding the material at a macro-level and the implications for law and society more generally. In other words, you may not be able to approach every class the exact same way. Caveat: You should still approach outlining and studying the exact same way (i.e., the way I told you about earlier).

2. Your Professor Is Not Your Friend

I've noticed that some students have taken to oversharing with their professors. This is not just a "me" thing. I've heard it from many of my colleagues as well.

Students, please be mindful that your professors are your professors. They are not your friends. Now, there are situations that call for sharing information. For instance, if you have a medical condition that interferes with your ability to take a test, then you should probably share that information with your professor (or the relevant Dean).

I am talking about something different. I am talking about sharing too much personal information with professors, including specific medical conditions, relationship issues, family or friend drama, or other non-law school

---

1. I can never remember the end of that saying, but I know it fits here.

related issues. I do not need to hear about your irritable bowel syndrome and how it was the reason you weren't able to attend class. I do not need to know about your on-again-off-again relationship with your high school sweetheart. I do not need to know that your child's favorite game is peek-a-boo, and his favorite book is "Goodnight, Moon." I am making all these up, but they are not very far from reality (and in some cases, the reality is even worse than what I've written here).[2]

Law school is a professional environment. And while your professors are here to help you succeed, you need to be mindful of the line between appropriate and inappropriate. I have seen far too many students stray over that line.

I realize that things are perhaps more casual in undergrad, and that you may have called your professors by their first name and hung out with them after class. But that is generally not the norm in law schools—nor should it be, I think. When you enter the workforce, there will be these same lines that you need to be cognizant of.

I'll share a story with you. I had a former student who was applying for a clerkship. She was a superstar. She went into the interview and, by all accounts, did a good job. But she referred to her boyfriend several times during the interview. The judge reached out, concerned about the maturity level of this student: Did she really think she should be talking about her "boyfriend" in an interview for a prestigious clerkship? While the student ended up getting the job, she almost didn't. To this day, she doesn't even know that.

You want to be careful about what you share and with whom. To you, it might be perfectly natural to talk about your boyfriend or girlfriend. Or your cat, dog, or guinea pig.[3] To a judge, a professor, or an employer, not so much.

---

2. I had one student email me about draining her "Bartholin abscess." I had to google it. I beg of you, don't google it yourself. I did not need this level of specificity. An email saying "I was in the hospital this weekend" would have sufficed.

3. I have residual trauma from babysitting our neighbors' guinea pig. They had a one-page list of instructions for my husband and me which included "holding and petting" the guinea pig. As they were explaining the instructions, they gave us a blanket to use in case the guinea pig tried to bite us or pee on us. *Are you f**king kidding me?* Needless to say, the guinea pig did not get held and petted.

3. Your Professor Is Not Your Private Tutor

It amazes me how many students act as though the professor is their own personal tutor. Back when *I* went to school (yes, when I trudged through ten kilometers[4] of snow. . .) we did not ask our professors questions. We figured things out ourselves.

Very occasionally, I would timidly raise my hand in class and ask for clarification. I never spoke to a professor after class or in their office. I never emailed a professor for help or clarification.[5] The prevailing sentiment was that class was *done*; now it's on you.

I am not advocating for a return to those days. But I do think we've gone way too far in the other direction. Instead of trying to figure things out themselves—even basic things—students automatically contact the professor for assistance. *What page was the quote you mentioned on? I missed the fifth element of the doctrine you talked about at the end of class—can you tell me what it is? How do you spell "impracticability"?* I mean, good grief. . . *seriously*? I would say that at least a third of the questions I get are like this. Questions that I would have been mortified to ask as a student. For questions like this, ask a friend or figure it out yourself. Do not bother your professor. It will make you look bad and, frankly, you should know better.

There are also the students who feel like the professor is their own personal Wikipedia. A question pops into their head and their first instinct is "I'm going to ask the professor about this." There's a textbook; there's the internet; there's actual Wikipedia; there's a library. I am not your "go to" source for all things Contracts.

Finally, there are students who are working hard trying to understand the material and want to meet with the professor to "go over" their understanding.

---

4. Americans: The rest of the world uses the metric system. Get on board.

5. I recall sending two emails to professors in my law school career, both of which I should not have sent. The first was after my Business Associations exam. I thought one of the questions on the exam was unfair because the professor had not taught the material. The professor assured me that she had indeed taught the material and provided dates for when she had covered the material. She told me to just wait for my grade and not to panic. I ended up getting an A+, so it was a wee bit obnoxious to have sent that email. As a professor now, I *hate* students like me (but also secretly respect them). The second email I sent was to my Family Law professor after I got a B+ on a paper. I was devastated and was looking to her for moral support, something I now realize I should not have been doing (see the very next section). She was also very kind and told me that the paper was only worth 30% of the grade and I could still do very well in the class. I did. I ended up with an A+. Again, so obnoxious.

Most professors are very indulgent of these requests. I, however, am less indulgent than most. If I spent two full classes (i.e., 150 minutes) teaching battle of the forms, I'm not going to spend another 60 minutes verifying that you have the correct understanding or re-explaining the material to you personally. Please realize *you are not my only student*. A fair professor will treat every student equally, and that means providing the same access, help, resources, and accommodations across the board. A professor cannot teach full lessons in class and then re-teach them again privately in his or her office. Do not put the professor in that position.

My husband, who I mentioned is also an adjunct professor, recently received an email from a student saying that she might be absent from class and was hoping to set up a meeting to talk through the material and go over everything she missed. Think about what you're asking. You are asking to sit down with a professor so he can privately re-teach what you missed in class. *Are you kidding me?* The answer is a definitive no. If you miss class, you miss class. It's on *you* to figure it out. Not on the professor to give you a private lesson.

It might sound like I don't think students should ever go to a professor for help. *Au contraire*. If you have struggled with the material on your own, talked to classmates, re-read the material in the book, and consulted supplementary materials and *you still don't understand*, then by all means go see the professor. But the self-sufficiency piece of this is the most important. You need to learn how to learn, and automatically going to the professor every time you don't "get" something is not furthering that skill in the slightest.

4. Your Professor Is Not Your Mom

There is a phenomenon afoot in higher education called "academic momism." There is an expectation from students that the professor will act as their academic mom. The professor will remind the students of impending deadlines, be forgiving when it comes to late assignments, comfort a student when he or she does not do well, and make life otherwise easier and more comfortable for students.

The problem exists not just because students have these expectations but because professors (both male and female) cater to these expectations.[6] I am all

---

6. I cringe every time I see a female professor bring cookies or other treats to their class. I want to scream, "You know this is not helping, right?!"

for being kind and supportive to students. I am not for pandering to students. *Late assignment, no problem! You think you deserve an extra 0.5 points on the assignment—let me regrade that for you! You were 20 minutes late, but you want to be marked present for attendance purposes? Sure, I can do that!*

The sentiment I've heard expressed is that we, professors, are here to *serve* students. They pay our paychecks. Therefore, we must accommodate them in any way we can.[7] This customer-service model of legal education gives me serious *agita*.

I am not here to *serve* students; I am here to educate students. And part of educating students involves enforcing boundaries and rules. Law students will become tomorrow's lawyers. And nobody in the "real world" is going to give a rat's a** that your second cousin is getting married and you're in the bridal party and that's why you need an extension on your brief.

There's also something else I want to bring to your attention that is intrinsically related to this academic mom-ism. Students hold their female professors to a different standard than their male professors.

Most of you will scoff at this.

I would never do that.

I'm female, so I'm pretty sure I'm not biased against females.

Oh, this sexism stuff—I'm so over it. It's not 1950.

Yeah, I don't think that I'm harboring stereotypes against female professors.

Let me clarify what I mean by holding female professors to a different standard. There are a variety of ways that this happens, but let me focus on two.

First, students make greater demands of their female professors than of their male professors. By "demands," I don't mean "I demand you review my exam with me" (though that happens). I mean that students seek help from their female professors more than they do their male professors. And students request emotional support from female professors in a way they don't with male professors. In short, students are far more likely to make demands on a female professor's time than they are on a male professor's time. If you walk down

---

7. I recently heard a presentation where the speaker advocated for a model of legal education premised on *professor as therapist*. Pass me an Advil.

the faculty hallway at almost any school, you will largely see female professors working one-on-one with students and male professors alone in their offices.

Much of the extra work which falls disproportionately on female professors' shoulders involves what is referred to as "emotional labor." It is not work that is directly related to being a teacher, but instead is work that perhaps a social worker or psychologist would take on. I would estimate that about half a dozen students per semester sit in my office crying. I have no problem with that and am happy to provide emotional support where I can. By contrast, a male colleague of mine remarked that in his 30+ years of teaching, he's not sure he can ever recall a student crying in his office.

From a female professor's perspective, I will say that the additional labor that is expected of females takes its toll. It is very time intensive to be so available for so many students. It is frustrating—I'm not going to lie—to see that male professors do not share in these burdens. Granted, it's not their fault. Students simply don't make as many demands on male professors or have the same expectations of them.

This brings me to my next point. Students tend to judge their female professors by an unfair standard. There have been several studies that have documented disparities in student evaluations of male vs. female faculty members.[8] The majority of these studies showed that female professors fared worse on evaluations than their male counterparts. I do not think overt sexism is at play here. Instead, I think it is something far more subtle.

Like it or not, students (both male and female) have expectations that their female professors act a certain way. What way is that? Kind, supportive, nurturing, caring. They want their female professors to act in ways and to exhibit characteristics that are traditionally associated with being female. The more a female professor deviates from this paradigm, the more students will judge her harshly. Not because she is a bad teacher, but because she is not who students want her to be.[9]

---

8. There are also documented disparities between evaluations of white professors and professors of color.

9. Here is a perfect illustration of this from a Rate my Professor evaluation of me: "She plays off being as kind and approachable but she's the exact opposite. Is she good at teaching contracts? Yes. Does she care about her students? NO." The student acknowledges that I am "good at teaching" but laments that I am not "kind and approachable" and I do not "care" enough about students.

All of this is well documented in the literature. There's even a name for it: role congruence theory. Role congruence theory posits that women face backlash when the characteristics they exhibit deviate from their prescribed gender role. The more assertive and agentic a woman is (the opposite of what people expect) the more hostility there is toward her. One student even said to me that he wished I would be "more pleasant," like another female professor. Ironically, males are *rewarded* when they exhibit characteristics not in conformity with their gender role (supportive, caring, nurturing).

I have witnessed this double standard on too many occasions to count. Let me give you one example. Last year, I gave a closed book Contracts exam. The Torts professor, a male, also gave a closed book Torts exam. My class went sort of crazy on me. *Why do we have to have a closed book exam? It's not fair! Please make it open book! You don't know the toll this is taking on us!* I was, frankly, a little surprised at the backlash. I checked in with the male Torts professor, assuming that he was having similar issues since we taught the same students. Not a peep from the students. Not one student complained about the closed book exam or asked him to change it.

So why the uproar in my class? I guess I will never know for sure. But my guess is that the class expected me, a female, to be accommodating and cater to their emotional requests ("we're so stressed"). When I did not, the class did not "accept" my answer. They began a bargaining process with me, asking for more time on the exam instead. Again, they didn't ask the Torts professor for more time, even though he was providing less time for the exam than I was.

The example here illustrates both facets of the implicit bias that I have described: (1) More demands are made of women; and (2) When women hold their ground and don't accommodate students like women are "supposed" to do, students become angry and judge them more harshly.

Lest you think I'm making this all up, here is an excerpt from an excellent article on gendered expectations in academia:

> Consequently, female professors may undergo extra burdens in their careers simply as a result of their gender. In order to please students, female professors must walk a line between warmth and agency, a fine balance not as strictly required of male professors. They may need to display more communal behaviors to be viewed favorably.
>
> However, doing so by exhibiting behaviors such as dedicating more time to students is still not a guarantee of fair evaluation. Bennett showed that despite

students' reports of receiving more office hour time and personal attention from female professors than from male professors, students still rated their female professors as less available. These increased expectations of nurturance are likely to increase female professors' workload, with students expecting or demanding more help and favors from them.

Bernard's term, "academic momism," describes these gendered expectations aptly. In expecting and perceiving female professors to be more nurturing, students are essentially expecting them to function like academic mothers. Increased nurturance demands on women in academia may cause them to perform more emotional labor with their students. Emotional labor involves performing extra emotional work in the context of one's employment, which often goes unnoticed and uncounted in work evaluations.

Female professors may find that they must take on extra burdens, such as helping students cope with stress or insecurities, having to set personal boundaries with them, or providing gentler feedback to them to avoid being perceived as excessively harsh.

This leaves women at a disadvantage in terms of having and exerting authority in the classroom. Much like female businesswomen, they must deal with the potentially negative consequences that result from exerting authority. For example, when female professors exercise power, including in standard educational ways such as managing the classroom, students seem to perceive them as pushy. Female professors are also expected to assign a lower workload and give higher grades than their male counterparts do, and women are judged more negatively when they do not.

At the same time, women must also work harder to demonstrate competence in order to be seen as being on equal footing with men. For students to consider female professors competent, they must exhibit greater evidence of expertise and skill than do male professors.

Why am I telling you all this? Because there is very little that can be done—or will be done—at the institutional level to change these dynamics. Trust me, I've tried. For years.

Instead, the only way to effect change is to educate students and raise awareness of these potential biases. The next time you're inclined to lament that Female Professor is such a witch for not extending the deadline, check yourself and ask whether you would have said the same thing about Male Professor. If not, keep your mouth shut and get back to work.

5. Your Professor Is Not There to Entertain You

Students love to be entertained. Let's face it, who doesn't want to be entertained? But it's a lot to put on professors to expect them to be entertaining.

One of the ways that students love to be entertained—and that professors seek to entertain students—is through storytelling. Students *love* storytelling. The more stories, the better. There are two reasons students love stories. First, they take time away from class (i.e., less substantive material to cover). Second, they give students an insight into the professor's world.

I don't tell a lot of stories in my class.[10] I feel like this works to my disadvantage, especially compared to other professors who are master storytellers, including my husband. I have several reasons for not telling stories.

First, stories take up a lot of time. Students don't necessarily appreciate this, but professors must get through a ton of material in a fairly short period of time. If ten to 15 minutes per class is taken up with stories, this amounts to about 300 minutes. Three hundred minutes wasted. *I can't even.* You are paying an inordinate amount of money to go to law school. You need to learn about consequential damages, not hear me drone on about what shows I like on Hulu.[11]

Second, I am a bad storyteller. I'm the person who gets sidetracked on small, irrelevant details and isn't able to build up a story to its crescendo. My husband's favorite thing to say when I tell stories (in real life) is "Land the plane." I *hate* it when he says that.

Third, my life is pretty boring, so I don't feel like I have a lot of interesting stories to tell my students. I was the girl who organized an anti-drug campaign in high school. I called it "Why Die for a High?" I was going for dramatic. Clearly, I am not the right person to regale you with stories.

Fourth, I feel like stories are more for the storyteller. Some professors love capturing students' attention with their stories. It's like their opportunity to be Kevin Hart for ten minutes. It feels good to have everyone listening rapturously (is that a word?).

---

10. One of my Research Assistants who helped edit this book said to me that my book persona is a little different than my class persona. It's sort of true. I'm pretty much "all business" in the classroom. I feel much more comfortable expressing some personality in writing than in front of a class of students. For the small number of you who are reading this book and scheduled to be in my class, rein in your expectations. Seriously.

11. I recently cancelled my subscription. There's not much on there after you've watched *The Handmaid's Tale*. Canadian author, by the way.

I've focused on storytelling, but there are other expectations that students might have. Professor So-and-So shows funny videos. Professor So-and-So has memes in her Power Points. Professor So-and-So dressed up like a chicken when he taught the *Frigaliment* case (this is an actual *thing*—google it). Law professors have become the source of infotainment. I'm guilty of occasionally playing into this expectation as well.

But my message to you is to recognize that your law professor is your *law* professor. Do not equate good teaching with entertaining teaching. Certainly, a good teacher can be entertaining. But an entertaining teacher is not necessarily a good teacher. Just like your professor is not your friend, your mom, or your tutor, your professor is not a source of entertainment. Law classes shouldn't be fun. Don't expect them to be.

6. Don't Try to "Get to Know" Your Professor

Apparently, students are sometimes told to visit their professors' office just to introduce themselves and to get to know the professor. I don't know who's telling students this. But it is not a professor who teaches many students or a professor who publishes regularly.

Your professor doesn't have time to chit-chat with each of her students. Picture this. Your professor teaches 100 1Ls. Each one of those 1Ls drops by "just to say hi." That's a lot of chit-chatting for your professor. I got asked by my 1Ls about this advice earlier this semester. When I explained that it is too much to expect a professor to meet one-on-one to shoot the sh*t with you, I got blank stares. I got the feeling that the class was like, *why wouldn't you want to do this?* Because, uh, I have a job.

And think about it outside the law context. There's no other professional person in your life that you'd drop by and "visit" with. Would you stop by your dentist or doctor's office just to say hi? Your accountant? Your professor is no different.

Even if you're not picking up what I'm putting down,[12] consider this: It is very awkward for both you and the professor to have a stilted conversation that

---

12. I had never heard that expression until Matteo used it in class one day. You can read about Matteo's law school experience in Chapter 21. Matteo's a blunt guy. I don't remember exactly what I was teaching, but Matteo put up his hand and said, "I'm not picking up what you're putting down." The class inhaled sharply. Most students would never have dared to

starts with, "I just came by to say hi." If you want to meet your professor and you genuinely don't have any questions for them, *make something up*. Say, "I wanted to ask you a question about X," and take it from there. This makes the conversation much more organic. If the professor wants to continue to have a conversation after answering the question, then great. If not, and the professor wraps up the conversation, then you're not left there feeling like an idiot.

Your goal should not be to get to know your professor or have them get to know you. Your goal should be to do well in their class. I guarantee that if you do well in their class, they will get to know you (or certainly they will know enough about you to write a letter of reference for you).

7. Seriously, Read the Syllabus

There is no worse question that a student can ask than something that is plainly laid out in the syllabus. I know many law professors say that there's no such thing as a dumb question. Bullsh*t. There are dumb questions. And at the top of the "dumb questions" list is any question that has already been answered *in writing* by the professor.[13]

Your syllabus is one-stop shopping for any logistical questions pertaining to the course: attendance, assessments, midterms, exams, office hours, books, etc. If your question falls into the logistical category, re-read the syllabus before reaching out to the professor. Every professor I know is annoyed to high heaven[14] having to re-answer questions they've already answered.

And, in the interest of full disclosure (cause that's why you bought the book), here are some additional pet peeves I have, which may be reflective of other professors' pet peeves as well. I'll give you five, though I am sure I can think of more than that.

---

speak that way to me. A number of my students are pretty scared of me, but I'm not scary, right? *Right?!* I paused and said to Matteo, "What did you say?" He said, "I'm not picking up what you're putting down." I replied, "I love that expression! I've never heard it before. Let me write it down." So, I did. The class exhaled. And we proceeded.

13. Apparently, not reading the syllabus is a universal student reality. A professor recently hid $50 in a locker to see if his students read the syllabus (he had placed the combination to the locker in the middle of the syllabus). Not one student in the class read the syllabus and the $50 went unclaimed. Sigh.

14. This is yet another old person expression, isn't it?

Pet Peeve #1: When a student doesn't answer the question I asked, but instead answers a question completely of their own choosing. You'd be surprised, but this happens all the time. Students feel like if they are in the "zone" of the topic at hand, they should put up their hand and say something. No. If I ask a specific question, answer that question—not the question you want to answer. For instance, I might ask, "Can you explain how revocation of an offer works in unilateral contract?" And a student would respond, "A unilateral contract is a promise in exchange for a performance." True, but that's not what I asked.

Pet Peeve #2: When students give the same wrong answers. Sometimes I will call on Student 1 and he will get it wrong. Then I call on Student 2 and she will say the exact same thing. Still wrong. Then I move to on to Student 3 and…you guessed it…same thing. I have no problem with wrong answers. I have a problem with five people giving me the same wrong answer. Phrasing it slightly differently does not make it less wrong.

Pet Peeve #3: When a student says, "I don't know if this is what you're looking for…". Like nails on a chalkboard. What I'm looking for is the correct answer. It's not some esoteric answer that's in my head that you need to guess. For example, I might ask, "What does it mean to rescind a contract?" and a student says, "Well, I don't know if this is what you're looking for, but…". That's not really an "I don't know if this is what you're looking for" question.

Pet Peeve #4: When a student does not take the time to process feedback. Professors spend a lot of time marking up papers, quizzes, assignments, and exams. The least students could do is look at them before asking for more feedback (that they are not going to implement).

Pet Peeve #5: When a student makes a mistake on a basic legal concept that I repeated 20 times (or more) during the semester. For instance, I have now said the following sentence hundreds, if not thousands, of times in my academic career: *Article 2 applies to all contracts for the sale of goods. Not just contracts involving merchants.* Invariably, three or four students every year write on their exam that Article 2 only applies if you have a merchant buying or selling goods. This year, it was more like 20 students.

I think it's helpful as a student to at least be aware of some of the things that drive us crazy and hopefully avoid them. I'm sure you all have, or will have, your own list of pet peeves (such as when a professor lists her pet peeves). I get it. Everyone has things that drive them nuts-o. Hopefully there can be a happy mid-point where you're not driving the professor crazy, and they are not driving you crazy.

8. Your Professors Do More Than Just Teach

I had a meeting with a student recently in my office. As part of the conversation, I mentioned something about writing and gestured at the publications on my shelf. The student was confused. "You *wrote* all those?" she asked. "What are they, exactly?" I explained the concept of law review articles and how a large portion of a professor's job is to engage in "scholarship." She had no idea that this was the case. I guess she thought that professors just teach.

Professors don't just teach. Teaching is probably only about a third of what professors do. Typically, professors are expected to engage in scholarship, as I mentioned, and in "service." The latter is a broad term that captures things like serving on committees, taking on leadership roles in the law school and the community, directing programs, and rendering legal services to the public. I would probably add another thing that law professors do: administrative sh*t. Much of a law professor's job, especially nowadays, is taken up with figuring out course management platforms, tracking attendance, fighting with Zoom, filling out paperwork, responding to "I will not be in class today because I have a dentist appointment" emails, and the like. This takes up an inordinate amount of time.

You might be thinking, "That's nice, but why do I need to know this?" You need to know this because you need to scale back the expectations you have of your professor. Teaching you, and 150 other students, is not your professor's only job. Just like Contracts is not your only course. Knowing this might help you curb your indignation when your quiz isn't graded three days after you took it, or the professor tells you to first look for the answer on your own before coming to them for help.

9. Your Professors Are People Too

There is this weird thing where students see professors as only a professor. It's hard to imagine the professor doing something *other than* professor-ing. It's like running into your doctor at the supermarket. It's weird and it just doesn't feel right.

The first time I encountered this was in my second year of teaching. I was at school on a day I didn't teach. I was wearing jeans. A student in my class walked right by me as I said hello. He turned and realized who I was. He said, "Oh hi! I didn't recognize you. I didn't realize you owned jeans." He wasn't kidding. I think law students have this image of us where we sit at home in our tweed jackets in our comfy leather armchairs reading the Restatement for fun.[15]

Even students who I know quite well have a difficult time picturing me outside of work. I was visiting my family in Canada last summer and had a call scheduled with my Research Assistant. When he called, I mentioned that I was a little winded from teaching my toddler niece the chicken dance. The image of me doing the chicken dance has stuck with him ever since. Professor = classroom = serious = chicken dance. It just did not compute.

I'm not just trying to say that professors have a life outside of school—i.e., they wear jeans and dance around the living room with toddlers. I'm saying something much more profound (if I do say so myself): Professors are human.

Professors have life sh*t they are dealing with and maybe can't always be 100% accessible to you. And maybe can't always be peppy and entertaining in class for you. And maybe can't always tell you really *nicely* that you got the wrong answer, but good try anyway.

Here's an example of what I mean. My very first year teaching, my (now) husband got deployed to Iraq. Every day, I lived on pins and needles, worrying about his safety. I was lucky because I was able to speak to him by phone almost every day. But, some days, "coms" were down on his end. And I would have no idea what was going on. *Did something bad happen? Was his base hit? Is he still alive?*[16] I would google "Baghdad, Forward Operating Base Hamer" to see if I could figure out what was going on. It was an awful eight months. Yet, during this time, I had to go into work every day and teach. I did my best to put my "real life" aside and be fully present for my students. I'm sure, though, that some days my stress showed, and that I didn't handle things in the exact right way or in the exact right tone of voice.

Professors are people too. Professors have kids that they take care of. They have parents for whom they are the primary caregiver. They have health problems of their own. They have deaths in the family. They have depression, anxiety, and other mental health problems. Students: You do not have a monopoly on life problems. When you recognize that, perhaps you can cut your professor a little slack occasionally.

---

15. My favorite authors, by the way, are Elin Hilderbrand and Emily Giffin. I'm a sucker for chick-lit with a pastel pink, yellow, or blue cover.

16. Yes, I go to worst-case scenario really fast.

Also, I would ask that you remember that most professors do read your course evaluations. It is really awful for us when you cross the line from constructive criticism to downright mean and degrading comments.[17] I have witnessed one of my colleagues in tears over some of the hateful things that were said in her student evaluations. I, myself, have gotten some of these hateful evaluations over the years, and it is very upsetting. We get it: maybe you don't like the course or the professor or how the professor taught the course. But that's no excuse for being unnecessarily cruel to another human being. If you would not have made the comment to the professor's face, you should not write it in an anonymous evaluation.[18]

10. (After All This) Do Not Be Scared of Office Hours

Didn't she say somewhere else that students shouldn't go to office hours? Nope. You weren't reading carefully. I said students should not go to office hours just to "say hi" or get to know the professor. Students should also not go to office hours to ask questions that are already answered on the syllabus. Or to ask questions that should be not be directed at the professor.[19]

However, if you have struggled with the material on your own and you're still not understanding, then you *should* go to office hours. Many students are nervous about this. Especially if they are shy and reserved.

Just walking into the office can be intimidating. Some professors' offices are filled from top to bottom with books and papers. Undoubtedly, you will be thinking, "This professor is really smart and has a lot going on." Other professors' offices are neat and tidy, and this may be even more intimidating because you'll be thinking, "Wow, this person really has their act together." And other professors will have walls of awards and publications and you'll be thinking, "I'll never be that accomplished." I completely understand the intimidation factor of going into a professor's office.

---

17. One student wrote on an evaluation, "I hate you." That sh*t is uncalled for.

18. If I could say just one thing to the students who make these cruel, anonymous comments, it would be this: *Is the third time the charm for the bar exam?* Two can play at this game. My Research Assistant said this comment was "too savage," but you guys know I'm (mainly) kidding.

19. For example, what section of Article 2 deals with cover damages? The professor will have said it in class. If you missed it, ask a friend, or look it up. It's not rocket science.

Please don't let that stop you. And try to re-frame your thoughts about the physical space. For instance, for the professor who has papers everywhere, you might think, "Wow. They are disorganized," or, "This is a fire hazard." Or the professor who has all their publications on display, you might think, "They must be insecure if they have to broadcast their accomplishments to the world." Pure digression: I have all my publications on display. I read once that the average law review article only gets read by seven people. I figured that after pouring approximately 12 months into each article, I should at least look at the cover of the article on a regular basis. Plus, I had like 100 copies of each article just sitting in boxes.

Another concern is that you're going to come across as nervous or "stupid." With respect to the latter, students worry that they have stupid questions, and the professor will just roll their eyes, briefly provide an incomprehensible answer, and then kick them out of the office. So rather than risk embarrassment, and still be no better off understanding the material, students often avoid office hours like the plague.

Now I will say that not all students fall into this camp. Some students *love* hanging out in their professors' offices. I had a Research Assistant once, Kyle, who commented that "the professors' corridor" was his "natural habitat." This section is aimed at those who are the antithesis of Kyle.[20]

Here is my advice to you. Bite the bullet. Face your fear. For several reasons.

First, you can't avoid people you're scared of for the rest of your life. Better to start trying to conquer your fears now rather than waiting until your first meeting with opposing counsel.

Second, if you need help, your priority must be getting help. Your goal is to get an A on the exam. If utilizing your professor's office hours helps you accomplish that goal, then you need to put your fears and insecurities aside and get help.

Third, you may learn that the professor is not that scary. You may even become—dare I say it?—friendly with that professor. As I just told you, professors are normal people. They sometimes drive on Empty. They own jeans (maybe mom or dad jeans, but still). They watch *Real Housewives* (but will deny it to their death).

---

20. Note to these students: Scale back your office visits.

Fourth, what is the worst that can happen? You get into the office. You're nervous. You stammer. The professor seems annoyed. The meeting doesn't last very long and you leave. I can tell you that this encounter will likely not register for the professor—or not register in the way that you think. They will not think you're stupid. They will not hate you. They will not hold this against you. Most professors have a lot going on and this will be just one of hundreds of meetings with students they have that semester.

One final piece of advice. If you are going to visit your professor, there *is* a way that you will make a bad impression: if you haven't planned out your questions in advance. I have had students who decide that they want to flip through their outlines to talk about random questions they have. It then takes them minutes to locate or remember the questions. I guarantee that this will make a bad impression. Not because the professor will think you're stupid, but because you are not considerate of the professor's time.

TEN

Choosing Your Courses and Extracurriculars

Education is what remains after one has forgotten what one has learned in school.

ALBERT EINSTEIN

1. Don't Plan Based on Having Fridays Off

When course registration rolls around, students tend to panic. *What do I take? Should I take Professional Responsibility with Professor X or Professor Y? Should I do an externship or a clinic? What about bar courses?* It feels very overwhelming. And it feels like you've got to fit a lot in, and you don't want to make the wrong decision.

It is important to be thoughtful and deliberate about your approach to course selection. Do not just cobble a potential schedule together the night before registration. Have a back-up plan and a back-up to the back-up plan. For instance, if Federal Tax fills up, then I'll take Commercial Law instead. But that means I can't take Wills & Trusts because it conflicts with Commercial Law, so I'm going to take Copyright instead. It's annoying and confusing. But it's life.

Scheduling needs to be a consideration in course selection. It is probably not ideal to jam all your courses into two or three days. Because those days will be hell. Most students like having Fridays off (I get it). But if there is a course on Friday that you want to take, don't let the day it's scheduled deter you. The most important thing is to try to take the courses you need or want to take—even if it's not the ideal schedule.

One more thing. Before you commit to a course (even in terms of just registering for it), find out what that course entails. It always surprises me that students don't read the course descriptions or know what the course is about. I have seen more than a few students take Administrative Law because they thought it was on the bar (it's not). And I've had a number of students take Conflict of Laws with me, not knowing what in the world it was about. I get that law schools have curricular "tracks" or "concentrations," but don't just pick courses blindly. Do a little bit of homework.

2. Consider the Bar Exam (But Not Exclusively)

I hate to even bring this up, but you will have to take the bar exam in a few years. That means you will have to know certain subject areas like Business Organizations, Evidence, Wills & Trusts, and Sales. The bar exam is currently in a bit of a state of flux, so some subjects are going to be nixed in upcoming years (like Secured Transactions and Conflict of Laws[1]).

You should consider taking some of these bar courses in law school, rather than waiting for BarBri or Themis to teach them to you six weeks before the bar exam. But, if there are one or two courses that you have less than zero interest in and you don't think you will ever use in real life, consider skipping out on these and learning them during bar review.

It goes without saying, but you should take courses in your area of interest. But don't go crazy with this. You want to come out of law school with a broad base of education—not just having taken every criminal law course under the sun.

I would also recommend that you consider courses that will help you improve your writing skills. I know that for most of you, this will sound awful. But as I mentioned before, writing is what you're going to be doing for the rest of your life. Seize on opportunities that allow you to practice that skill.

Finally, consider GPA boosters. I don't live under a rock. I realize that some students take courses that are known to be GPA boosters (and that are perhaps not as difficult as Federal Courts). I don't think it's a terrible idea to consider some...less challenging...courses. But don't let these make up too much of

---

1. So sad!

your schedule. You really do need to learn bread-and-butter legal skills. You will deal with Contracts in your life, but you may never need to know about Animal Law. I'm not saying Animal Law doesn't have its place in the law school curriculum. But try not to load up on too many Animal Laws.

3. The Professor Makes All the Difference

I said this before. You are not taking Evidence. You are taking Evidence with Professor X, or Evidence with Professor Y. Your professor can really impact your experience.

If you had a professor before and had a terrible experience (e.g., they were disorganized, cancelled classes arbitrarily, didn't seem to even know the law really well[2]) then you can probably expect a repeat. In that case, you need to weigh the utility of the course with your anticipated experience of the professor. If you absolutely need to take Business Organizations *and* you are in your last semester of law school *and* Professor Arrogant is the only one teaching it, then so be it. Bite the bullet and take the course.

One thing I would caution against is putting too much stock in chatter from other students concerning a professor or a course. Certainly, there could be (and often is) a grain of truth to this chatter, but it is probably not a great idea to plan your academic schedule based on what Brent in Criminal Procedure thinks of Professor Z who teaches Wills & Trusts. I say this because I am Professor Z. No, I don't teach Wills & Trusts, but there is chatter about me.

I often hear from 3Ls who oh-so-bravely register for my courses that they were advised to avoid my classes because I am "so hard" and my expectations are "too high." Every student who has told me about this has subsequently said that they were very happy they did not heed the advice. I can think of two students who said that they were "kicking themselves" because they missed out on the opportunity to take other upper-level classes with me.

What I'm saying (other than I'm a really good professor) is that you should not believe everything you hear.

---

2. Yes, this happens.

4. Experiential Education Eats Up a Lot of Credits

There has been a big push in recent years toward experiential education—essentially, hands-on legal experience. Learning by doing. Almost every law school touts the number of clinics, externships, and field placements they provide. Almost every law school will have a photo of a student in an experiential setting on the homepage of its website. And almost every law school will have a brochure with a picture of the most photogenic student on earth saying how the [insert name of experiential program here] changed her life. How it was law in motion. How it made the law come alive. Yada yada yada.

You guessed it. I'm not a huge fan of experiential education. Actually, that's not true. I think experiential education—done right and in moderation—is a good thing. The problem is that not all experiential education is great, and some students do too much of it at the expense of other things in law school.

I am *certain* that I am going to get nasty emails from professors sending me a ton of literature on the value of experiential education. I'll save you the time. I've read it. And I still think what I think.

First, let's talk about the outsized credit load that many experiential courses carry. Some schools offer 10, 12, or 14 credits (or more) for experiential courses. That is a lot of credits. It's also usually an easy A and a GPA booster. Some quick math. Let's say you need 90 credits to graduate. Thirty are mandatory in your first year; another 15 credits are upper-level required courses. This leaves 45 for electives. What this means is that over 25% or 30% of your electives could be eaten up by experiential credits.[3] This means fewer bar courses, fewer writing opportunities, fewer courses of general interest or application. It's a trade-off.

In some cases, it is totally worth it. There are clinics where you get a robust educational experience, you get one-on-one supervision from a faculty member, and you are learning substantive areas of law in a clinical setting. There are externships where you get to work for a prominent judge and immerse yourself in legal research and writing.

But not all externships, clinics, and field placements are created equal. Particularly with the latter, it can be hit or miss. A field placement is what it sounds

---

3. I've seen students load up on so many experiential courses, broadly construed, that they barely took any doctrinal courses outside the required curriculum. This is probably not great for their breadth of knowledge as a lawyer.

like. You go and work "in the field" with a real lawyer. This experience will usually be completely idiosyncratic. You'll have lawyers who provide you with real legal work and show you the ropes. And you'll have lawyers who expect you to get them coffee and do administrative work.[4]

I had a former student who did an externship at a large multinational company (by large, I mean traded on the stock exchange and with revenues in the billions). She said she sat in her cubicle and surfed the internet all day. She had a couple of assignments here and there, but she was essentially just being babysat by the legal department. I wish I could say that this student was an outlier, but I suspect she's not.[5]

The other thing I would say is to not "spend" your credits (recall: you are paying for this) on areas of law that you have no intention of practicing in. For instance, there are often very specialized clinics at law school (e.g., Domestic Violence Clinics, Immigration Clinics, Housing Law Clinics). If you intend to practice business law at a big firm, then it doesn't make much sense to pay thousands of dollars to do the Housing Law Clinic. Your money is probably best spent elsewhere. Students think they need to do some sort of a clinic or externship because it is a "good experience" or because the law school is encouraging it. Remember, you are *paying for this*. Do not pay for something you don't need or don't want.

5. You Should Probably Try Out for Law Review

I have mixed reactions to a question I get a lot: *Should I try out for law review?* The common wisdom is that law review is super prestigious, it is a great resume booster, and it will help with future employment. By and large, that is good advice. Law review is still seen as a brass ring by a lot of employers. And your very membership on law review—even if you did a terrible job or bluebooked only one article—is enough to give you a gold star.

This is a little unfair in a way. Selection for law review usually turns largely (though not exclusively) on your GPA. This means that the top students get a

---

4. How do you tell the difference? You need to do your homework. Find out how the program is structured, who will be supervising you, what other students say about the quality of the experience (students will usually readily admit to other students if the experience was a cake walk).

5. Not many students admit this to professors at their school because it's a complete boondoggle.

double bonus for the same thing: good grades. They get to say they are ranked fifth in the class, for instance, *and* say that they are on law review. Such is the world we live in.

If you want this double accolade, try out for law review.[6] But know what law review entails: a lot of tedious work. You're going to be bluebooking for two years. You're going to become an expert in when to use "that" versus when to use "which." You're going to know the difference between an "em" dash and an "en" dash. Riveting stuff. You might get to work on a cool law review article and maybe do some research or make some comments on it. But most law review articles are pretty boring, so prepare yourself for that reality.

If you plan to clerk, then you should absolutely try out for law review. It will be good practice for the clerkship. If you plan to work at a big city firm, you should probably also try out for law review—those sorts of firms like the law review feather in your cap. If you plan to work as a public defender, at a small local firm, or open your own law practice, I'm not sure you should do law review. It takes up a lot of time and it might not be worth it for you. All of this to say: Make decisions based on you and your own personal circumstances. Don't just try out for law review because everyone else is doing it and you feel like you have to.

6. Employers Don't Care About Extracurriculars

I have to think of catchy titles for each section to get your attention, so that's why I titled this section as I did. However, is it a huge overgeneralization to say that "employers" don't care about extracurriculars.

What I mean by this is that, in my experience, the primary criterion for hiring a law student is grades. You could be President of the Sports Law Society and Treasurer of the Student Bar Association. But if you have a 2.5 GPA, you are going to have an uphill battle. I could certainly be wrong, but I suspect that most employers don't really care if you are "well rounded." They care if you are smart, diligent, and hardworking. Good grades certainly don't mean you are all those things, but they are the best proxies that employers have to go by.

---

6. There is usually what's referred to as a "write on" competition, which is what it sounds like. Your performance on the written portion is combined with your grades (and maybe some other factors) to select membership for law review.

My advice is this: If you want to do extracurricular activities, have at it! But don't do them because you think they will "look good" on your resume. Do them because they interest you and you think they will be fun (maybe too strong a word—but you know what I mean). If you are doing extracurriculars with the hope that they will make up for bad grades, I think you'll be disappointed.

I will also say that the more extracurriculars you do, the more likely it is that your grades will suffer. If grades are not the most important thing to you, then okay, so be it. But if grades are important to you (as they tend to be to most law students), then choose your extracurriculars wisely.

I was probably a bit of an outlier in law school. I was on a full scholarship, and I was really worried I would lose it. Because of that, all I did was work hard and study. I literally did not do one extracurricular activity. This made me a bit nervous because other students were doing this and that—and I wasn't. Ultimately, though, it did not matter. No employer ever asked me why I didn't join any clubs or organizations at school.

Maybe things are changing (in fact, I think that they are). There is a move toward looking at candidates more holistically. As more than just their grades. But we are not there yet. We are still in a place where grades matter a great deal. Proceed accordingly.

ELEVEN

Dealing with Life Stuff

Life is what happens to us while we are busy making other plans.

HENRY COOKE

1. Life Doesn't Stop Because You Are in Law School

I t sounds trite, but life doesn't stop because you are in law school. Bills still need to be paid, your apartment still needs to be cleaned, you still need to take care of your mental and physical health, and you still have personal relationships you need to maintain. Some of these are readily dealt with by good time management (e.g., I do my grocery shopping on Saturday mornings; I clean my apartment on Sunday afternoons). Other things are not so amenable to scheduling.

Your personal relationships—your relationships with your significant other, your parents, your children, your friends—will be impacted by the fact that you are in law school. I think it's fair to say that many relationships suffer while a student is in law school. Law students tend to be irritable, stressed, and very stingy with their time. It's no wonder that many personal relationships become strained.

A law student's relationship with their significant other is the relationship that often takes the greatest hit. It is difficult to have a relationship thrive in law school. Sometimes if your partner is also in law school, it helps—though you have the problem of what happens if you break up. If your partner is not in law school, they will likely not be thrilled about getting only scraps of your time. Many relationships do not survive law school. I don't mean to be all doom and gloom. Many relationships *do* survive law school. If you want your relationship to be in the latter camp, then you need to give it adequate attention. By that, I don't mean that you must devote gobs and gobs of time to speaking on the phone (or texting, cause apparently speaking on the phone is not actually "a thing" with you guys), or having date nights twice a week. It means that when you are with your significant other, you are *fully present*. Do not bring the stress and aggravation of law school into the relationship. Do not make things all about you.

2. Use Your Support Network

By this, I mean both your personal support network and your law school support network. If you are having a particularly hard week, maybe call up your mom and ask if she wouldn't mind bringing over some food for you. Or maybe you could ask your brother to take your car to the mechanic, so you're not sitting there trying to work on your outline while the technician is loudly unscrewing the bolts on your tires. Don't fear asking for help when you need it.

Additionally, law schools have a large support infrastructure nowadays (they didn't when I was in school). Most law schools have an academic support department, whose job it is to...well, support you academically. Some law schools have a writing specialist who, you guessed it, can help you with your writing. Law schools that are part of larger universities have counselling centers to help with mental health issues. And all schools have a Dean of Students who is the point person for almost everything student related. You are *paying for these services*. Use them if and when you need them.

3. Bad Stuff Happens

This is a depressing thing to say, but bad stuff happens. Having taught for as many years as I have, I've seen it all: death of a parent, death of a spouse, critical illness, abuse, severe mental health issues, homelessness, food insecurity, and suicide. It can be hard to go through a traumatic life event as a law student.

I have seen students persevere in the face of great adversity. I can't tell you how much I admire these students. I had a student who lost both his father and his brother within one week. He refused to take a leave of absence. He kept on keeping on. He graduated with Honors and is currently a successful attorney out West.

It is not always the best idea to fight through the pain and remain enrolled in law school when experiencing a traumatic event. Sometimes the best thing to do is to take a temporary leave of absence. This will give you the opportunity to deal with far more important things than the rule against perpetuities and the nuances of the character evidence rule.

Pushing yourself too hard through these sorts of things can be the wrong decision. I had a student whose mother was diagnosed with terminal cancer. She wanted to stay enrolled in my class because she felt that maintaining consistency was the best decision for her, which I understood. During a quiz, her nose started bleeding due to all the stress she was experiencing. I told her to go home and take the time she needed to deal with what was going on. We figured out the logistics of the grading later.

If something bad happens to you in law school, which I pray it doesn't, do not feel like you *need* to keep pushing through. Focus on what's important in life. Law school will always be there to go back to when you're ready.

4. You Should Sometimes Tell Professors About Your Personal Circumstances

I said before that you should not overshare. And you shouldn't. You should not tell me which actress is your "hall pass."[1] You should not send me a sonogram of your unborn baby.[2] And you should not tell me that you just got off the birth control pill and are having cramps.[3] But there probably *are* some things you should tell your professors about.

If you have a significant life issue that may impact your performance in a course, it is probably a good idea to let your professor, or the Dean of Students, know what is going on. For instance, I taught a student once who had just been the victim of a violent crime. It was September of his 1L year. He was physically okay but still emotionally scarred from what had happened. He contacted the Dean of Students who, with the student's permission, shared what happened with his professors. I am very grateful that I knew that. I avoided calling on him for several weeks until he was feeling ready to fully participate in class.

---

1. This is not made up.
2. Also not made up.
3. You guessed it.

By contrast, I had a student who did not tell me that something serious was going on in her life. During class, I saw her texting (something that, as you can guess, is not allowed). At first, I gave her the benefit of the doubt and did not say anything. But the texting continued throughout class. It was very obvious. I felt I needed to say something, so I did. She burst out crying and said that her mom was in the hospital, and she was checking in on the surgery. Maybe that would have been good to know ahead of time. Or what would probably have been more appropriate would have been for the student not come to class that day and instead attend to more important matters.

Professors are not mind-readers. If there is something going on that we should know about, please tell us. Most professors are very understanding and accommodating of legitimate life issues. With that said, where professors draw the line between legitimate and illegitimate may differ. I personally am not going to give you a pass from getting called on for a week because your bird died, or you didn't get to prepare because you were at your kid's kindergarten orientation.

5. The Non-Traditional Law Student Is a Superhero

Most students starting law school will be 24-year-olds right out of undergrad. Law school is simply the next step in their educational journey. Some students, though, will not fit this mold. Some students will be what schools call "non-traditional" students. Students who have been out in the real world for a while and lived to tell about it. Students who are married and have children—sometimes even children older than most students in the class. I really admire these non-traditional students. It takes a lot of courage to upend your life, put everything on hold, and commit to law school for three years.

Some of these students have given up high-paying and secure jobs to pursue a legal career. A career that they can't know 100% will pay off for them. That's courageous. In my experience, these students almost always have the right frame of mind in law school. They are hard workers, they crave knowledge, they accept criticism and learn from it, and they are self-starters. These are all critical traits for being successful in law school.

Some non-traditional students are in their 30s, 40s or 50s. They have families at home that they are responsible for. I have taught quite a few students with newborns or toddlers at home. I can't imagine what it's like to spend all day in school and then go home and take care of a baby. *Where do you find the time? When do you sleep?* I am in awe of these students. You would think that these students would just get by in law school. After all, they don't really have the time that the typical law student does. Nope. You would be wrong. These students tend to overperform in law school, often graduating at the top of their class. They somehow find superhuman strength to parent and to be full-time law students. For the traditional law student reading this, the message should be clear: *If they can do it, you can do it.* If someone can excel in law school while raising a newborn and a toddler in their "spare" time, you can excel in law school when all you have to take care of is yourself and the succulent plant your mom bought you from Home Depot as a housewarming present.

Now that I've told you how great non-traditional students are, I want to direct my comments to these students, in particular. You will probably enter law school with more than your fair share of worries. You will be worried about whether you made the right choice. Whether you can financially afford to do this. Whether you are a bad parent. Whether your relationship will survive. Whether you can physically and emotionally handle the pressure that comes with law school and raising a family. These are all normal worries. It would be naïve not to have these worries. But take solace in the fact that this road has been trodden before. And students *like you* end up doing well in law school and in life.

Two other things you'll be concerned about. One, will I "fit in" with these 20-year-olds? And two, do I remember how to "do" school? The answer is yes and yes. You'd be surprised, but non-traditional students find "their people" in law school.[4] They tend to be very well liked and very well respected. Sometimes they take on sort of an academic mom or dad role, which they tend to relish (better them than me). In terms of these students not knowing how to do school, that's just silly. No student nowadays knows how to "do" law school. In fact, a non-traditional student is probably better equipped to do school than a student who is entering law school out of undergrad. Because they will have gone to school at a time when schools taught grammar, focused on critical thinking, and did not have mass standardized testing.

One of my biggest non-traditional student success stories is William. William had a 25-year career before he went to law school. He had two full-grown children as well as grandchildren. He was an amateur pilot and lived a very

---

4. *Grey's Anatomy* reference.

full life. But something was missing; he wanted a new challenge. So, William enrolled in law school. He was in the first class that I taught in the United States and one of my absolute favorite students. Always did the work. And very sweet, very polite. This is probably because he is Southern (full on Southern accent, which I love—I think at one point, he called me "ma'am" by accident). William did well in all his courses and graduated near the top of his class. He went to work in-house at a large corporation and has since lateralled to another corporation. In his late 50s. He no longer lives locally but comes to visit me when he's in town. He also has a ton of friends from law school—all 20 to 30 years younger than him.

This story is not an aberration. It is the story of most non-traditional law students. If you are in this category, don't be fearful as you start law school. Or at least don't be extra fearful. It will be okay. Probably even better than okay.

TWELVE

Getting a Job

If people are doubting how far you can go,
go so far that you can't hear them anymore.

MICHELLE RUIZ

1. You Are Not Going to "Work at the United Nations," "Be an Entertainment Attorney," or "Go into Fashion Law"

I f I had a quarter for every time I heard a student say they want to one of the following things, I would be a very rich woman (and maybe my dad would get off my back):

- ➢ Be an Entertainment Lawyer
- ➢ Work for NATO or the UN
- ➢ Practice "International Law"
- ➢ Be a Judge
- ➢ Be a Law Professor
- ➢ Be a Sports Lawyer
- ➢ Work for a Thinktank
- ➢ Do Policy Work
- ➢ Practice "Fashion Law"
- ➢ Do Civil Rights Work

➢ Go Into Politics

➢ Work In-House

I'm sure there is a lot more I've left off the list. I hate to crush your hopes and dreams, but it is very unlikely that you will do any of these things—at least in the way that you are picturing them in your mind.[1]

Most law students do not end up doing glamorous or high-profile legal work. What you see on television is nowhere close to what the real practice of law looks like. Much of what you will be doing (certainly in your early years) can be characterized as "grunt work." You will be the one researching some fine point of law, switching out names on templates, doing document review, writing the "whereas" clauses in a contract, and coordinating discovery. You will likely not have a "You can't handle the truth" moment in your entire legal career.

I'm not saying this to get you down.[2] I'm saying this because you should go into law school with eyes wide open. And if you truly are going to law school only because you want to practice "fashion law" and you *literally* cannot see yourself doing anything else, you might want to think deeply about whether law school is for you.

Sincerely,

Your Dream Crusher

2. Do Not Rely on Career Services to Get You a Job

If you have forgiven me for raining on your parade, thank you. Let's proceed....

You are all going to law school with one goal in mind: to get a job. Getting a job in law will sometimes *feel* like a full-time job. There are a lot of things to think about and a lot of missteps that you can make.

Most law schools (probably all law schools, actually) have an office of career services that is designed to help students get jobs. You have to remember that these offices have to help sometimes in excess of 1000 students. In most cases, you are not going to get a great deal of individual time and attention from the staff at these offices. And sometimes, you may even get bad advice. Accordingly, it is important that you do your homework. Figure out how

---

1. Unlikely does not mean impossible ("So you're saying there's a chance!").
2. Is it too late to get your seat deposit back?

to craft a good resume, how to draft a cover letter, what you need to do to prepare for an interview, and the like. Getting a job is *on you*—not on your school. Be smart about it.

When it comes to finding a job, whether a summer position or a real-lawyer job, you need to take the bull by the horns. You cannot and should not wait by passively while Molly in the career office sends you a list of weekly job openings (a list which is going to go out to every other student in the school). *You* need to be actively searching for jobs. *You* need to be checking out law firm websites to figure out if they are hiring and how to apply. I guarantee you: Molly will not be privy to every job out there.

Two additional things:

First, if you are really interested in working somewhere, you should reach out and apply even if they are not actively hiring. Best case scenario, things work out. Worst case scenario, they don't. In either event, you haven't lost anything except some time. Also, even if they are not hiring now, that's not to say that they will not be hiring in the future. Putting yourself on someone's radar is almost always a good idea.

Second, be open to different job possibilities. If you focus too narrowly, you might not get a job. And you might miss out on good career opportunities. It often happens that students come into law school thinking they absolutely want to do one thing, and then they end up doing something completely different. Do not pigeonhole yourself.

3. Your Resume Needs to Look Pretty

Your resume (also known as your *curriculum vitae*—CV, for short) needs to look pretty. I don't mean Elle Woods "pink paper and scented" pretty. I mean professional pretty.

Your resume is the first thing a prospective employer sees. Like it or not, the employer will get an impression about you from the very "look" of your resume. Obviously, the employer doesn't sit down and say, "Oh look, the alignment is off. This person lacks attention to detail." But, where your resume looks *strapazzato*,[3] the employer will make implicit judgments about you.

---

3. This is an Italian word that means "worn out" or "unkempt." One might say "janky." As an aside, I'm pretty sure that a resume can't be *strapazzato*, but it has become one of my husband's favorite words, so we use it a lot.

Let me give you an analogy. If you went to a job interview, you wouldn't show up with a wrinkly suit with a stain on the lapel and shoes that have scuffs on them. If you were to show up looking like that, it would not inspire confidence.[4] That doesn't mean that you're not the smartest, most capable person in the room. It just means that people judge. It is human instinct.

Knowing this, you need to dress up your resume in the same way that you would dress up for a job interview. It needs to not only contain all the relevant information, but it needs to look nice at first glance. It needs to look professional, clean, and crisp. You never get a second chance to make a first impression.

I have very particular rules about resumes. Which is not surprising because I have very particular rules about everything. As with everything I write, follow my advice, or don't—totally up to you. But if you choose to follow my advice, do it because *you* think it's best, not just because I said to do it.

Here are some concrete rules of thumb pertaining to presentation and content that I think you should consider in crafting your resume:

A. Presentation Tips

1. FONT

Use a nice font. By nice, I mean one that is not ugly. It does not have to be Garamond (my font of choice), but it should not be Times New Roman. It should be 12-point font (with rare exceptions). Headings should be in larger font.

2. FULLY JUSTIFY

Fully justify the resume.[5] I know justification is a matter of personal preference and some people hate it. But I love it. It makes everything look so much neater.

---

4. This has become one of my favorite expressions. I first heard it when a senior partner said to my law school boyfriend, Adam, that his "work product did not inspire confidence." Adam was devastated by the comment, as well he should have been. And I was, of course, supportive. *How dare he say that to you?* It stuck in my mind ever since and I now sometimes trot out the expression when I can make it work for me.

5. https://en.wikipedia.org/wiki/Typographic_alignment ("A common type of text alignment in print media is 'justification,' where the spaces between words and between glyphs or letters are stretched or compressed in order to align both the left and right ends of consecutive lines of text.").

3. APPROPRIATE MARGINS AND SPACING

Have appropriate margins and spacing. I've seen *waaay* too many students have 0.5-inch margins (or less) and extremely cramped spacing. Don't do this. Have normal margins and normal spacing.

4. THE SECOND PAGE

If you go onto a second page, use it. The almost sacrosanct wisdom conveyed to law students is to fit everything onto one page. This rule is not set in stone. If you need two pages, use two pages. But what you should *not do* is to use one page and three lines on a second page. If you're using anything less than half a page on the second page, either add more, or make it fit on one page.

5. SPELLING AND GRAMMAR

Check and double check spelling and grammar. I can't emphasize this enough.

6. ENSURE CONSISTENCY

Ensure consistency. Seriously. If you use periods after your job descriptions, do it *all the time*. Make sure headings are identical. Make sure your alignment is consistent. For instance, if you have one indentation where you list job responsibilities for one position, make sure it is identical for another listed job.

7. MATCH SIMILAR CONTENT

Have similar content "match" in terms of length. Do not have one job description that is eight words long and another that is ten sentences long.

8. HAVE WHITE SPACE

Have appropriate amounts of white space. This is somewhat related to the point above about not squishing everything together. Make sure that there is white space dispersed throughout the resume. Try not to have a pocket of your resume (usually the upper right quadrant) have too much white space where the resume looks lopsided.

9. BE ORIGINAL—WITHIN LIMITS

Be original, but not too original. You can play around *a little* with fonts, small caps (if you don't know what that is, look it up—it will change your life!), extended spacing, and all that fun stuff.

10. DO NOT OVER-FORMAT

Do not over-format. Be careful with too much bolding, underlining, all caps, small caps, and italics. It can quickly look cluttered.

11. USE A PROFESSIONAL (PREFERABLY SCHOOL) EMAIL ADDRESS

For your name and contact information at the top of the resume, be mindful of your email address. Preferably, use your school email address. If you are using a personal email address, it should not be something like bills_fan91@gmail.com.

12. USE NICE BULLET POINTS, NOT ROUND DOTS

If you're going to use bullet points, consider an upgraded bullet point, rather than the traditional black dot. Whatever do I mean by that? Figure it out—see Chapter 7 on Learning How to Learn.

13. PDF YOUR RESUME

If your resume is going out the door to an employer, send it in PDF format. Every computer is different, which means that how your resume looks on *your* computer may not be how it looks on *their* computer. To avoid your resume looking messed up (and I've seen this before too many times), PDF it. That way, it will look to them exactly how it looks to you.

14. USE A SIMPLE FILE NAME

Use a simple and straightforward file name. For instance, "Joaquin Jones – Resume" is fine. "JJ Resume-updated as of 7.11.21-version 2" is not fine. The latter looks like a work in progress, while the former looks like a completed product.

15. DO NOT PUT AN ACCENT ANYWHERE ON RESUME

It's resume. Not resumé. Not résumé.[6]

---

6. *See* https://novoresume.com/career-blog/how-to-spell-resume. Resumé is not grammatically correct. And résumé, while grammatically correct, looks douchey.

B. Content Tips

1. BE MINDFUL OF TENSES

When you describe your previous jobs, they should all have the same tense. Do not say that your job responsibilities included: tending to customers, inventory management, and reports to the president. All the tenses need to be the same. You should say that your responsibilities included: tend__ing__ to customers, manag__ing__ inventory, and report__ing__ to the president.

2. JOBS YOU HAVEN'T STARTED

If you have an important or impressive job that hasn't started yet, you should list it. For instance, if you have secured a clerkship that doesn't start until a year from now, it should be on your resume. So that it doesn't look strange with no job description, I would probably include something like "Anticipated responsibilities include: [x, y, z]." Otherwise, you have five jobs with three lines each and one job with nothing, which just looks weird.

3. OMIT HOBBIES AND INTERESTS

I know this is controversial, but I do not think students should list their hobbies and interests on a resume. It's nice that you rock-climb, swim, and travel. Good for you. But, as an employer, I don't really give a sh*t.

I know some people say that the hobbies can be a way of showcasing your personality and provide a springboard for conversation. I get that. In some (limited) cases, this is true. For instance, one of my former students was a professional ballerina. I wouldn't have known that unless she put it on her resume, which I reviewed. In that case, the interest worked to her advantage: she had a cool and memorable thing that she was able to broadcast on her resume.

If you have a cool and memorable thing, you might want to consider putting it on your resume. But remember that one person's cool and memorable is another person's weird and/or creepy. For instance, you might want to think twice about listing hobbies like hot dog eating champion, collector of vintage Star Wars figurines, or cosplay enthusiast. I am not judging these hobbies,[7] but your employer will.

---

7. I am.

4. DO NOT ADVERTISE OBVIOUS PROFICIENCIES

You should not advertise that you are proficient in Lexis and Westlaw. Of course you are—or should be. Under no circumstances should you say you are proficient in Word, Power Point or Excel. I would nix that applicant on the spot.

5. INCLUDE GPA (IF GOOD)

You should include GPA and rank if it's good or pretty good (B or above). If not so good, then don't include it.

6. YOU DON'T HAVE TO LIST EVERY JOB YOU'VE EVER HAD

Consider which jobs you want on your resume. Just because you had a job in high school or college does not mean that you have to list it. If you think that listing it will potentially work to your disadvantage (e.g., "Worked at a gun range" or "Worked at a sports bar"),[8] then don't list it.

7. CONSIDER HOW POLITICAL YOU WANT YOUR RESUME TO BE

This is a touchy one. Employers will read into your resume. As such, you should consider how political you want your resume to be. For instance, if you are applying to a very liberal public interest organization, you might not want to include that you were president of the college republicans. Or, if you are applying to a conservative law firm, you might not want to broadcast that you organized a day of protest at your law school. Just know your audience.

* * *

It does not take much to put your best foot forward. Once you've put in the time in creating a professional-looking resume, you'll have it forever. You can just build on it, adjust, and tweak as necessary.

One final piece of advice you might want to consider. I suggest that you scour the internet and find resume samples you like and then copy them.

---

8. I say this as someone who worked at a sports bar for several years. There's good money in it, and I'm not casting aspersions here.

There's no copyright protection on resumes! You do not have to use the template that you're given in law school. In fact, I would deliberately not use whatever template your career services staff gives you. Not that it's bad. But every single student at your school will be using it. You'd like your resume to stand out a bit.

I want to give you an actual before and after of a student resume. No substantive content was changed. Things were just moved around a bit.

Julia Smith
(XXX) XXX-XXXX
Juliasmith@lawschool.edu

EDUCATION

Whatever University School of Law, City, State
Candidate for Juris Doctor, May 2023
GPA: 3.5
Rank: 40/170
Honors: *Member*, Moot Court Board
Activities: *Treasurer*, Tax and Business Law Society

Different University, City, State
Bachelors of Arts in Political Science and Administration of Justice, May 2019
Activities: Women's Softball

EXPERIENCE

City District Court City, State *Judicial Intern for the Honorable Fancy Judge, City District Court, May 2021-August 2021*

Assisted all judges in the City District Court. Conducted extensive legal research on criminal and civil matters. Drafted bench memoranda and briefs in preparation of trial. Observed court proceedings and magistrate hearings.

Firm Firm & Firm City, State *Claims Advocate, October 2019- March 2020*

Managed a high-volume caseload. Drafted legal correspondence to clients and the Department of Federal Affairs. Completed forms and releases with clients. Completed applications for claims and appeals.

State Office of the Attorney General City, State *Legal Intern, January 2019- April 2019*

Conducted extensive legal research on civil matters. Organized and assisted with legal documents and case files in preparation of trial. Observed numerous court proceedings and legal practice. Reviewed trial records and transcripts in preparation of trial.

Different City Third District Court Different City, State *Legal Intern, September 2017- December 2017*

Observed court proceedings and magistrate hearings. Organized files and maintained confidentiality. Reviewed trial records and transcripts.

ADDITIONAL EXPERIENCE

Bed Bath and Beyond. City, State *Customer Experience Manager*, August 2017 - Present
Provide online and in-person customer service. Oversee in-store and online transactions to ensure customer satisfaction. Assist with training new employees.

Before

JULIA SMITH
(XXX) XXX-XXXX
juliasmith@lawschool.edu

EDUCATION

Whatever University School of Law   City, State
Candidate for Juris Doctor, May 2023
    GPA: 3.5/4.00
    Rank: 40/170
    Honors: *Member,* Moot Court Board
    Activities: *Treasurer,* Tax and Business Law Society

Different University   City, State
Bachelors of Arts in Political Science and Administration of Justice, May 2019
    Activities: Women's Softball

EXPERIENCE

City District Court, City, State   May 2021- August 2021
Judicial Intern for the Honorable Fancy Judge, City District Court

Assisted all judges in the City District Court. Conducted extensive legal research on criminal and civil matters. Drafted bench memoranda and briefs in preparation of trial. Observed court proceedings and magistrate hearings.

Firm Firm & Firm, City, State   October 2019- March 2020
Claims Advocate

Managed a high-volume caseload. Drafted legal correspondence to clients and the Department of Federal Affairs. Completed forms and releases with clients. Completed applications for claims and appeals.

State Office of the Attorney General, City, State   January 2019- April 2019
Legal Intern

Conducted extensive legal research on civil matters. Organized and assisted with legal documents and case files in preparation of trial. Observed numerous court proceedings and legal practice. Reviewed trial records and transcripts in preparation of trial.

Different City Third District Court, Different City, State   September 2017- December 2017
Legal Intern

Observed court proceedings and magistrate hearings. Organized files and maintained confidentiality. Reviewed trial records and transcripts.

ADDITIONAL EXPERIENCE

Bed Bath and Beyond, City, State   August 2017 - Present
Customer Experience Manager

Provide online and in-person customer service. Oversee in-store and online transactions to ensure customer satisfaction. Assist with training new employees.

After

Maybe you don't see much of a difference, but I do. I would be far more inclined to hire Julia #2 over Julia #1.

4. Your Cover Letter Is About
What You Can Do for Them

Everyone dreads writing cover letters, me included. You have to talk about how great you are. You have to sell yourself to a prospective employer on paper. Ick. Unfortunately, you're going to be writing your fair share of cover letters as a law student. Here's what you need to know.

First, make sure it is pristine. Everything is spelled correctly. There are no grammatical mistakes. It is fully justified. And it is in Garamond font. We'll talk more about this in a little while.

Second, be mindful that the letter is about what you can do for the prospective employer, not what they can do for you. This is one of the biggest mistakes I see students make. Students will say, "This position will afford me the opportunity to hone my research and writing abilities." Why would the employer give a crap about how they can help *you*?

Third, you need to engage in self-promotion, but not in an overly egocentric way. This one is tough. You want the subtext to be "I am fabulous" without saying it outright. Students struggle with finding the right tone here. For instance, I had one student who was a superstar, but he was very humble about his accomplishments. His cover letter did not showcase how amazing he was. I told him he needed to go back to the drawing board and be a little less modest. But then he went completely in the opposite direction. This made him sound full of himself, which he wasn't. Eventually, he got it right, but it took a while.

Fourth, focus on concrete skills or experiences that make you well suited to the position. If you are applying for a position as a tax attorney, and you used to be a financial advisor in a prior life, play that up. Focus on things that will set you apart. But do not reach too far to make connections. If your uncle is a tax attorney, do not write about how that makes you well suited to being a tax attorney.

Fifth, repeat important parts of your resume, such as your GPA and class rank (if good), any relevant awards, etc. You never know if a prospective employer is going to read the resume, the cover letter or both. It can't hurt to have it be a little duplicative.

Sixth, keep the tone very professional. No exclamation marks! No contractions (don't use). But don't go overboard with stock professional phrases such as "at your earliest convenience," "To whom it may concern," and "I wish to convey my interest." Do not speak like a robot. Speak like a human being.

I know that writing a cover letter sucks, but it's an important part of the job-hunting process. Plus, once you have crafted a good sample template, you can use that as a basis for future letters, so you don't have to start from scratch.

5. Dress for an Interview Like You're Going to Church

You will go on a lot of interviews as a law student. One of the most important pieces of advice I can give you is that the interview is not the time to express yourself creatively. Do not show up to the interview with purple hair, a Hello Kitty bag, or pastel blue suit. Whatever it is might be on trend, but it is a very risky move.

Obviously, how you dress is up to you. But I suggest that you bear in mind that lawyers, by and large, are a conservative bunch. Many of the lawyers, judges or employers that are potentially hiring you will be older than you and may not be huge fans of your super-trendy Zara dress or flowered bowtie. To be clear, once you *get the job*, then dress however you want. Well, not *however you want*, but you know what I mean.

A good piece of advice that I am going to borrow from a colleague (shout out to Jenna!) is that when you are going on a job interview, you should dress as boring as possible. You should dress like you're going to church. The interview is not the time to break out your leopard print pumps. I can say that because I own leopard print pumps.

I want to provide some concrete guideposts to those of you who are still on the fence about what to wear.

A. Should You Wear a Suit?

In most cases, you should wear a suit. Women may have more flexibility in terms of wearing a blouse/skirt/pant combo, or a dress. In any event, make sure that your suit fits you well and is the appropriate length. You don't want to look like you're a kid playing dress-up in your parents' closet.

B. Colors

Pick a basic color, preferably navy blue, or dark gray. Black suits for men tend not to be favored. Black looks too somber (funeral) or too dressy (black-tie). For whatever reason, black suits for women are fine.

C. Shirts/Blouses

Men: Do not get creative with your shirt and tie. Wear a white or light blue shirt with a matching tie. The tie should not be a statement piece. You should stick with conservative colors (navy, red, burgundy, gray, etc.).

Women: If you're wearing an outfit with a blouse, stick with neutral colors (white, cream, blush, etc.).

D. Shoes

Men's shoes should be polished black or brown dress shoes. Women should wear dress shoes in black, brown, navy, or nude. If you wear heels, try to aim for a reasonable—and easily walkable—height. There is nothing worse that teetering around on sky-high stilettos as a partner is showing you around the firm.

E. Jewelry and Makeup

Keep this to a minimum. You do not want your employer staring at your too-long eyelash extensions slathered with mascara. And do not wear perfume or cologne. While you might love the smell, the interviewer might not. You don't need anything distracting them from the interview.

F. Hair

Your hair should be neat and kept out of your face. If you tend to play with your hair or flip your hair, maybe consider wearing it tied back. You don't want to be the "hair flipping" girl (or guy, I guess).

G. Additional Guidance for Women

I think women should wear nude pantyhose if they are going on an interview and are wearing a dress or skirt. I'm old school that way. I know the trend now is to go bare-legged, but please, not for an interview. There was once a woman who interviewed at my former school wearing a skirt suit with no panty hose. The whole time, I kept thinking, *Really, doesn't she know she's on a job interview?* I remember her bare legs almost a decade later.[9]

I also would caution women against wearing anything sleeveless (except under a jacket). While you may love that Wendy Rhoades sheath dress look from *Billions*, the interview may not be the place for it. Wait until after you get the job to (gasp!) bare your arms. I know the bare arms thing is going to sound overly conservative, especially if you are interviewing in the summer. However, I had a former student who wore a sleeveless blouse as a summer associate, and it caused a huge uproar at her firm. I wish I were kidding.

With all that said, I want to be clear that I am talking about what you should wear or not wear to an interview. I am a huge fan of dressing however you want and feeling comfortable at your job, so long as it is professional. I own more than my fair share of pink heels (four different shades). I have a dress with feathers on it. And I have a top with zebras on it and another one with owls.

---

9. She was also wearing platform heels, which in my mind is a total no-no for a job interview. Cause I'm not super judge-y, right?

Oh, and one with…skulls. I'm so edgy. I'm not saying not to be you. I'm saying, "Wait to be you until after you *get* the job."

Also, in typical law professor style, I want to put a caveat on my general recommendations. If you are applying for a position that values creativity and individuality (e.g., legal position at a tech firm, a job in fashion law,[10] etc.), then maybe you can and should break the rules. In most cases, however, I think it's better to initially err on the side of caution.[11]

6. Prepare for an Interview

I probably don't need to tell you this, but still, I will: Prepare for an interview. This means the following:

1. Knowing a little bit about the place you are interviewing, the people you are interviewing with, and what the position entails.
2. Having stock answers for questions they will ask you: *Why do you want this position? What makes you qualified for this position?*
3. Preparing (non-objectionable) questions to ask them.

First, do some research on the firm, the practice, and the people who will be interviewing you. There is nothing worse than not knowing basic things that you should know. I can tell you that it is mortifying. It happened to me twice. I'm almost too embarrassed to share my experiences with you. But I will because everyone loves reading about cringeworthy moments.

The first happened when I was interviewing at Skadden Arps as a 1L. They flew me out to New York and had me meet a bunch of different people. Now, the details are a little hazy, but I was scheduled to meet with the attorney who presided over the mass tort litigation group. She was a really big deal, but I did not know that at the time. She asked me what I knew about mass torts, and I remember thinking, "nothing." I knew what "mass" meant and I knew what "torts" were, but I didn't know what the words meant when put together. I wanted to die. I would like to say that I didn't get an offer. That way, you can take this as a word of warning ("be prepared"). But I did get an offer, so I think my story is less impactful.

---

10. Ha!
11. Told you, lawyers use this a lot!

The second time this happened was in a different context. I was applying for a very sizeable scholarship to pursue my master's in law (LL.M.). The scholarship was named after a person—let's call it the Earl Grey Scholarship (I don't want to give away too much information). It did not occur to me, for whatever reason, to look up who "Earl Grey" was. The scholarship committee, which was composed of eight law professors, asked me about the scholarship's namesake. I turned bright red and wanted to melt into the floor. You literally cannot B.S. your way around this question. In this case, I did *not* get the scholarship. That was a good call on the committee's part. I wouldn't have given it to me either. Incidentally, a friend of mine received the scholarship that year, so all's well that ends well.

I think I've made my point about being prepared. There is such a thing, however, as being over-prepared. Over-prepared can turn creepy real quick. Let me give you an example. Say you find out that you will be interviewing with Michael Thompson, a junior associate at the law firm you've applied to. You look up Michael's profile (so far, so good). You see that he went to Case Western. Hmmm. You google Michael Thompson and Case Western and you see that he wrote a law review note that was published when he was in school. You pull it up and read it on Westlaw. You see in the acknowledgment line that he thanks his wife, Jillian, for all her love and support. You go to the interview and ask Michael about his wife Jillian—that's totally creepster. Feel free to snoop all you want; just don't let the interviewer know you snooped.

There is also another way that you need to be prepared. You need to have both prepared answers and questions (and yes, I deliberately phrased it that way). Let's take each in turn.

You have to expect that the interviewer is going to ask you certain questions. Consequently, you need to think about how you want to answer those standard questions. You do not want to be struggling and "ummm"-ing over a basic question like, "Why do you want this job?"

Every single interviewer in the history of interviews has asked a candidate, "Do you have any questions for me?" It is never acceptable to say "no" even though that is usually the honest answer. If you say that you do not have questions, that will signal two things. First, it will signal that you have no idea how interviews work. Second, it will signal that you don't really care about getting the job. So, have questions ready. The questions should be medium softball questions. Not really basic questions, but not really involved questions. Under no circumstances should you ask about the pay. Focus on things like job responsibilities, opportunities, and stuff like that. Also, do not ask about "workload." That makes you sound lazy.

Of course, these are all just generalizations since I am writing for a mass audience (even using the word "mass" here touches my Skadden nerve). If, for instance, you are a single mother who has significant childcare responsibilities, then asking about workload might be advisable. As with all things, context matters.

7. Bring Water (and Some Other Stuff) to an Interview

Let's get into the weeds here. Lots of professors give you advice on what to say or not say during an interview, but not a lot of professors tell you what to bring and not bring. So here it is:

A. What to Bring

1. WATER

Not a giant Yeti container, but rather a plastic water bottle or a plain reusable water bottle. If you have a bag or a purse, try to keep the water discreetly tucked inside.

2. SNACK FOOD

Think almonds or trail mix or something like that. The last thing you want is your stomach growling during your interview. Have some easy to eat food handy just in case. And to be clear, do not pull out the snack food and eat it when anyone is around. Duck discretely into the restroom, take a mouthful, and then go back to the interview.

3. KLEENEX

You would think this one would be obvious, but it's not. You don't want to be without Kleenex if you sneeze or your nose starts running.

4. PAPER AND PEN

You should have a simple notepad and pen to take notes, if necessary. Under no circumstances should it be a pencil. You're not in third grade.

5. EXTRA COPIES OF STUFF

You should have extra copies of your resume, cover letter, writing sample, etc. handy in case someone asks for one.

6. BREATH MINTS

Preferably easy-dissolve ones. This one is self-explanatory.

B. What Not to Bring

1. YOUR PHONE

Well, you can bring it, but it should not be anywhere where it can be seen or heard. Do not forget to turn it off.

2. LARGE, BULKY BAG OR BACKPACK

You should not have a bulky bag where it looks like you're carrying half your personal belongings. Under no circumstances should you bring a backpack (think Steve Urkel…and if you don't know that reference, thanks for making me feel old).

3. COFFEE OR SODA

I'm sure there will be pushback on this one, but something feels a little off about bringing coffee or soda to an interview. Do so at your own risk.

8. How to Ask for a Reference Letter

Asking for a reference letter is awful. It feels so awkward, especially when you're not even sure that the professor knows who you are. I get it. First of all, rest assured that the professor probably does know who you are. And even if they don't, they'll figure it out and will agree to write you the letter anyway.

Nonetheless, it's so weird to have to write, "I'm not sure if you know me, but I'm in your class. And, um, well, I was wondering if…". Fair enough. But you're just going to have to suck up the awkwardness.

So how do you ask for a reference letter?

1. Choose someone that you think probably does know you and will do a good job writing the reference letter.

2. Send a polite email requesting the professor to write the reference. The email should state what you need the reference for and the timeline. The email should probably also state something like, "If you don't feel comfortable writing this letter, or the timeline is too tight, I completely understand." No professor is uncomfortable writing the letter (save in

exceptional circumstances), and no timeline is too tight. The email should also indicate that you will send along *additional* information if the professor agrees to write the letter.

3. When the professor agrees to write the letter, make it as easy as possible for them. Have the contact information for the employer listed out, the deadlines, and provide them the materials they need to write a good letter (this usually includes your resume, list of grades, and any relevant information about the job). Make sure that what you email the professor is organized and professionally formatted. After all, this will influence their perception of you, especially if they don't know you very well.

4. Follow up with professors. Make sure that they sent your letter of reference in.[12] You don't want this to fall through the cracks.

And, finally, if you get the job, touch base with your professor to tell them—let them share your joy! I always feel a little dejected when I hear job news from LinkedIn. That's cause, of course, it's all about me...and I need sufficient recognition that my reference letter played a role in you getting the job.

9. Law School Connections and Networking Are Overrated

There is a lot of talk in law school about "making connections" and "networking." There are events set up by schools for the express purpose of networking and introducing you to alums and members of the legal community. They are sent around in email blasts, they appear on the television sets that have popped up in law schools everywhere, they are pushed by administrators, and they are hyped up by students.

These events are perfect for the stereotypical law student: the assertive, extroverted, and confident law student. Not all law students are like that. Some law students prefer not to be the center of attention. I was one of these students. So, I speak from experience. For the introverted student, this sort of networking is a particular kind of excruciating. The idea of walking up to a lawyer at a big firm, introducing yourself, and making small talk makes the introverted student want to up-chuck.

---

12. To be clear, *I* would never let this slip through the cracks. But I have seen other professors agree to write letters and then totally forget about it.

But that's not the worst part. The worst part is that you feel like you are sabotaging yourself if you don't network. The inner dialogue will go something like this: *Why are you paying $40,000 to go to school if you're not even going to try to get a job? You know, law will involve talking? If you can't talk to someone at a cocktail party, maybe you're not in the right profession.*

You'll see all your friends and classmates chatting people up as though it's no big deal. They will be drinking white wine (never red),[13] laughing, and regaling their conversation partner with interesting stories. You—the introverted law student—have nothing interesting to say. Your mouth is dry as a bone. You are drinking water because you don't need the wine to go to your head and make you say something stupid. You are hovering near the cheese board, trying to look engrossed in the brie and taking your time loading up your plate. You feel like a total loser.

I assure you that you are *not* a total loser. Or, if you are, then I am one too. It is okay to be scared of networking. And it's okay to opt out. Certainly, it is not a great long-term strategy to just opt-out of things you don't like. In fact, it's the opposite of what psychologists will tell you to do.[14] But Rome wasn't built in a day. Take the pressure off yourself. In time, you will feel more comfortable in crowded rooms full of people who intimidate you. (Okay, maybe not).

Here is something no one will tell you. Those networking events don't do much good in securing you a job. You'll get a job because you have good grades and good references. Full stop.[15] No amount of schmoozing is going to con-

---

13. It stains your teeth. Also, avoid ordering beer—it makes you look like a frat boy or sorority girl.

14. One critical theory in behavioral psychology involves what is called exposure therapy. From the American Psychiatric Association website:

Exposure therapy is a psychological treatment that was developed to help people confront their fears. When people are fearful of something, they tend to avoid the feared objects, activities or situations. Although this avoidance might help reduce feelings of fear in the short term, over the long term it can make the fear become even worse. In such situations, a psychologist might recommend a program of exposure therapy in order to help break the pattern of avoidance and fear. In this form of therapy, psychologists create a safe environment in which to "expose" individuals to the things they fear and avoid. The exposure to the feared objects, activities or situations in a safe environment helps reduce fear and decrease avoidance.

https://www.apa.org/ptsd-guideline/patients-and-families/exposure-therapy.

15. One of my students recently sent me this message: "So, I thought of you today! I was drafting an opinion and I used one of your terms—full stop. Anyway, it just made me

vince the hiring partner at Sullivan & Cromwell[16] to hire the student ranked in the bottom 10% of the class simply because she was captivating at a law school cocktail party.

10. It's Okay Not to Know What Type of Law You Want to Practice

The worst question you can ask a law student is "What type of law do you want to practice?" Whenever I ask this question (which I should really stop doing) most students hesitate, turn red, and say they are not sure. I would say that 80% of students I've encountered don't know what they want to do after they graduate.

It is completely normal to not know what area of law you want to practice when you graduate law school. It is completely normal to have different areas of law that interest you, even if these areas are quite different (e.g., contracts and criminal law). It is completely normal not to be in the 20% of students who seem to have their career trajectory mapped out. But it is the source of great insecurity. I sense from students the guilt and trepidation associated with "not knowing." There is nothing wrong with not knowing. Absolutely nothing. Don't feel bad about it. Just try to embrace the possibilities that lie ahead.

Most students know what they *don't like* (e.g., "I don't want to do immigration law," or, "I really don't have the stomach for family law"). This is a very good start. It is important to cull out the areas that you don't like, and then to explore the areas that you do like. This means seeking out different opportunities that will allow you to test drive different practice areas. Maybe an externship, a clinic, a simulation course, whatever. Be open to possibilities. And then cross them off your list if they are not for you.

Students often ask me how I knew I wanted to be a professor. There was not one defining moment. Again, it was more about what I didn't want to do. Even though I had the option, I didn't want to be working 16-hour days at a stuffy law firm. When that was off the table, the possibility of an academic career

---

think of all of your 'Canadian terminology'. Lol." I had to break it to him that "full stop" is not Canadian.

16. Am I allowed to use real firm names? I'll proceed on the assumption I can until I get some sort of a cease-and-desist letter. I worked at S&C for six weeks one summer, so I feel like they wouldn't do that to one of their own.

emerged. But there was not one moment that I woke up and said, "I'm going to be a professor!"

I don't think you should be looking for the "ah-ha!" moment when, suddenly, you just know that wills and trusts is your calling. Instead, try to be comfortable with some level of uncertainty about the future (I know—it's scary!), and try to put feelers out in different areas.

But the most important thing I want you to take away from this section is that *it is okay not to know.*

THIRTEEN

Money Matters

Do not save what is left after spending,
but spend what is left after saving.

WARREN BUFFETT

1. Financial Aid Is a Loan You Have to Repay

I hate the term "financial aid." I would abolish it from our vocabulary if I could. The term is deceptive. It's not "aid." It's a loan you must repay. It's the same as a mortgage. And maybe even more expensive than one.

What you call something matters. It affects your mindset and your decisions. Let me give you an example. Banks offer what is commonly referred to as "overdraft protection." Do you know what that is? Probably not. If you had to guess, you'd think it's some sort of insurance that the bank is giving you. It's something *good*, in other words. For those of you who don't know, let me tell you what overdraft protection is. Overdraft protection is a "service" where banks allow you to spend money you don't have. And then they charge you a $30 fee for overdrawing your account. Shouldn't overdraft protection be the opposite? Where the bank "protects" you from going below zero? You would think. But the label makes customers much less likely to opt out of overdraft "protection," thus generating billions of dollars in fees for banks.

An analogy can be drawn to the term "financial aid." This is a soft and palatable term. It's not harsh like "loan" or "mortgage." It even makes it seem like someone's doing you a favor ("aid"). What this means is that you are more likely to spend financial aid money without regarding it as real money.

Here's a perfect illustration. At my former school, students who received scholarships were not able to apply them to summer classes. Not sure why, but that's beside the point. This means that if they were to take Family Law during the academic year, they would get to pay reduced tuition. If they took Family Law in the summer, they would pay full freight. I had countless conversations with students on scholarship about whether they should take summer school classes. Almost every one of them said that it didn't matter to them whether they took the course in the summer or during the year. They would just get "financial aid" for the summer class. *Seriously?!*

When you don't look at something as real money that you have to pay back (with interest), it's super easy to spend it. If you had to part with cold, hard cash, I doubt that you would be so willing.

What I'm imploring you to do is to look at financial aid as real money. Do your own "Big Mac" conversion and see what it's worth to you. Only those who read the footnotes will understand that reference.

2. Make Good Money Decisions

I'm sorry to be all up in your biz about money, but you really need to hear it: Make good money decisions. If you don't, you'll be paying the price (pun intended) for years.

The biggest money decision you'll make, of course, is choosing where to go to law school. You may have to decide between paying full-price tuition at your dream school and accepting a full-ride scholarship somewhere other than your dream school. I am not saying that finances should be your only consideration, but they should be a major consideration.

This is probably not a story that many of you are going to empathize with (#firstworldproblems), but I was faced with this choice in selecting what school I wanted to get my LL.M. from. My dream school had always been Harvard. I had been voted most likely to attend Harvard Law School in high school, and Harvard represented the pinnacle of academic achievement in my mind. I got into Harvard. But apparently Harvard does not give scholarships. They do give "financial aid."[1] I also got a Commonwealth Scholarship, which gave me a full ride to any school in the British Commonwealth. I got into both Oxford

---

1. This was the first time I'd encountered the term and thought it was bullsh*t even then.

and Cambridge. I had the choice to go to Oxbridge for free or to Harvard for $55,000 plus living expenses.

Being a 25-year-old brat, the choice was not immediately obvious to me. After all, Harvard was my *dream school*. And I could wear a cute little maroon sweatshirt with a big "H" on it. I could be like Elle Woods, except brunette. And England was cold and rainy.

I remember being in my apartment in Ottawa and talking to my dad on the phone about the decision. Yes, people used to use phones for *talking* back in the day. I was going on about how much I wanted to go to Harvard, how this was such a tough decision, and so on. And he said to me, "If you really want to go to Harvard, we will pay for you to go to Harvard." Right then and there, I decided not to go to Harvard. The thought of my dad spending his hard-earned money to indulge my whim—when there was a fully paid-for, comparable option on the table—solidified it for me. I had been operating in fake money land. My dad shelling out what probably would have amounted to $70,000 U.S. (which was about $100,000 Canadian dollars) really made me wake up.

It is very hard to quantify what a law degree from *fill in the blank* school is worth. That's what makes this so tricky. If I pay full price and get a degree from Cornell, is that better than paying heavily discounted tuition at Michigan State? I don't know. But think long and hard about whether a degree from a more prestigious school (with a more prestigious price tag) is necessary to end up where you want to end up. For example, if you want to do public interest work, maybe you shouldn't spend $250,000 on a law degree from Stanford. That's $250,000 that will take you 30 years or more to pay back.

Of course, some people have the luxury of not worrying about money. But for the rest of us, it is appropriate to assess the true value that a law school provides. If you can get from point A to point B in a Honda, why buy a Rolls Royce?[2]

3. Seek Out Scholarships

From what I've seen, students are not as proactive about seeking out scholarships as they should be. There is free money out there—go find it! Maybe the

---

2. Speaking of cars, I know of a student who just graduated and is in her first year of practice. She makes about $70,000 a year and has close to $200,000 in student loans. She drives an Audi Q5. Is that really the best judgment call?

reason for this lackadaisicalness[3] is related to students' view that none of this is real money anyway. Whether it's financial aid or a scholarship, it's all going toward paying tuition and not going in my pocket. Totally wrong way to look at it.

Financial aid, as we have established, is a loan. Anything that can help in reducing the amount of loans you need is a good thing. If you get a scholarship, you need less financial aid, and therefore, there is less to pay back. Simple.

As you can probably guess, I'm pretty militant about finances. I think those of you who grew up with immigrant parents can probably relate. My dad and I were walking through a parking lot once when I was a teenager. There was a penny on the ground, and he told me to pick it up. I said, "Don't worry about it, it's just a penny." I will never forget what he said back, "If you won't pick up a penny, you're not worth a penny." Yeah, my dad is harsh. You already knew that. But what he said was really deep. It reflects an ethos of hard work and sacrifice that I will never be able to fully appreciate. A couple of years ago, I shared this story with my husband when he too refused to pick up a penny. Since then, any time my husband sees a penny on the ground, no matter how battered and dirty, he picks it up. He feels guilty not picking it up. There is really something powerful about the penny sentiment.

I feel the same way about scholarships. Someone is going to potentially give you free money. And you don't "have time" to apply? Maybe you're not worth the penny. I said that for dramatic effect. But I appreciate it might have been a *tad* bit harsh.

4. Negotiate

I think this is the Italian in me, but I recommend that you always try to negotiate with a law school for more money. My dad is an expert negotiator. Two quick stories to show you what I mean.

First, it was early January, and my parents needed a new TV. We went to Best Buy to look around. My dad, unbeknownst to me, had brought along a flyer advertising a Black Friday sale. When he saw the television he wanted, he whipped out the flyer and said to the salesperson that he wanted the Black Friday price. The salesperson was like, *But it's not Black Friday. That was a month and a half ago.* My dad's position was, "If you could offer that price then, you

---

3. Is this even a word? Spell check isn't flagging it, so I guess we're good to go.

can offer it now." I mean, he had a point. Although I wanted to die of embarrassment, you gotta admire someone with that amount of gumption.

Next story. My dad has a ritual every summer. In late July/early August, he gets the renewal form for his home and auto insurance. Every year, he gets angry that his rates have increased, usually by about $100. Every year, he calls up the insurance broker, Sujata, and b*tches about his rate increase. Dad and Sujata are on a first-name basis. Every year, Sujata finds a way to keep his insurance premiums the same. But she gives Dad the opportunity to vent and threaten to switch insurance companies. Thank you, Sujata. You are doing God's work.

My husband, by contrast, is terrible at negotiating. Anytime we hire someone to do work at the house, he gets me to do the negotiating. If it were up to him, he'd pay everyone *more* than they asked for. I'm not kidding. We once had some guys come and clear our driveway of snow. They wanted $75. My husband gave them $100. His logic was that if we treat them well, they'll come back and do a good job for us next time. First off, I was *so not happy* about the $25 tip. Second off, they never came back.

I feel like I had a point here and then got off topic. Sorry. Back to you. My point is that when a school admits you, you should try to see if more money is available. If another school you have been accepted to has offered you a 50% scholarship, ask your chosen school to match that. Obviously, don't tell them that they are the chosen school. In other words, play hard to get.

Schools compete for students, and one of the ways that they make themselves attractive is through their scholarship offers. You are in the best position to ask for increased scholarship funding before you have committed to a school. However, you should also consider asking again after your 1L year if you did well. Every school will have a different policy about whether to award or increase scholarship funding after your 1L year. Regardless of what your school's policy is, reach out to the relevant contact person (it might take a while to figure out who that is) and make your case. They don't want you to...God forbid...transfer.[4]

I know this is awkward. Nobody likes asking for more money. But you really should do it. Be polite and explain why you think the school should consider increasing your scholarship. Do not take the "I deserve" approach. Not because

---

4. Nothing strikes fear in the hearts of law school administrators more than the prospect of students transferring.

it won't be effective, but because it's kind of obnoxious. I have a visceral hatred of the expression "I deserve." I guess I should tell you why.

I have a "friend" (and I use the term very loosely) who often says she "deserves" stuff. *I deserve a spa day. I deserve to buy this $150 cashmere sweater. I deserve to drive a nice car.* For me, "I deserve" is an expression I've never uttered in my life. My friend was recently offered a tenure-track position at a prominent undergraduate university. Instead of being thrilled she had been chosen for the position, as most people would have been, she took the view that she "deserved" the position. She even referred to herself as "a unicorn." Since then, I grimace every time I hear someone say, "I deserve." Apologies for the "I deserve" digression... back to you and scholarship funding.

Look at it this way. If you ask for more money, what's the worst thing they can say? No. And the person saying no will likely be an administrator. Your professors and anyone you see face-to-face on a regular basis won't be the one making the financial decisions. There's really no downside to it.

Take the plunge... and maybe it will pay off (pun intended again).

5. It's Okay to Work During Law School

I did not work during law school, but I worked during undergrad, so I feel like I have something to go on. And back then, undergrad was not the "joke" I'm hearing that it is today. In undergrad, I worked several nights a week at a sports bar. I would go to school during the day, do some reading and homework in the late afternoon, and then work from about 7:00 p.m. to close (usually around 1:00 a.m.). The bar owner was really good about letting me schedule my work shifts around school and giving me weeks off to study for exams. Looking back, I'm not sure how I did it all. But I'm sure it "built character."[5] That was a big thing in my house. My dad made me mow the lawn when I was 12 because it "built character." My dad insisted I become a lector at our local church—also starting at age 12—because it "built character." My dad and Tom got me a job working as a data entry clerk at a steel company when I was 16. I had to take four busses to get there every morning. You guessed it, "built character."

---

5. And it provided me with money that I saved up to go on my Italian summer vacation. You know, the one before law school I told you about.

Some students need to work during law school. Not working is simply not an option. For those students, I would offer the following advice. First, try not to overextend yourself. It is virtually impossible to have two full time jobs. Try to work, at most, 10-20 hours per week. Second, try to find a job that might allow you to get some schoolwork in. For example, students who work in the library often have downtime and can do some reading when things are quiet. Third, find a job where you work hours that would otherwise be "fun" hours. For example, a lot of students do not do schoolwork on Friday and Saturday nights. If you find a job (say, bartending) where you work Friday and Saturday nights, you are not sacrificing schoolwork hours. Fourth, be honest with your employer about your limitations. Ask for extra time off to study for exams. In law school, exams are everything. You do not want to get a bad grade because you did not have enough time to study.

With all that said, I recommend that you try not to work during law school. If anything, work harder during the summer and hopefully that money can tide you over for the academic year.

.

FOURTEEN

Professionalism

*My idea of professionalism is probably
a lot of people's idea of obsessive.*

DAVID FINCHER

1. Acknowledge Receipt

One of my pet peeves is when students do not confirm receipt of emails.[1] I'll give you an example. I have had many amazing Research Assistants over the years. And God knows, I'm not an easy person to work for. But, oftentimes, these students fail to confirm receipt of an email. So, days later, I'm left wondering whether they got the research assignment I sent them and are on top of it. Then I have to send the "Did you get my message from the other day?" email. It's awkward. You can avoid all this. Just confirm receipt and that you're on top of stuff. Then your professor can cross this off their mental to-do list and move on.

To be clear, I'm not just talking about Research Assistants confirming receipt of an email. I'm talking about anything. For instance, when I supervise independent study projects, I extensively mark-up students' papers. There tends to be a lot of red ink and marginal comments. I'll send them off to the student with some global comments in the text of the email. And then ... radio silence.[2]

---

1. You may wonder why I didn't include that in my list of pet peeves from Chapter 9. Didn't want to be duplicative because I knew I would be covering it here.
2. Military reference!

When you get something like this from a professor, *please* just write back. In a timely manner. It's the polite and professional thing to do.

This advice is not just about your interactions with professors. These are best practices for the real world. When you are working for a judge, a senior associate, a partner, or the general counsel of a company, these are the same habits that will serve you well.

2. Say Thank You

Two easy words. Use them. Often. It takes so little to say "thank you," and it means so much.

I often get emails from students asking for clarification on such and such, inquiring whether they can use my name as a reference, or seeking some sort of law school or career guidance. I would say that most students are appreciative—or, more accurately, express appreciation. But a number of them fail to even say "thank you." This does not go unnoticed. If I just spent the past 15 minutes explaining how you've misunderstood the bargained-for exchange theory of consideration, the least you can do is say thank you. If not, I will remember. And you're not going to get as detailed or quick an answer next time.

What's particularly off-putting is students not thanking you when you go out of your way for them (e.g., to write a reference, conduct a mock interview, or make a phone call on their behalf). This happened to me recently. I wrote a reference letter for a student, after waiting a while for the student to get me the relevant contact information and his resume. After I drafted the reference letter and sent it to him—nothing. I mean how hard is it to click "reply" and type "Thank you very much for the letter. I appreciate that you took the time to do this"? Basic courtesies are important as a matter of professional legal norms. *But also, didn't your mom teach you better than that?*

I've focused on saying thank you to your professors for what they do for you. But my message goes beyond that. Say thank you to anyone who assists you and makes your life easier: secretaries, career services personnel, cafeteria workers, staff in the registrar's office. Not only will it make them feel valued (because you should value them), it is just the right thing to do.

You would think from this chapter that law students, by and large, don't say thank you. That's not true at all. Most students are very appreciative for efforts expended on their behalf. I've even received the most amazing thank you gifts from students. Among these...

> A giant bouquet of flowers delivered to my office that made other professors jealous.

> A bottle of wine with the engraving "For my favorite professors." I apparently had to share the honor with my husband.

> A mug with the words "Best. Professor. Ever." written on it.

> A handmade collage with three years of law school memories.

> A trophy for "Professor of the Year" in a year that I did not actually win that honor.

> Lavender essential oils. Because the student knew I needed to chill out a bit.

> A sweatshirt with the following emblazoned on it: "I'm not arguing with you. I'm just explaining why I'm right." Students know me so well.

Now that I'm writing about all these, I'm wondering if I should have declared them on my taxes? I'm sure there's some sort of *de minimis* gift exemption. Not to imply that the gifts were *de minimis* in my heart. Okay, let's hope no one with connections to the IRS is reading this.

I am not saying that you need to make or buy gifts for your professors. I am saying that it is nice to be appreciated. And any token of appreciation is more valuable to your professors than you will ever know.

3. Don't Be Late (Or, Worse, a No-Show)

Growing up, there was no such thing as being late. You had to be on time. My dad was, and is, a stickler for timeliness. He always shows up early, in fact. Especially if food is involved. During my childhood, I distinctly remember a scene that played out all the time. My dad would put on his coat and go wait in the car for the three of us. Within a minute—or two, max—the honking would begin. There was the warning honk. And then the "Get your a**es in the car" honk.

My dad has mellowed out a bit as he has aged. But not much. Last year, my dad and husband were going to my brother's house to do some tile work. My dad got it in his head that he wanted to leave at 8:00 a.m. to be at Dennis's house by 8:15 a.m. Cause that's great timing for someone who is taking a toddler to school. Whatever. At 8:00 a.m., dad put on his shoes and shouted to David, "I'm gone." That's what he says when he wants you to hurry. David grew up on American time, not Northern Italian time. He still needed to finish getting ready and, as my dad would say, "beautify" himself. After waiting a few minutes in the car, my dad left without David.

Now remember, there was no reason they needed to be at Dennis's house at 8:15 a.m.—and in fact, Dennis had told them to come at 9:00 a.m. But my dad had other plans. He did not want to be "late." Because my entire family is passive-aggressive, David decided to *walk* to Dennis's house, which was about five miles away. He walked quickly and got there by about 9:00 a.m. My dad was like, "Who dropped you off?" David replied, "No one. I walked." My dad didn't believe him. He called my mom who verified that David had walked. The walk was intended to be a big "take that" to my dad. Instead, my dad said, "Good. I'm proud of you." David didn't even get the satisfaction of being passive-aggressive that time.

All of this to say, in a totally roundabout way, that being late is a huge non-starter in my family. Which makes it particularly ironic that I'm writing this section as I am not-so-patiently waiting on a Zoom call for a student to show up. The student specifically reached out to me to set up the meeting and she picked the time. She is currently seven minutes late. I'm about to sign off. You would think this is an aberration. You would think. Students routinely schedule meetings and calls and then just fail to show up. It's the epitome of unprofessional. I'm not talking about an emergency happened and they couldn't be there. I'm talking about plain old "I just forgot." Or they show up ten to 15 minutes late with some silly excuse.

Nothing says "I don't respect you or your time" more than not showing up for a meeting that was scheduled to benefit you. The student I was supposed to meet with today set up the meeting to talk about "career advising." Here's my career advice: F**king show up. Sorry, I'm a little irritated, as you can tell.

I think I also have PTSD on this issue based on something that happened to me almost 20 years ago. It wasn't a late or not showing up scenario—but it was similar enough.

I had recently met and started seeing this guy, and I thought things were going well. One Saturday night, we went out for dinner in Stamford, Connecticut, which is where I was living at the time. We got done around 10:00 p.m. I suggested, as one does, that we go for drinks afterward. He got all hesitant and weird. *I mean, literally, there's a bar next door.* Then he said, "Well, I told some friends from college that I'd meet up with them in the city tonight." *You what? You're meeting friends in New York after our date? You double booked?! Are you kidding me?* I never saw him again after that night. But I did occasionally cyber-stalk him after that. He became sick rich after selling his software company for $450 million. Yeah, so, there's that.

But the double booking has left an indelible impact—and it spills over to being late and being a no-show. It's just not a good look.

Post-script: It's now 48 minutes later. Student never showed up and never emailed me. Nice.

Post-post-script: It's now 48 hours later. I sent the student an email about the no-show. No response.

Final post-script: The student never reached out. Instead, she went to see my husband, her Evidence professor, after his class. She said, "I think your wife hates me because I blew her off. Twice." My husband told her that the professional thing to do would be to reach out and apologize. Did she reach out? No.

4. Think Twice Before Sending an Email

A very good rule to live by is not to send emails when you are angry or irritated. I try my best to abide by this one but have not always been successful. There is precious little communication that can't wait until tomorrow. So, if you must, draft an email—but do not send it. Leave it in your draft folder and then re-read it the next day. When you write an email while angry, upset, or irritated, it will have an edge to it, no matter how neutral you try to make it sound. It is also often helpful to have someone you trust look the email over before you send it.

For instance, let's assume you just got a grade back. You received a 50% and are so pissed off that you barely even read the comments. Instead, you go straight to your computer and write, "Professor, I think there's been a mistake. I studied for days and there is no way I deserved this score. I want to meet with you asap. Please advise." That is not an appropriate email. You sound like a spoiled brat. That's not the vibe you want to be projecting. Your professors and eventual employers won't forget communications like this. Once it's sent, it's sent. You will forever be a brat in their mind.

The other thing that is worth mentioning is that you only know your side of things. You don't know what is going on with the other person. This can make an angry or irritated email especially bad. There is one email I truly regret sending in my life. I was working on a short article for a journal and the editor gave me a very tight timeline. I worked my butt off to get the article done. I then learned that the article wouldn't be published for another eight months. I did not follow my golden rule. I sent a complain-y email to the editor. It wasn't rude or unprofessional. But I did convey my surprise and (let's say) displeasure at the timeline. She replied defensively. She was the sole editor and was working on multiple articles at once. The timeline she gave me wasn't arbitrary, but necessary considering the circumstances. Our email communication ended there.

The article was eventually published, and I did not give the conversation that much more thought. Until about a year later. When I read the editor's obituary. Unbeknownst to me, the editor had been living with a chronic illness that eventually took her life. She was editing this journal, all by herself, while battling her illness. And I had sent her a whiny email, which is the last thing this woman should have been dealing with. That email haunts me to this day. Please, I beg of you: Press pause on irate emails. You can thank me later.

5. Don't Go Whining to the Dean

There is nothing worse, from a professor's perspective, than the tattletale student. The student who runs to the Dean's Office to "tell on" the professor. It's one of the most childish things I've seen with law students. But I see it happen regularly. Instead, how about I suggest this: If you have a gripe about the professor or the class, maybe go talk to *the professor* first? I know, crazy right?

To be clear, there are legitimate issues that students should raise with the relevant Dean. If the professor refuses to make a reasonable accommodation for a documented disability, that is a problem. If a professor has cancelled six classes in the past month without explanation, maybe that's worth bringing to the administration's attention. I'm talking about something different.

I'm talking about you not liking some aspect of the course or something about how the professor teaches and trying to go above the professor's head to get it changed or perhaps to get the professor "in trouble." Students who do that have no business being in law school. Apply again when you've grown up.

I'll give you some examples. I had a student call the school anonymously to complain that I gave low grades to the whole class on a quiz worth 5% of the grade. The student's view was that everyone did badly (which wasn't true), so there must be a problem with the professor. I had another student insist on a meeting with the Dean because the student did not like my "teaching style." And another student who complained that I did not "let her" ask questions in an online class because I required that questions be submitted prior to class so I could address them all in an organized way.[3] I think there's a sense that if you complain and whine enough, you'll get your way. The squeaky wheel gets the grease.

But no one likes a whiner. And everyone knows who the whiner is. Your reputation will precede you. This is true in law school and in life. Dad story time! I went to the pharmacy to pick up a prescription for my dad about a year ago. I said, "I'm here to pick up the prescription for Graziano Monestier. Do you need me to spell the name?" The pharmacist said, "No, we know who that is." I said, "Oh, you know my dad?" She said, "Yes, he always comes in and complains about how high the drug prices are. We all know him." I wanted to die. Running to the Dean is the equivalent of complaining about the high drug prices at the pharmacy. Don't be a Graziano.

One more thing. The whiner not only gets a reputation for complaining, but the whiner also alienates the professor or staff member she complained about. Someone who otherwise could have been a professional asset.

As professors, we do not like our day-to-day decisions being questioned and micro-managed by students. This reminds me a little of Jack Nicholson's famous speech in *A Few Good Men,* which I'm sure almost none of you has seen:

> I have neither the time nor the inclination to explain myself to a man who rises and sleeps under the blanket of the very freedom that I provide and then questions the manner in which I provide it.
>
> I would rather that you just said "thank you" and went on your way. Otherwise, I suggest you pick up a weapon and stand the post. Either way, I don't give a DAMN what you think you're entitled to!

All that to say, let the professor fly the plane. And stay in your seat.

---

3. This makes it seem like a lot of students complain about me. They don't (at least not as a percentage of the number of students I teach). This all happened in the past couple of years.

6. Do Not Send Emails Addressed, "Hey Prof., Happy Monday!"

Almost all your professors will use email as the preferred means of communication. Treat emails as a professional form of correspondence. Emails are *not* *texts*. They are more like letters. Proceed accordingly.

Your email should address your professor as "Dear Professor X" or simply "Professor X." It should not say, "Hey prof", "Prof", "Hi!", "Happy Monday!" or anything like that, unless you know the professor really well. And even then, I'd steer clear of that sort of salutation. You are in a professional environment, and you need to treat it as such.

The text of your email should be clear and to the point. It should not contain any spelling and grammar errors. It should be polite and thank the professor, if appropriate.

It should end with your preferred way of signing off: "Best," "All the best," "Thank you," or whatever (you need to pay attention to how people end their emails and copy which expression you like best).

Chances are that students reading this are in one of two camps:

Camp 1: The "obviously" students. These are the students who read this and think, "Obviously...tell me something I don't know." This section is not for you. You can stop reading now.

Camp 2: The "you need to chill out" students. These students think that my approach to email communication is unduly formal and that maybe I have a God complex. This section is for you.

For the "you need to chill out" students, let me tell you why I am recommending the overly formal approach. Your professors are not your friends. They are your professors. They will be grading you. They will be writing letters of reference. They may be connecting you with alums or prospective employers. You want to make a good impression on them. You want to project competence and professionalism. Nothing says "I'm not serious about being a lawyer" more than "Hey prof...(sent from iPhone)." We teach dozens of students per year. In some cases, maybe even hundreds of students per year. You don't want to be the "Hey prof" student.[4]

Also, when you get into the real world, you will be expected to engage in professional correspondence. At some point, you will not be texting like you're

---

4. Or the "Cool Beans" student. I had a student write that to me once.

a teenager. Why not get a head start on that? And for those of you not convinced, let me suggest you look at it this way. What is the downside to my recommendation? There is none. Except it takes more time and attention to detail. What is the downside to the "Hey prof" approach? Well, I don't know that it's worth finding out.

And if you're still not convinced, I'm not the only one who feels this way. From an op-ed in the *Washington Post*:

> [B]eing too familiar with your instructors in your initial interactions does not make the best first impression. Erring on the side of formality is always the safer signal to send. As Laura Portwood-Stacer explained a few years ago: "Whether or not you, as a student, actually respect your professor's authority or position, it's a good idea to act like you do."[5]

7. If You Talk Sh*t About Your Professor, They Will Hear About It

Law school leaks like a sieve. Remember that. Anything you say can and will be held against you. Students vent about their professors all the time—to other students, to other professors, and to academic support staff. You should assume that you will be ratted out and that your professor will hear that you talked smack about them. I have had this happen a few times. And it's usually the students who are the nicest and sweetest to your face. I guarantee that once a professor hears that you've been trash-talking them, they are not going to go out of their way to help you with your career.

How do you avoid this problem? Uh...don't bad-mouth your professor. If you have a problem that you'd like to discuss with the professor (e.g., a bad grade, feeling like the professor embarrassed you in class, or whatever), go talk to them. Like a grown up. It might not be a fun conversation to have, but it will be a worthwhile one.

If you choose to go a different route (i.e., you're going to tell everyone who will listen that your professor is a real you-know-what), then be prepared for the professor to know about it. And let the chips fall where they may.

---

5. https://www.washingtonpost.com/outlook/2021/07/21/my-completely-uncontroversial-take-what-call-your-professor/.

One final point. If you're going to talk sh*t about a class or a professor, please make sure that the professor is not in earshot. I've had this happen on several occasions, and I can tell you, it's wicked mortifying for the student. Quick story. I had just finished teaching my Contracts class and was walking out to the parking lot. Two students were maybe ten feet ahead of me. I couldn't hear what they were saying and didn't know who they were (since I could only see their backs). As I got closer, I realized that they were two students from the class I had just taught. I heard the girl say to the guy, "And then she called on me…" and I piped in jokingly, "Hey, are you guys talking about me?" Little did I realize that they actually *were* trash-talking me. I got home and there were two emails waiting for me in my inbox. In them, each of the students apologized profusely for a lack of professionalism and tried to explain why they said what they said (which, unbeknownst to them, I didn't actually overhear).

I imagine that the parking lot students were permanently scarred from that encounter. And, frankly, so was I. These were two students I thought I had a good relationship with. Had they just come to me with their concern, we could have had an actual conversation about it.

I get that sometimes students just need to vent. I do. But if you're going to vent, just don't do it in front of the professor.

8. Do Not Wait Until the Last Minute

All the academic support books will tell you the same thing. You need to work on "time management." You should not be waiting until the last minute to do your assignments or study for exams. As someone who did all her assignments weeks in advance and studied for exams at least six weeks out, I just can't fathom any other way of doing things. But I know I'm perhaps in the minority here. I'm not going to preach on this one because I think—in your heart of hearts—you *know* you shouldn't be procrastinating and that it will reflect in your grade.

So, I want to make a different point…. Pause for dramatic effect.

Your professors and your eventual bosses take note of *when* you hand something in. And the timing creates an initial impression of the ultimate work product. Let's take this into the real-world context. When I was in private practice,[6] I would often get tasked with drafting memos or preparing dispositive

---

6. I worked in-house at a pharmaceutical company.

motions or motions *in limine* (don't worry about what the latter two mean). I would ask my supervisors what their timeline was[7] and would always complete the assignment *well in advance* of that timeline. In short order, I had them convinced I was a superstar. I wasn't.

I know it won't always be possible to do things well in advance, especially when you are juggling multiple assignments and responsibilities. But you should never (ever ever!) wait until the last minute to submit an assignment. It just *looks* bad.

As a professor, I have given assignments that are due on Sundays at 5:00 p.m. I have a great many students who wait until Sunday at 4:58 p.m. to upload their assignment. Could that be the best assignment ever? Maybe (doubtful). But seeing the upload at 4:58 p.m. really taps in to my spidey-sense that perhaps this student just phoned it in at the last minute.

Here's an analogy. You have a job interview at 9:00 a.m. What time do you show up? 9:00 a.m.? Maybe. But I think most of you would say 8:50 a.m. at the latest. You get my point.

9. Do Things the Right Way

In my household, there is a right way to do things and a wrong way to do things. You might have guessed that about my dad already. But my mom is also the same way. *That is not how you load the dishwasher. You are stirring the sauce incorrectly. You're folding the plastic grocery bags the wrong way.* You heard me correctly on the last one. My mom neatly folds all her plastic grocery bags. By extension, so do I. I didn't realize that most other people didn't fold their plastic bags until I was well into my twenties.[8]

My father is worse than my mom about doing things the right way. One of his favorite expressions is "That is not proper." You have to picture it being said with an eye squint and a thick Italian accent. My husband, David, has been on the receiving end of "That is not proper" on many occasions the past few years. Every time David embarks on a house project, he gets the squinty eyes and the

---

7. Always do this!

8. In case you're wondering what the right way is to fold a plastic bag, here you go (you're welcome). Lay it flat and smooth out air pockets. Then have the two handles meet. Then fold the middle portions of the bag inward. Then fold in four so you end up with a small rectangle.

"That is not proper" admonition. David is a very patient person, but even he has his limits. One time, the two of them were painting the downstairs. When Dad saw how David was painting, he said, "That is not proper," and showed him how to do it (long up and down strokes). David was not impressed and replied, "There is no proper way to do it!" Fast forward six months. David was visiting his mom in Idaho. Along with his two sisters, they were all painting his mom's bedroom. When he saw how his sisters were painting, he almost lost his mind. *That is not proper.* He finally understood.

If you'll indulge me a second, my dad's "That is not proper" refrain is not limited to the Monestier household. My dad believes that *everyone* needs to know when things are not proper. Last week, my dad was going for his hour-long morning walk. He loves his walks because he gets to check out construction projects in the neighborhood. He is on a first-name basis with every foreman on every job (Frank and Tony are always safe bets).

In any event, he was walking by Vancho Crescent, a street in his neighborhood. A city inspector was supervising a repaving project. My dad stopped and observed what was going on. He noticed that the construction workers did not put tar down before laying the asphalt. Apparently, this is a no-no. My dad called over the city inspector. *Chief, why aren't you putting down tar?*[9] The inspector said that the machine was broken. My dad was like, *You can't do that. That is not proper.* The inspector shrugged. My dad rushed home. He came into the house yelling, *Oriiiiiiannnna!!* He marched into the kitchen with his shoes on. This is *not done* in our house. My mom was like, "What's going on?" My dad said, "How do I take a picture with the phone?" My mom showed him how and asked what was going on. My dad said that he was going back to Vancho Crescent to get proof that they were doing the repaving wrong. He was going to, in his own words, "catch them."

My dad went back and took pictures. Here is one of them (try not to laugh too hard):

---

9. "Chief" is one of my dad's favorite salutations. Along with "young fella" which applies to anyone under the age of 55.

My dad asked for the inspector's name, which he wouldn't give. My dad said, "Fine I'm just going to take a picture of you." Empty threat because, as you can see, my dad can't take a picture to save his life. My dad was not happy that he wasn't able to get "proof" that they were doing it wrong. Nonetheless, he was undeterred. He called the City of Toronto the next week to let them know *this is not proper.*

What was this long diatribe about? It's about not cutting corners. There sometimes is a right way and a wrong way to do something. When you take shortcuts, you don't get a good result. If you're going to do something, do it right. Don't half-a** it.

Let me give you a concrete example in the law school context. You might be writing a paper and you've found a quote from a case that you want to use. But it's not actually a quote from that case; it's a quote from a different case that is cited within your case. In case I lost you, this is what I mean: You are reading *Smith v. Jones*, which says, "In *Peterson v. Miller*, the court said that 'silence can never equal acceptance.'" Instead of going to the *actual* case that the quote came from (*Peterson v. Miller*), you half-a** it and just cut-and-paste the quote that's in front of you. After all, the court probably quoted it accurately.

That is the wrong way to do this. The right way is going to the actual case, making sure the quote says what you want it to say, and checking to see how it was used. It might be saying the absolute opposite of what you want it to say. For instance, you might go to *Peterson v. Miller* and see that the quote says, "although courts have sometimes held that *silence can never equal acceptance*, we think this view is outmoded." Completely different thing, right?

Back to my title: Do things the right way.

FIFTEEN

Don't Be Stupid

*The two most common elements in the universe
are hydrogen and stupidity.*

HARLAN ELLISON

1. Social Media Lives Forever

I'm going to give you advice that you've probably heard a million times before: Be careful what you post online. What happens in Vegas does not stay in Vegas. It lives on in the cloud forever. I realize that all of you have grown up in the social media generation, where you share every photo, every thought, every gripe, every everything with the world. But the "rest of us" just aren't like that. Your employers will largely be of a different generation. One that does not feel it necessary to share what they had for breakfast with complete strangers. I realize that there is a generational gap here and that I might not be able to convince you of my views on this. You might remain firmly embedded in the "This is me. And if a potential employer doesn't like me for me, too fricken bad" camp. Oh well, I tried.

Photos and posts on social media can come back to bite you in the a**, and you probably don't even know it. They influence how people see you. And if your professors, employers, or colleagues see things they can't unsee, it will impact their perception of you.

Here's a true story. I came across a student's social media feed. In the feed, she had posted a bunch of sexy pictures of herself. You know, the mirror selfies and the duck-lips, or whatever it's called nowadays. The images bothered me. Not because of what she was wearing (or more accurately, not wearing). But because, for me, it called into question her judgment. Did she really think it was a good idea, as a law student, to be putting this out there into the world? To be clear, I'm not picking on women here. My advice applies equally across the board. I'm an equal opportunity downer.

Now, some of you will think I'm prudish. Maybe I am. Maybe this is the same generational dynamic as my Italian grandmother being horrified that I would wear short cutoff jean shorts in public (what will people say?!). I'm not discounting the possibility that I'm just getting old. Like "get off my lawn" old. But there could be some wisdom to what I'm saying.

I want to be clear that that what I'm saying isn't just about inappropriate photos. It's about everything you put out on social media. Just today, I saw a student's Twitter post, and it said something like: "I'm feeling sick today. Staying home, drinking lots of hot tea with honey, snuggling with my dog, and taking a warm shower." Really? What happened to the days where you just stayed home sick?[1] Why do you need to put this into the Twitterverse? So that random people can mindlessly say "feel better soon" and send you "lots of love"? I just don't get it. And if *I* don't get it, some other people won't get it as well.

2. Avoid Drama

There is a lot of drama in law school. It's like high school but with grown adults. There will be relationship drama. Exam drama. Friend drama. Job drama. Political drama. You name it. It's sometimes hard to avoid drama, but please try. It's a drain on your time and mental health that you just don't need. Sometimes you don't go looking for drama; it just finds you. If this happens, then just soldier on (I already mentioned my love of military jargon).

In law school, I was quiet, kept to myself, and was the least drama-seeking person you could find. In my first year of law school, I started dating a 3L—let's call him Adam. Adam was really accomplished. He was a former NHL hockey player and he had "summered" at a top law firm in New York (which was a big

---

1. Also—FYI—nobody wants the image of you in the shower in their head.

deal at Canadian law schools at the time). Other 1Ls did not like that I was dating Adam. They thought this gave me an "unfair advantage." When I got straight A's first semester, there was a lot of talk that I didn't deserve the grades. That I just got them because Adam helped me (he didn't). I would hear that so-and-so overheard so-and-so saying that I only did well in Tax Law because I had Adam's outline or that Adam helped me with my legal writing assignments. Of course, none of this was true, but it didn't matter. It became the story that students preferred. This was difficult for me. I didn't need public credit for my success, but I also didn't want my success attributed to someone else. And there's really no way to dispute the narrative and to quell the rumors. Eventually, this all died down—especially given that Adam moved to the United States in my second year of law school. At a certain point, it's hard to argue that the person getting the top grade in virtually every class is only doing so because she has (or had) a smart boyfriend.

There is one form of drama that I see a lot, particularly with female students: *the frenemy*. It's the friend who is also an enemy. The person who sits next to you in class but then gossips about you behind your back or is secretly resentful of your success. It's bizarre. The first time I heard about something like this was about six or seven years ago. My response to the student was, *Why would you continue to be friends with her?* She just shrugged it off like it's just the way things were. NBD.

Another student recently relayed the following story to me. She had interned over the summer for a few male judges. She had done good work, and the judges had given her very positive feedback. When she told a "friend" about this (thinking the friend would be happy for her), the reaction she got was unexpected. The friend warned her that she should be careful and that these judges were either "interested in something else" or liked her only because of how she looked. A friend indeed....

If someone is not truly your friend, why bother?[2] Law school can be a toxic enough place without your friends also being your nemeses. Bottom line advice: Cut loose the frenemy.

---

2. There is an expression in Italian that is apt here: *meglio soli che male accompagnati*. Better alone than in bad company.

3. Never, Ever Lie

Right is right even if no one is doing it
and wrong is wrong even if everyone is doing it.

ST. AUGUSTINE

Integrity is when you care more for the hard truth than the easy lie.

MAXIME LAGACÉ[3]

As a lawyer, your word is everything. Your reputation is everything. Your integrity is everything. Do not put any of those things in jeopardy by lying—even about something small.

I know you might find this hard to believe, but professors have a very good bullsh*t meter. Let me give you some examples.

Food poisoning doesn't happen really often. That's why when I hear of three different students in three different classes at three different times in the semester having "food poisoning," I get a little suspicious. Um...the lie detector determined that was a lie.

I recently had different student who was "too sick" to attend an online morning zoom class. She emailed me later that day *from work* to ask what she missed. *You were sick, huh?* The lie detector determined that was also a lie.

I had a student log into a Zoom class and then leave for large portions of it, only to claim that he momentarily stepped out. The student recalled no specific details about the class. The lie detector...yeah, we get it.

If a student lies about anything, that automatically tells me something about the student. Even white lies. If you're inclined to lie about something small and trivial, you will be inclined to lie about something significant.

---

3. Who is this? I googled the name and it brought up a 28-year-old hockey player. I mean, it's not impossible that it's him, but it seems unlikely. The most observant among you may also be wondering why there is a quote within a sub-chapter (not just at the start of the chapter). I thought this topic was sufficiently important that it deserved its own special quotes.

I was involved in a case a few years back where the judge asked questions of the witnesses. The client had already testified and told a very detailed story about the relevant sequence of events. When subsequent witnesses testified, the judge asked them about small details of the client's story. Largely irrelevant details. The witnesses would have no reason to answer anything but truthfully. Through this line of questioning, it became apparent what the judge was doing: she was testing the veracity of the client's story. Very clever. Turns out, the client may have embellished (or, more accurately, misrepresented) the small details. This was a huge black eye for the client's credibility. Let's just say the client did not fare well.

4. Do Not Surf the Internet During Class

I am sure you have heard it time and again. Play attention in class; don't go on the internet. It is disrespectful to the professor to surf the internet during class. And it is disrespectful to your classmates, who don't want to be distracted by you scrolling through Buzzfeed. I'm going to offer another reason why you should not surf the internet during class that is consistent with the theme of this chapter: *Because it's stupid.*

We've already established that for many students in their early 20s, money isn't a real thing that they fully understand the value of. But again, and at the risk of beating a dead horse, when you take out loans for school, you are paying money—and a sh*t ton of it—to be able to sit in each and every class. Tuition at different schools varies dramatically, but I think you can take it to the bank (pun intended, yet again!) that you're probably paying between $200-500 per class session for the privilege to sit there. The idea that you're paying money to be there and ignoring what's going on makes zero sense to me. It's like going to the world's most expensive movie and then sitting there playing on your phone. It's just dumb.

I'm sure that if you could communicate with me, there would be a chorus of: *I can multitask. I already understand the material and I don't need to sit there and listen to the professor repeat it again. I don't need to listen when other students are asking stupid questions. I don't learn from class, I learn on my own.* My answer to this is: bullsh*t times four.

There is always something of value to be gleaned from class. And, by the way, science says you cannot multitask, so please stop saying that you can.

5. Don't Be a Tool

I was trying to think of an appropriate title for this section and went with "Don't Be a Tool." I wanted it to be harsher, but I settled on the more generic descriptor. If you want a more accurate title, see Matteo's Advice in Chapter 21.

What do I mean by "tool"? A tool is a student who is arrogant, braggy, and immature. Let me give you two real-life examples of "tool" things to do in law school.

I had a conversation with a 1L recently who proudly announced that she "disagreed with a lot of stuff in criminal law." I mean, you've covered *actus reus* and *mens rea* so far. What the f**k is there to disagree with? More importantly, you've been in school for seven weeks. You don't *get* to "disagree" with "a lot of stuff" in "criminal law."

There is another student I know of who posted screenshots of all his grades on Twitter and Instagram. I can't even. Why would you do this? I am not saying you should not be proud of your grades. By all means, be proud. Tell your family and friends. But bragging online so that everyone in your class—including the 85% of students who did worse than you—can see how well you did strikes me as gratuitous. This goes back the judgment thing I mentioned before. No matter how good this guy's grades were, if I knew he publicized them online, I would *never* hire him.

My broader point is this. You are in a professional environment. Be a professional. Hubris and obliviousness are not a good look.

Okay, before we move on, I have a public service announcement for the one person reading this book who goes to Harvard. It's actually a two-part public service announcement.

Part 1: When someone asks where you go to school, say Harvard. Don't say "I go to school in Cambridge." We all know that's code for Harvard. And *you know* that *we know* that's code for Harvard. It's all so tool-y.

Part 2: Do not throw in "I go to Harvard" in every conversation possible. I have a friend who does this. More like an acquaintance, truth be told. At every opportunity, there's a "When I was at Harvard" or "My supervisor at Harvard" or "I went to alumni weekend at Harvard." We get it. You went to f**king Harvard. Guess what? I didn't go to Harvard. Because I *turned down* Harvard.[4]

---

4. I actually got a phone call from the Harvard admissions department asking why I decided not to attend. Apparently, they are not used to hearing "no" very often.

6. Don't Phone It In

There are more than a few students I've encountered who are simply looking to phone it in. These are probably not the students who are reading this book. Or maybe they are because they are looking for tips and tricks and shortcuts. I guess those are the students who will give this book one star on Amazon.[5]

I'm talking about the students who put in next to zero effort, toss together their assignments at the last minute, don't do the readings, etc. They live by the motto: "C's are degrees." They just want to graduate and get out there and practice.

One thing that I want to say about these students is that the half-hearted attitude toward law school is a facade. I think these students *do* want to do well—they just don't believe they can.[6] So rather than engage, they opt out.

If you fall into the "C's are degrees" camp, I would suggest that you re-orient your mindset. You are paying an *awful lot of money* for your law degree. If all you are getting out of it is (literally) a piece of paper, then you might want to rethink your choices.

For some reason, these students think that they can skate by in law school and then become superstar trial attorneys. Uh, it doesn't work that way. I'm not saying that you need to be super successful in law school to be super successful in the real world. But I am saying that law school is designed to give you the tools you need out there in practice. If you don't ever get those tools, there's no way you can be a good lawyer.

Just take it outside the law context for a second. I'm sure there are medical students who get by with the least amount of effort possible. Terrifying, but probably true. Do you think that somehow these medical students are going to become the country's leading orthopedic surgeons?

You are paying to *learn*. You are paying to get the groundwork that you need to have a successful career. Why in the world would you phone it in?

---

5. Instead of giving the book one star on Amazon, I suggest you burn copies of the book in protest. I'm definitely not suggesting this in order to reduce the number of used copies of this book in circulation.

6. Yes, I'm a part-time psychologist as well.

SIXTEEN

Make Good Decisions

Good decisions come from experience.
Experience comes from making bad decisions.

MARK TWAIN

Make good decisions.

EVERY MOM EVER

1. Do Not Make Decisions Based on Fear

Law school is a scary place. We've established that already. But don't be afraid. Don't be afraid of professors, of particular courses, of things you're not familiar with. Do not let fear guide your decisions.

Example time! Several years ago, I taught a course called Contract Law Practicum: *In the Matter of Dr. Burton.* Sounds enthralling, I know. One of my students, Jessica, was really excited about taking the course. She even had to get special permission to register since it was an Honors-only course, and she wasn't in Honors. The week before the course was scheduled to begin, I got the following email from Jessica:

Hi Professor Monestier,

I wanted to let you know that I decided to drop the Contract Practicum this morning. I'm fearful that I will not be able to keep up with the demand of this course and devote the amount of time it deserves. Thank you for extending the

243

opportunity to me. I'm disappointed that I will not be taking a course with you this semester but hope there is an opportunity in the future to take another one of your classes.

I was very surprised to receive this email, especially because she had petitioned to take this course. I wrote back:

I'm very surprised to hear this, especially since you were really enthusiastic about taking the course. As I've told you before, I think this course is an incredibly valuable opportunity (and I'm not just saying that because I teach it). If you'd like to talk before making a final decision, I'll be in my office all morning until 12:00.

Jessica came by that morning to talk. I could tell that she felt bad about dropping the course. Jessica is a very shy person by nature, so I had to do some coaxing to figure out what was really going on. Jessica had freaked herself out. She got it in her head that she wasn't smart enough to take the course and that she would disappoint me by not doing well. Rather than try, she decided to opt out. I encouraged her to rethink her decision. Not because I cared whether she took the *Dr. Burton* course or not. But because I don't think it's good to make decisions based upon fear. If you make decisions based on what you think you can't do, you'll never prove to yourself what you *can* do. Jessica ultimately decided to take the class and says it was one of the best experiences she had in law school. Jessica and I are still in touch to this day, and she frequently brings up the *Dr. Burton* course as one of her formative experiences as a law student.

Let me give you another example of decisions being guided by fear. Many law students avoid certain courses like the plague. The courses tend to be those that undeservedly get a bad reputation like Conflict of Laws or Federal Courts, and those that involve numbers or math, like Tax, Law and Economics, Secured Transactions, and Accounting for Lawyers. Students will stay away from anything that scares them. Don't do this. Do not let your course selection be influenced by your perceived fear of something.

Let's talk specifically about math. Law students tend to hate math. They went to law school to avoid math. Now they discover that there's math in law school. In Contracts, Remedies, Tax, and Family Law. Oh no! Math is everywhere. Normally, the sight of a number causes law students to break out in a cold sweat. Having to compute anything more complicated than 2 + 2 provokes extreme anxiety. I get it. I'm not a math person either. I mean, don't get me wrong, I did well in math. But I found it hard. And it wasn't among my favorite subjects.[1]

As a lawyer, you are sometimes going to have to work with numbers. I know, why didn't anyone tell you this before you applied to law school?! Don't panic. It's usually not very complicated math. If you have any complicated math, you can hire an accountant or some other math expert to do it for you. But, as a lawyer, you do need to understand some basic formulas and do some simple math.

Here is my advice when math crops up in law school: Don't be scared. Forget the numbers initially. Focus on the concepts. For instance, when a seller breaches a sale of goods contract, the buyer is entitled to "cover" damages, the difference between the contract price and the cost of replacement goods. Work on understanding what that means using simple examples.

The example I use in my class involves a poison dart frog. If you don't know what that is, I didn't either—until I met Brian. Brian is who I have dubbed "the most interesting man in the world." He was a student in my Contracts class a couple of years ago. First semester, he was very shy. Didn't say a word shy. Second semester, I got him to come to my office hours. There, he finally opened up. And it all started with this seemingly innocuous compliment: "That's a really nice anthurium you have there." *Excuse me?* The 6-foot-7 guy[2] in my Contracts class wearing a Balenciaga sweatshirt knows what an anthurium is?

I learned over time that Brian is an amateur MMA fighter, he collects rare carnivorous plants and poisonous dart frogs, and he has travelled the world. Like I said, most interesting man in the world. Back to the dart frogs. I asked Brian for an example of a "good" he might buy—he said, "poisonous dart frog." Okay. Most people would have said TV, or bike, or car. But *you do you.* I

---

1. One day, my 12th grade calculus teacher was not feeling well, so he asked me to teach the class for him. *What was I supposed to say?* So, I did. As you can guess, this made me *really* popular among my classmates.

2. Before I included this narrative in the book, I checked with Brian. In my original draft, I called him Jerome because he kind of looks like my brother's next door neighbor, Jerome. I did not say I was creative. The story said something about the 6'4" guy commenting on the anthurium in my office. Brian told me to feel free to use his real name. And he politely informed me that "Jerome" was actually three inches shorter than he was. Clever. I also sent him a sample chapter of the book, to which he responded, "I'm surprised you didn't have me sign an NDA." First, Brian knows me so well. Second, I should have asked Brian to help with the book. He's legit funny.

worked with him on an example of cover damages involving a poisonous dart frog. Let's say that you enter into a contract to buy a poisonous dart frog for, what, $50? Who the hell knows how much these frogs cost? Then, the seller backs out. What do you, the buyer, do? Brian replied, "I guess I'd go find another frog if I still wanted one." Exactly. You'd go find another seller. And, Brian, how much is this seller going to charge you? Brian was like, "Maybe $70." Okay, great—thanks for making my life easier. So, Brian, how much do you, the innocent buyer, get in damages from the first seller. Brian was like, $20. Bingo. That's cover damages. It's not rocket science.

The lesson here is don't get dizzy when you see numbers. Don't freeze in fear and assume you can't do this. I've seen it happen time and again: deer in the headlights. Students see numbers and panic, not knowing what to do with them. When you see a number, slow down, *breathe*, and focus on the law, not the math.

You may surprise yourself and end up loving Tax or Federal Courts, which you initially thought was the scariest thing imaginable. I've had students terrified of Contracts when they come in only to end up practicing business law four years later. You never know unless you try. My mom says that a lot in an attempt to get me to try new food.[3] I'm not exactly an adventurous eater. I don't need to try fried octopus to know it's gross. Sorry, off track there.

2. You Should Clerk (Probably, Maybe)

Should you do a clerkship? Yes! I have never heard of a student regret doing a clerkship. I'm going to somewhat walk back the very enthusiastic "yes" above. If you want to do a clerkship, and you get offered a clerkship, then you should take it. If you have no interest in a clerkship and think it sounds like the worst job in the world, then no, don't do one just to put it on your resume or tick the "clerkship" box.

A clerkship is time limited. It will not derail future career plans. Most firms and other organizations are very happy to have clerks in their ranks, so they will often hold jobs open for you while you are clerking.

A clerkship is a wonderful opportunity to see the law through a different lens. Though an insider's lens. It will enable you to play a small part in crafting

---

3. Why do parents do that? I think the "try new food" refrain should stop after you've moved out of the house.

the law. It will challenge your analytical reasoning skills. And it will make you a better writer.

The cherry on top is that you will develop a relationship, hopefully a close one, with "your" judge. That is how they will forever be known to you: "your" judge." My judge and his wife came to my wedding. The same is true of many other people I know.

Enjoy your year clerking. There will never be another one like it. Unless, of course, you get the ultimate dream job, permanent clerk! I once asked "my judge" if I could clerk for him forever. He was amused. I was only half-kidding.

Me and "my" judge! There's no hi-res version since this is a picture using actual film (what we used before digital cameras and phones).

3. Yes, You Should Transfer (Or Maybe You Shouldn't)

At the end of 1L year, several students come to me and say that they are thinking of transferring. The reasons are varied: they want to be closer to home; they think the new school affords better career opportunities; they want to go to a law school that puts them in closer proximity to their significant other; they want the prestige associated with a higher ranked school. Should you transfer? Maybe. Maybe not. Or as my dad would say, "Probably yes. Probably no."

The decision to transfer is not an easy one. Every case is unique, and it is important for students to think through the decision from all angles. I would recommend that students seek out several people they trust and try to talk through the pros and cons.

The biggest thing I think students should be thinking about is finances. Strangely, this almost always seems to be the *last thing* on students' minds. Students just tend to take the view that they'll add the cost to the huge amount of money they already owe. I suggest that students look at the decision in more concrete terms and really consider the cost/benefit ratio of transferring to a new school.

For instance, a student approached me the year before last about wanting to potentially transfer to a school in California. Let's call this student Miguel. Miguel had fairly vague reasons for transferring: it might be "better" experience, he'd be close to the ocean (well, a different ocean), etc. I asked Miguel how much scholarship money he was getting currently. The amount was significant. If I recall correctly, he was on something like a 75% scholarship, which means he was paying very little for a law school education. I asked him how much tuition was at the other school. It was over $50,000/year. There would be no scholarship money available there. Basically, it would cost him almost $100,000 *more* to go to the California school than to stay at his current institution. I told him to look at that as real money. That is a Ferrari! That is a house in some parts of the country! It is a lot of money that would take a *loooong* time to pay back.

Would it be worth it to transfer? In that case, probably not. The reasons for wanting to transfer weren't super-compelling. Miguel was happy where he was. He was getting close to a full ride. He had good friends. He was doing well in school. He enjoyed his classes and his professors. The other school was marginally better than his current school (but it wasn't exactly Stanford). In that case, I advised that it probably wouldn't be a good decision to transfer.

You have to realize that there is an apparent conflict of interest here. No school wants its professors to advise students to transfer (it's not good for business). So, you may be thinking that *of course* a professor is going to suggest you stay at the current institution. Not true, at least in my case. I personally look at each student's situation individually and advise, based on my own independent judgment, what I think is best for that student. In some cases, I have advised the student to stay. In other cases, I have advised the student to go. The latter is always tough, but necessary.

Another student, Damien, approached me about a potential transfer two years ago. He was torn. He had made two good friends at school and didn't want to leave them. Damien also did well in his courses and really liked his professors. I told him to transfer. The school he transferred to is a top-25 school that offered opportunities in his area of interest. Staying with his friends and professors he liked wasn't worth giving up such a good opportunity. So, Damien went. And he thrived (he's currently clerking). And he still stayed in touch with his friends and his professors (or at least one professor—me!).

I would say that in considering whether to transfer, students should assess the following.

First, how much "better" is the new school compared to the current school? "Better" is a loaded term, but what I mean is that you should consider rankings and career prospects. With respect to the latter, I don't mean "Do they have an internship program that you like?" I mean "Is the chance of getting hired where you want to get hired *significantly* better at the new school than at your current school?"

Second, how much more would it cost to go there? Is that worth it? In making this assessment, you also need to consider cost of living. For instance, if you move to a place like New York, your cost of living will likely increase exponentially. Focus on the bottom-line number: *If I stay here, I will pay $X. If I transfer, I will pay $X + $100,000.*

Third, do I need to be closer to home? If there is a particular reason you need to be close to home (e.g., to care for a family member), then this needs to factor into the equation. If you just miss home, this is probably not a good enough reason to transfer.

Fourth, am I unhappy at my current institution? Now, all law students are unhappy. Being a law student kind of sucks. So I'm not talking regular unhappiness. I'm talking next-level unhappiness. If you are profoundly unhappy where you are, then it is worth considering a move.

Things that should probably not factor into the equation:

Friends. You will likely have made friends in your 1L year. That can't be a factor in your decision to transfer. After all, you will be leaving those friends in two years anyway, so don't let those connections tie you to a school.

Professors. You may be close to some of your professors. You may be eager to take Conflict of Laws with them. But guess what? There are good professors at the new school too. And you can always stay in touch with the connections you've made at your current school.

Social Life. If you feel like you would be happier at another school because it is in a city, or near a beach, or whatever, this is probably not a good enough reason to make the move. Think about it this way: is it worth it to pay $100,000 just to *be in* a particular city for two years?

One Particular Course or Internship/Externship. Schools offer varying curricular programs. It may be that you really want to participate in a Veteran's Law clinic, say, and your current school does not offer one. If this is your only, or predominant, reason for wanting to transfer, that's probably not a good enough reason. A clinic or internship is a time-limited deal, and there are probably similar curricular offerings at your current school. I wouldn't pay a huge premium for one particular course (cause that's what it is).

I know that the decision to transfer or not transfer feels like an enormous one. It feels like if you make the "wrong" decision, your life and career will be ruined. You need to take some pressure off yourself. Whatever will be will be. If you don't transfer, it will be okay. If you do transfer, it will be okay.

I was once debating an issue that was very important to me at the time. I kept going back and forth. A friend said to me, "Listen, I get that this is stressful. But this is not the choice between chemo and radiation." Put things in perspective.

4. You Might Have Made a Mistake Going to Law School

There comes a point with some students where they feel like they made a mistake in going to law school. This usually happens sometime in their first year of law school. I'm not talking about "Law school is hard" or "I got bad grades so this might not be for me." I'm talking about "I don't think I want to be a lawyer" and "Nothing about law remotely interests me." If you're feeling this way, then it's time for a serious conversation. With yourself.

You will undoubtedly feel "pot committed." For those of you who don't know anything about poker, it's the idea that you've invested a lot of money in the game already and therefore, you should not back out now, even if you have a bad hand. In behavioral economics, it is called the sunk cost fallacy. I mentioned it earlier in the book in relation to case briefing.

Although it goes against everything we believe, you should not let what you've put into something (the poker game, law school) dictate whether you continue with it. I came across an article that does a great job explaining this. The article says,

> The sunk cost fallacy sinks a lot of people. How many friends do you know who have stuck-it-out with a job or relationship or house or so-so daycare provider because they'd already invested in it? There are many reasons a person remains committed, as notions of ego, pride, fear of failure, and more come into play. But there are ways to think about such situations and poker players can teach us all a lot. Good players know when it's time to move on to the next hand.
>
> . . .

Sometimes you need to get out.... [I]n life, like at the table, it's crucial to think about the decision that you want, not about the ones you've made. It could be any big choice, but let's say it's a job. Do some mental time travel and imagine, If I stayed, what would it look like a year from now? Would there be opportunities? Would I be any less unhappy?...[It's] also important to think about what's missing from your current situation, which helps focus on the issue.

After you do this, ask, "What would a new situation look like?" It might be great. It might be terrible, but if your current situation has no reason to improve, your pot odds are better by changing, and,...you're now evaluating the value and risk of an opportunity.[4]

Sometimes the right thing to do is to be honest with yourself and move on. Even if that decision is painful right now. It will be a blow to your pride, your finances, your imagined identity. But you should not continue down a track that you are 99% sure *you don't actually want* just because you feel like it's too late in the game to back out now.

Disclaimer from the Contracts professor in me: I am not encouraging you to quit law school. I am saying that if you have serious doubts, then be aware of the sunk cost fallacy and think really hard about what is best for you.

5. You Might Be Making a Mistake by Going to Law School

Wait, didn't we just cover this? No. Read the title carefully. This section is for those students who haven't started law school yet, not those who started law school and then realized it was not for them.

There are some students who should not be in law school. Every time I say this (or something like this), I have colleagues freak the f**k out. *How dare you suggest that there are some students who shouldn't be in law school?* I'm sorry, but it's true. Just like there are some students who shouldn't be in medical school or engineering school. Not everyone is cut out for law school. I don't know why saying that out loud is considered blasphemous. If someone said I wasn't cut out for dance school, I would agree with them—not deride them for pointing out the obvious.

---

4. https://www.fatherly.com/love-money/make-better-decisions-poker-players/.

In the United States, pretty much any student who applies to a law school can get in. That's a problem. Some schools have an 80% or a 90% acceptance rate. So "getting in" to law school doesn't signal much other than these schools want your tuition dollars.

By now, you're probably having an aneurysm...*am I one of the students she's talking about potentially making a mistake by going to law school?* Maybe.

If you scored between 145-146 on the LSAT, you are considered at "very high risk" of failing the bar. If you scored anything lower than 144, you are at "extreme risk" of failing the bar.[5] This is very worrisome. Why would you spend over $100,000 (and maybe over $200,000) and three years of your life doing something that may not amount to anything? Now, I'm not saying that if you got a 146 or lower on the LSAT, you *will* fail the bar. I'm saying that it's a definite possibility. Certainly, students who bomb the LSAT can do well in law school and do pass the bar. And you may be one of those students. But you may not be.

Your LSAT score is one thing you should think about before you commit to law school. But there are other questions you should be asking yourself.

First, what is the bar passage rate at my chosen school? These numbers are publicly available on every law school website (and available here: https://www.abarequireddisclosures.org/).[6] Consider the numbers carefully. Consider how many graduating students took the bar versus how many students graduated. For instance, in a class of 200, maybe only 130 students took a bar exam and only 60% passed. While the bar pass rate doesn't look terrible in the abstract, you might want to consider what happened to the other 70 students. Presumably, at least some portion of these students decided they weren't going to pass the bar, which says something about what the pass rate would have been if they had taken the test.

Second, look at job placement statistics.[7] Again, look at them with a critical eye. What percentage of graduates get jobs? What kind of jobs? There is a category of jobs called "JD Advantage" which means you don't need a law degree to do them.[8] Is that the kind of job you want with a law degree? Also consider the number of students who are doing clerkships. Clerkships are a

---

5. https://data.lawschooltransparency.com/enrollment/admissions-standards/.
6. They are called 509 Required Disclosures.
7. https://www.abarequireddisclosures.org/EmploymentOutcomes.aspx.
8. But, as its name suggests, having a JD is an "advantage" (whatever that means exactly).

wonderful opportunity, but they are only usually a year long. When the school reports that 100 students are "Employed Full Time, Long Term" and 35 of these students are clerking, this really means that 65 students are employed full time, long term. The other students have a clerkship and then *hopefully* will be employed full time, long term thereafter. All I'm saying is look deeper into the numbers.

Third, be honest with yourself about your academic aptitude and level of commitment. I said before that intelligence is not an immutable characteristic—and that is true. But to do well in law school and to pass the bar, you need good study habits. If you know that you're a half-a**-it kind of person (and that isn't likely to change), you might want to re-think your decision to attend law school. If you hate reading and writing and have no tolerance for tedium, then law school may not be for you.

Fourth, be realistic about how far your chosen school can get you. Let's say that your dream is to become a partner at a big New York firm. Consider what it takes to get there. Usually, to get hired at one of these firms, you need top grades from top schools. There are exceptions, of course. And sometimes these firms hire from outside the top 20. But not usually. How realistic is it to expect that with a 146 LSAT and a degree from a school ranked #132 in the *U.S. News & World Report* Rankings, you will achieve your dream?[9] Is it worth three years of your life and well over $100,000 to figure it out?

I know that reading all of this is going to feel icky. You have probably been told your whole life that you can be *anything* you want to be! Accordingly, you may be approaching your law school decision with Pollyanna-ish naïveté. But you're an adult and I'm going to treat you as an adult. Whether to go to law school is a very big and very expensive decision and not one you should make because you "feel like it." Most students will be paying off law school debt for the rest of their lives. I don't want you to assume that crushing burden if there is going to be little to no payoff in the end.

---

9. To be clear, I am not saying that lower-ranked schools are not worth attending. I worked at a non-top tier school for over a decade and had the privilege of teaching many smart and talented students that I keep in touch with to this day.

SEVENTEEN

Technology Stuff

You can't upload love, you can't download time,
you can't google all of life's answers.
You must actually live some of your life.

SOURCE UNKNOWN

1. Figure Out Microsoft Word

Microsoft Word is the currency of the professional legal world. Learn how to use it. Learn all the functions (small caps, extended spacing); learn how to use track changes; learn how to change margins and adjust spacing between paragraphs; learn where the special symbols are located (like § € © ¶); learn how to hyperlink; learn how to insert page numbers and headers and footers; learn where the comment feature is and how it works; learn how to create tables and graphics; learn how to insert a page break; learn how to change your default font from Calibri (seriously, Microsoft?). I'm sure there's a ton of other stuff I've missed.

It's strange, but the most digitally savvy generations are the least word processing savvy. Or maybe they have just mastered whatever word processing software Apple uses or rely on GoogleDocs. Whatever the case, the legal world does not use Apple word processing software or GoogleDocs (except to share documents). Do yourself a favor now and learn how to use Word.

I know you think that whatever free or alternative word processing software you're using is the same as, or at least or compatible with, Word. No, it's not.

That's like saying that generic ketchup is the same as Heinz.[1] We all know that's not true.

If you insist on creating or editing documents in something other than Word, it's only a matter of time before something goes wrong. The document won't be compatible with your professor's computer, or the document will look like a three-year-old created it because the fonts and spacing will be off. Or, worse yet, you'll eff up someone else's document (like your boss's document). Once you start shifting between real Word and fake Word, bad things are going to happen. You've been warned.

At the very least, if you're going to use fake Word, then PDF your document before you send it (see #3 below). But, of course, that's not going to work if the recipient needs to edit the document. Which brings me back to my original point: Figure out Word.

2. Use Garamond

If there's one thing that students know about me, it's that I *love* Garamond font. If you don't know what Garamond is, you're missing out. Garamond is considered one of the most classic and readable fonts. In fact, I tried to get this book published in Garamond font, but alas, I was told that wasn't one of their "standard typefaces." Whatever. Also, in case I haven't sold you yet, Garamond is environmentally friendly. That should resonate with the Millen-Z crowd, right? It has been reported that if the U.S. Government switched over to Garamond, it would save thousands of trees a year (smaller font size, less ink, less paper being printed).

I encourage all my students to migrate their typed work over to Garamond, unless, of course, there are other prescribed font requirements. I mean, if a court says you have to use Times New Roman, then use Times New Roman. I suspect that many of the font rules were developed in the 1990s when TNR was literally the only game in town. Now, those are some rules that need revamping.

Why am I so particular about my font? Because as a lawyer, your work product says something about you. And Garamond says: professional, organized, neat, and reliable. Font matters:

---

1. And Heinz ketchup that you buy at the store is *not* the same as McDonald's Heinz ketchup. That stuff is *sooooooo* good. I load up on it every time I go to McDonald's and have a secret stash of it in my house.

Don't get me wrong, you don't have to use Garamond in particular. But, like, why would you not? It could be some other serif font. Google that. I'm not going to explain it.

Fonts such as Arial and Times New Roman are so ugly and (to use a word that I'm sure is out of style now) so *basic*. Times New Roman has been referred to by one publication as the "sweatpants" of fonts. You wouldn't go to an interview in sweatpants, so why would your resume and cover letter be in Times New Roman?

I promise you, once you've converted to Garamond, you will never go back. Times New Roman will hurt your eyes and you'll think, "How can anyone ever use that?" A funny story about Garamond: Two of my former students took the Garamond message to heart and got matching tattoos in Garamond font. Their tattoo artist had no idea what Garamond was. Both my students were incredulous: How can you *not* know Garamond? That is how you will feel when you make the switch.

3. PDF Your Documents

PDF all your documents. Okay, not all of them. But the important ones. If you are sending a cover letter, resume, and writing sample to a prospective employer, they should all be in PDF format. To be clear, I'm not talking about a scanned document—I'm talking about a file that is saved in PDF format.

Why is it such a big deal whether you send something in Word (or whatever the Apple/Mac equivalent is) or in PDF? It's because documents show up differently on everyone's screen. You don't want your potential employer to open your resume only to have it look "all jacked up" (that's one of my husband's expressions).

I know this happens because I've seen it happen too many times. When students send me their resumes, portions carry over to page two when they did not intend that. The alignment is off. It looks like you didn't even bother making the document look nice. When I've asked about it, students often say that it was originally a "Google docs" document or a "Mac" document.

What you want employers to see on their screen is *exactly* what you see on your screen. The only way to do this is to PDF the document. Plus, I personally think PDFs just look better than Word documents.

4. Your Phone Is F**king With Your Law School Success

The biggest impediment to your law school success is...your phone. If you want to do well in law school, you need to seriously rethink your relationship with your phone.

I'm not here to lecture you about how your addiction to your phone is bad for you, how you should be reading instead of texting, how watching TikTok videos is not the best use of your time. All that is true. But the problems with your phone run much deeper than that.

Students' addiction to their phones (let's admit, it is an addiction) has changed their capacity for learning—and not in a good way. And all of what I'm going to say below *applies to you*, even though you will vehemently deny it.

My dad has an expression that we always use in our family. He said it one day while playing poker at Christmas. Don't judge. He triumphantly put down a winning hand and exclaimed, "Mathematics is not an opinion." It is now a running joke in our family. Mathematics is not an opinion. Facts are facts. Whether you like them or not.

Here are two facts about you and your phone:

First, you cannot multitask. Because there is no such thing. I cannot tell you the number of times that I've heard from students "I am great at multitasking." When I hear that, it makes me cringe. *Nobody can multitask.* To go from one task to another means your brain has to turn off the first task, then go to the second, then go back to the first. This constant attention shifting has repercussions for memory. Some studies say that it can take up to 23 minutes for your brain to refocus after you check your phone.[2] This basically means that you are never working on full throttle.

Second, just having your cell phone near you—even turned off— affects attention and memory. This is crazy, but a study has found that students do not perform as well when their phone is *near* them.[3] The study involved participants completing certain tasks with their phones turned off. Some participants were asked to put their phones in front of them, face down. Others were asked to keep their phones in their pockets or bags. And others were asked not to bring their phones into the room. What was the result? You guessed it. Those participants whose phones were nowhere near them performed best. Followed by those whose phones were out of sight. And in last place...yup. Those students with phones near them. There is science behind why this is the case. Humans learn to "automatically pay attention to things that are habitually relevant to them, even when they are focused on a different task."[4] This is why, for example, you hear your name being said across the room even if you are deep in conversation with someone else. Same thing with your phone. There is going to be something on there that is relevant to you, so your brain is constantly monitoring for that.

Bottom line is that your phone is bad news for your ability to succeed in law school. This is not my opinion. This is a fact. As my dad would say, "Mathematics is not an opinion." The good news is that this is an eminently solvable problem. Turn off your phone. Put it in another room. At first, you'll probably have withdrawal symptoms. But in the long run, it is absolutely the best plan.

---

2. https://news.bloomberglaw.com/us-law-week/is-your-smartphone-making-you -less-smart-distraction-addiction-is-real.
3. https://hbr.org/2018/03/having-your-smartphone-nearby-takes-a-toll-on-your -thinking.
4. *Id.*

5. Lose the Bells and Whistles

There is technology for everything out there: for taking notes, for creating outlines, for retroactively footnoting,[5] for studying, for creating flashcards. Don't use any of it. The technology tends to detract from the task at hand. Instead of simplifying your life, it's going to make it harder.

I just did some online searching for note-taking programs. I got anxiety just looking at them. You don't need all that functionality. It is a waste of money, a waste of time, and will just complicate matters. If you're taking notes by computer, use a plain document (e.g., a Word document). Take notes without formatting. Do not waste your time in class bolding, numbering, underlining, tabbing, and spacing. The more you do of that, the less you are paying attention and the more you miss. Also, I've said this before, do *not* try to create your outlines in class. Outlines are outlines and notes are notes. Don't blur the two.

Students tend to think that if there is technology for something, it is automatically better. Do not fall into this trap. For instance, a smart TV is not better than a dumb TV if you are not planning on using any of the smart functions. It's the same with you and law school technology. You don't need and won't use so many of the bells and whistles that these programs provide. Don't bother with them.

6. Buy a Printer

Most of my pieces of advice are big picture. This is decidedly not that. I recommend that you buy a printer. You can buy a cheap laser printer for less than $100 and you can load up on paper when it's on sale. You will thank me for this advice.

In undergrad, many students get by doing schoolwork and studying based solely on what's on their screen. This is going to be tough to do in law school. Particularly with written assignments that you need to edit, it is much easier to catch errors on paper than on a screen. There is also something about the tactile nature of an assignment or outline in your hands... or maybe that's just me.

There will also occasionally be forms you'll need to print out, and it's just a pain to have to go to the library every time you want to do this.

---

5. Terrible f**king idea. I can't explain why (confidentiality issues) but trust me. Terrible f**king idea.

I might be preaching to the choir on this one. You might all have printers. But I have seen a number of students go through law school without one. And given the cost/benefit ratio, I don't think that's a good decision.

7. Set Up Email on Your Phone

There is a generational disconnect at play here. My generation's predominant method of communication is email. Yours views email as being for old people. I am surprised at how many students say that they "forget" to check email or that they don't have email on their phone. *What?* Neither one of those things computes with me. Frankly, checking email on my phone was one of the *only* reasons I got a phone. Go figure.

Whether you like email or not doesn't matter. That is how communication happens out there in the real world. Your boss will not text you; she will email you. You should get used to checking email all the time. It should be on your phone—which you are addicted to anyway. That way, you won't accidentally "forget" to check it.

To be clear, nothing I say here is intended to negate my previous comments about your phone messing with your law school success. That is all 100% true. But since there's a 0% chance you're going to give up your phone in any meaningful way, you might as well use you phone for good, like to make sure you're on top of your school email.

EIGHTEEN

Things You Should Hear
(But Probably Don't Want to Hear)

Life's not fair. Get used to it.

BILL GATES

1. Life Is Not Fair

Law students are drawn to the law for a variety of reasons, but chief among them is because they have a deep sense of what is fair and unfair. One of the things that you need to know about law school, the legal profession, and life in general, is that it's not always fair. Or, at least, it does not always meet *your* conception of fairness.

For example, I was speaking to a 2L student recently who was frustrated with how things have worked out for him so far. He told me that he was near the top of his class in every class. Yet other students who were nowhere close to him in the rankings got way better summer jobs. He surmised, but didn't know for sure, that it was because they had connections. He was also frustrated that some of these students had much more scholarship funding than he did. In his mind, the top student should get the highest funding and the best job.[1] I

---

1. I also recently encountered a student who did not think it was fair that her female professor had chosen two male Research Assistants over her, even though she was at the top of the class. She blamed it on sexism. I urged her not to make assumptions based on limited knowledge. I had it on good authority that the decision was based on myriad factors, none

263

get it. And rather than debate the merits and explain the nuances of why other people might have gotten better jobs or more money, I settled on, "Sometimes life is not fair." The sooner you learn that lesson, the better. If you spend your life adhering to a rigid moral conception of "fairness," you are going to be disappointed.

Let me give you another example. When my husband and I got married, he decided to leave active-duty military service. He applied for his dream job as a Federal Defender. He made it to the final round of interviews. The lawyer doing the hiring told my husband that she thought he was the best candidate. He got a good feeling that he was going to get the job. Guess what? He didn't. It went to an "internal" candidate instead. This sort of stuff happens all the time. Why? Because, like I told you, life is not always fair.

2. The Best Argument Does Not Always Win

This is an offshoot of the above. And I think if you bear it in mind, it'll save you a lot of heartache as you proceed throughout your legal career. The best argument does not always win. Sometimes *terrible* arguments win. Sometimes your client will go to jail when they did not deserve jail time. Sometimes your client will lose custody of her children even though she is a really good mom. Sometimes the greedy stepchildren of the decedent's estate will get the money intended for the decedent's biological children. The law is unpredictable.

I have experienced this firsthand, and I can tell you *it is hard*. It is hard to feel like you've made an incredibly compelling legal argument, the entire weight of the law is on your side, the other side's argument is a joke, and *still lose*. My husband was involved in a high-profile case some years back. I ended up teaming up with him to help with legal research and motion drafting. There was one issue—the interpretation of the *Computer Fraud and Abuse Act* (CFAA)—that I spent weeks on. I probably drafted over 100 pages of motions on the CFAA. I learned more about it than I ever needed, or wanted, to know. The other side's argument was so weak. Didn't matter. We lost. You know it's bad when opposing counsel says to you, "I know we won, but I'm not sure why." It was a hard pill to swallow.

---

of which had anything to do with the professor being sexist. I urge students who think that something is "not fair" to realize that there are many things they don't know. And while a decision may, on its face, not *seem* fair, that does not mean it *isn't* fair.

Fast forward seven years. The Supreme Court takes up the exact issue we litigated (with different parties, of course). The Supreme Court "sides" with us. I mean it wasn't literally us—our case was done. But they came down strongly in favor of the interpretation we had advanced and that our judge had rejected. There was more than some pleasure in knowing that our judge was told she had made a mistake. By the Supreme Court, no less.

3. Some Students Will Have Voted for the Other Guy

It surprises me how many students think that everyone in the class has the same political leaning that they do. Ditto for professors. Professors are probably worse than students in this respect. I don't think I'm going out on a limb here in saying that academia, including law school, is decidedly liberal. Something like 80% of law professors identify as liberal or very liberal.[2]

Because of this, it can be very difficult as a student to have, or to espouse, a view that differs from the liberal orthodoxy. In today's law school it feels like there are certain things you cannot believe and certain things you cannot say. Anyone who dares to step outside the ever-changing lines will be punished. This is really tough for students who don't hold the same political and social values as the majority. These students tend to feel alienated in law school and are constantly in fear that they are going to say the wrong thing.

Here are two different messages that students wrote anonymously at the bottom of their exams recently.

Lastly, and slightly off topic, but it is incredibly difficult and stressful to go to an institution pushing political views. After the election [where the Democrats won], teachers were making jokes about how great everything was. The worst part is at this school, I have felt that nobody wants to have a discussion. It is backlash immediately. I hope something can be done differently. It should be okay to lean right and not be alienated. At this point I feel as if … you do not preach the "new democratic" ideals then you are outcasted.

---

2. *See* Adam Bonica, Adam S. Chilton, Kyle Rozema, & Maya Sen, *The Legal Academy's Ideological Uniformity*, 47 J. LEGAL STUD. 1 (2018).

I found this class to be extremely focused on the material, which was a relief from the majority of the other classes at this school that are ultra-political and take away from learning the law. This was one of the few classes where I did not worry or feel the need to self-censor my views for fear of retribution from the class.

For students in the ideological minority, I ask that you find the moral courage to speak up for what you believe in. You do not need to weigh into the fray on every occasion. What I mean by this is *pick your battles*. But you do not need to lie about your political beliefs and who you are. If that means you lose "friends," then they weren't friends to begin with. Be true to yourself. You are the only one whose opinion matters.

For students in the ideological majority, please realize that not everyone shares your same views. And that is actually *a good thing*. I saw a headline recently that Sesame Street is planning on having a segment[3] where Oscar the Grouch has a conversation with someone who does not share his viewpoint. The lesson, of course, is to have children understand that not everyone thinks the same way. I never thought I'd be suggesting that law students watch Sesame Street, but *here we are*.

4. You Will Feel Pressure to Conform

You will feel a great deal of pressure to conform. To do what everyone else is doing, to sign every petition that is circulated, to agree with every idea that your club president throws out. Law school is a place that rewards conformity. And it is a place where conforming is the easiest option.

Here's an example. I taught at a school where law students started a petition to change the attendance policy. I was told that one of the organizers of the petition called students personally to ask them to sign. Several students did not think a change to the attendance policy was warranted but signed anyway because it was the path of least resistance. How do I know that several students

---

3. I didn't read the story, so it could have been "fake news" or an *Onion* story. The fact that I can't tell whether this was a real or fake story shows how jacked up society has become. Emilia overheard my husband use the expression "jacked up" once and understood what it meant based on the context. Can't wait for her parents to hear her proclaim, "The puzzle is all jacked up."

signed a petition they didn't agree with? Because they told me afterward. One student sent me the following message:

> I'm all for the change makers and the people who "see a need for change". But if I'm being frank, I've never been that person. I'm not saying I'm anti-activism, because that would be ludicrous and appalling as a black woman. I'm saying I shouldn't feel guilt to participate in every call for action. And I know that is an unpopular opinion and it might even be a character flaw, but I'm tired. Sometimes I just want to do what I can to make it through a situation. I know if I say this in public, I would be "cancelled" but again, I am tired.

I get these sorts of messages and have conversations like this all the time.[4]

> I didn't want to go along with what the Executive Editor of Law Review was suggesting, but it was the easiest thing. I didn't want to be the only one who didn't agree.

> I went to the Town Hall with the intention of speaking but decided against it because I didn't want to deal with any backlash for saying the wrong thing.

> I don't really want to put pronouns in my signature line, but everyone else does it so I think I should too. Otherwise, I'll get blowback and people will think I'm not an ally.

I am not going to tell you that you need to fight every battle or be a non-conformist. I'm going to tell you to *do you*. If you want to vote against a law review proposal, vote against it. If you want to speak at a Town Hall, speak. If you don't want to change your signature line, don't change it. You can choose to conform (that's fine). But you can also choose not to conform.

5. Empathy Is in Short Supply

I don't need to tell you that we live in a very divisive society. If you accidentally say the wrong thing, there is a good chance you'll live to regret it. Because of this, students (and some faculty) walk on eggshells, hoping that they won't get into trouble for having the wrong opinion, using the wrong words, or of-

---

4. These are not real messages. They are simply emblematic of the sorts of things students express to me.

fending someone inadvertently. If this happens, God forbid, the Twitter mobs will come after them.

Nowadays, *anything* can land you in hot water and potentially ruin your career. It's a sad state of affairs and one that should concern us all. For those of you who are not keeping up with "Cancel Culture: Academic Edition" I'll tell you that there have been far too many incidents of it in the past few years. What has happened to some of the "offenders" makes me question how we got to this place—where people are so cruel and inhuman. Can't we have a little more empathy, folks? Can't we have conversations instead of just seeking to silence people? Can't we try to see things from the other perspective? The answer seems to be no.

I've decided not to wade too deep into this chapter, except to say this. When someone does something wrong or something you disagree with, please resist the urge to go all "*Lord of the Flies*" on them. Remember that you are attacking a person. Maybe even a good person. Maybe a person who made a mistake. Or maybe a person who did absolutely nothing wrong. Before you try to take someone down, really think long and hard. Is that really who *you* want to be? And know that before long, the person being taken down could be you.

6. You Are Not Better Than Anyone Else Because You Are in Law School

Law students all go through a weird phase where they see legal issues everywhere: *Is the "Wet Floor" sign at Lowe's enough to avoid premises liability? Is this disclaimer conspicuous enough? Is this reward an example of an offer to enter into a unilateral contract?*[5] It's annoying for the people around you. But it's pretty harmless. Some students also develop a bit of an ego. *I'm a laaaaaw student. I'm special.* You may be a law student, but you are not special.

You are no better than anyone else because you are going to be a lawyer. My brother, Dennis, reminds me that he is more successful than me—a professor—every chance he gets. My brother was...how can I say it...not interested in school. He skated by, often by "borrowing" my old papers and "re-purpos-

---

5. This never goes away. I was at a kindergarten Christmas concert recently and the song they played for the finale that all the children sang along to was Mariah Carey's *All I Want for Christmas Is You*. I kid you not: my first thought was whether the kindergarten was violating copyright laws.

ing" them as his own. I did not know about this at the time, or I would have lost my mind. In high school, I had a teacher named Mr. Klaussen. He was one of my favorite teachers ever (yes, I have a list). Mr. Klaussen taught both me and my brother, albeit three years apart. Dennis handed in an essay to Mr. Klaussen and received something like 95% on it. I discovered the "borrowed" essay several years later. And since I was still in touch with Mr. Klaussen (don't judge), I asked him, "How could you not know that Dennis didn't write this?!" Mr. Klaussen said, "I figured it was yours. But you've got to appreciate the initiative."

Dennis has gotten by based on sheer luck and his blue eyes for the better part of 40 years. He has a sweet gig of a job as a sales representative that pays him *double what I make*. Sometimes more than double. At least once a month, he trots out, "How's that law professor thing working out for you?" When I told him that I was writing this book, he asked me how much I would make in royalties. I estimated about a few thousand dollars. He laughed and said, "That's like 10% of my Q1 bonus." Thanks, Dennis. I got it.

My dad is also one to keep me grounded. A couple of years ago, he came to sit in on one of my Contracts classes. He fell asleep. He claims he was "just resting his eyes." When the class was over, he said, "You are too tough on these students." *Really, Dad? I wonder where I get that from.*

He also seems to constantly forget that I'm a lawyer and Contracts professor. For instance, he recently hired one of my elementary school classmates, Nunzio, to draft his will. *Dad, I'm a lawyer. I could have drafted it for you.* Turns out my elementary school classmate completely screwed up the will and I had to re-draft it anyway. Don't worry, Dad didn't pay Nunzio for the crap will. He did, however, give Nunzio a piece of his mind. *That is not proper.*

And he'll argue with me about contract law. For example, he owns a commercial property that he rented to a flower shop. The flower shop installed some industrial refrigeration units. When the lease was over, the flower shop left them there, which was contrary to the lease terms. My dad was irate and wanted to sue the tenant for breaching the contract. I asked whether he lost any money. He said no. He found a new flower shop tenant that wanted the refrigerators. I told him that because he didn't have any "damages" he couldn't sue. He was like *Bullsh*t. They breached their contract.* To this day, I'm not sure he actually realizes that I know more about contracts than he does.

Why am I telling you all this? Because I have a daily reminder that I am not better than anyone else because I am a lawyer, professor, and now, an accomplished author. In case you don't have a Dennis or Graziano in your life, get one.

NINETEEN

A Chapter for the Girls

Real change, enduring change, happens one step at a time.

RUTH BADER GINSBURG

This chapter was not in the original plan, but I called an audible the month before the book was set to go to the publisher. I hope I used the term "audible" correctly and, for that reason alone, male readers will indulge me and read this chapter.[1]

1. The Face of Sexism has Changed

There has been incredible progress for women in the past 50 years. Women now comprise about half of the law student population. More and more women are partners in law firms and general counsel of large corporations. And women are quite well represented in legal academia. The overt sexism that women experienced in the past is not the norm today. And that is something worth celebrating.

That does not mean that sexism does not exist.[2] It just means that it takes on a more subtle form. Which is harder to deal with in many ways. One of my

---

1. Yes, I get it—female students like sports too, and this is a gendered comment. Sue me. It's called humor.

2. There are, of course, other "isms" in law school. By addressing sexism, I am not diminishing experiences of discrimination based on race, sexual orientation, religion, disability, or anything else. But I told you at the beginning of the book that my focus was going to

students puts it this way: Sexism nowadays doesn't look like "Shhh honey, the men are speaking." It's a lot quieter than that, but equally unsettling.

Let me give you an example. Early in my career, I worked in-house at a large company. I was hired after I completed my LL.M. degree, but before I had taken the bar exam. I negotiated with my company to give me from May to July off to study for the bar exam. The company originally wanted me to work part-time, but I said no. I told the company that I was happy to take the time off without pay because the important thing for me was to pass the bar exam on the first try. They eventually agreed to give me the two months off and paid me my salary during that time.

Unbeknownst to me, there were rumblings. Various support staff and paralegals didn't like that I got "time off." I don't know how it was any of their business or why they would feel like they could weigh in on this. I never talked about my arrangement with anyone. But somehow, I think they knew that I was being paid for (what they thought of as) my "time off." I took the bar exam in late July and then returned to work.

In October, I wanted to fly home to visit my family for Canadian Thanksgiving. I asked my boss if I could take a vacation day. He was very hesitant. He thought "other people" (meaning the support staff) would be upset if I had more time off. WT*? Since when are my vacation days anyone else's business? And since when does my male boss feel like his decisions need to be guided by keeping support staff happy? I was really confused. My boss did not give me the entire story, but I was able to piece enough of it together to tell you what I just told you. My boss let me have my vacation day but told me to "keep it quiet." Seriously?

How is sexism part of this? It just seems like you're dealing with really bizarre people. Fair enough. I can't say for sure that sexism was part of this—and that's what makes the new sexism so pernicious.

This is what I think. The support staff was entirely female. They were about a decade or two older than me and had been working at the company for a while. I don't think they liked the idea of a 25-year-old female graduate coming into the company and being treated like a lawyer, even though she was on her way

---

be only on stuff I had *direct* experience with, which is why I included the chapter on sexism. There are many great resources out there to help navigate issues related to diversity, inclusion, and belonging. In particular, I would recommend you check out Russell McClain, *The Guide to Belonging in Law School,* West Academic Publishing, 2020.

to becoming one. Lawyers were largely male, much older, and had earned their stripes. I, by contrast, did not fit their image of a "lawyer," and so they thought I was essentially one of them. One who was getting preferential treatment. My boss handled things clumsily. He did not want the other women to cause a fuss and make his life difficult. And he did not want to deny me a vacation day for no reason. Hence the "keep it quiet" admonition.

Frankly, this was bullsh*t. And I don't mean that after reflection I determined this was bullsh*t. I knew it was at the time, and I said so. Nonetheless, my boss did not do anything about it. *Were these women sexist? Was my boss sexist?* No. I don't think so. At least not in the traditional sense. Would this have happened if I were male? No. I can almost guarantee that 100%.

2. Or, Maybe the Face of Sexism Hasn't Changed

As I was preparing to write this chapter, I reached out to some female students to ask them whether they experienced what they would classify as "sexism" in law school. Several of them said no, which is awesome. But a number of them said yes. Here are some things they relayed to me.

Tamara, a 3L, told me that she was advised not to wear a skirt or makeup in court if she wanted to be taken seriously. She also said that judges often look "past her" to the males in the room, assuming that they are lawyers (they are not).

Mackenzie, a 2L student, recounted something that happened in her 1L year. She was doing her final oral argument for LRW. A male professor was acting as a judge. During his feedback, he told her that "a jury would not like a woman making such a forceful argument against another woman," and "you were a bit too assertive for a woman." Mackenzie recounts being in shock after these comments. Mackenzie met with her LRW professor privately to ask if she had done something wrong. The professor told her that the comments were completely unjustified and inappropriate. To Mackenzie's knowledge, the male professor was never told that his comments were out of bounds.

Laura worked on a research project with one of her professors. She had been selected for this project because she was one of the top students in the class. However, in an effort to undermine Laura's achievement, students spread rumors about her, intimating that she was "involved" with the professor, who is happily married and 30 years her senior.

Emily developed a friend group in her 1L year that was predominantly male. In part, this was by design—the females seemed really intimidating and like "mean girls." Emily would sit with the males in class. In her 2L year, she became more friendly with some of the girls in the class. They let her in on a little secret: they had initially thought she was a "whore" because she sat with the boys instead of the girls.[3]

Meaghan experienced what she calls "sneaky" sexism.[4] It's not quite something she could put her finger on, but it's something that she believed was related to gender. She gives this example. A friend of hers, Zoey, went to get help from a male professor. This male professor kept telling Zoey how much she looked like his wife. *Weird.* But let's leave that aside. The male professor also commented to Zoey that Meaghan was "uppity." *Weird. And unprofessional. And sexist?* Not surprisingly, the comment got back to Meaghan. Meaghan knew what the word meant but googled it anyway in case she was wrong and there was some other, less offensive, meaning that she didn't know about. There wasn't. The term is often used in relation to women. In fact, when I googled it just now, the way it was used in a sentence was "my sister-in-law is uppity." Interesting.[5] Was this professor just inappropriate and unprofessional? Or was this professor sexist? Don't know. Hence, sneaky sexism.

Erika describes how there was an interesting distinction she perceived between male and female "participators." You know, the students who put up their hands all the time in class. Both were judged by their peers but based on different criteria. She noticed that when someone commented about males, it was about *what they said*. When they commented about females, it was about *how they said it*. She remembers comments that were made about a friend of hers, a frequent contributor to class discussions: "Oh, is she the really shrill

---

3. You will see in a minute that "whore" seems to be a common refrain with some women.

4. A common theme from almost all the female students who provided me with feedback was that the sexism they encountered flew under the radar. Rose described it this way: "This form of sexism is difficult to confront because it's hard to call out something that's in the background. It's more of a low buzz as opposed to a bee flying in your face."

5. Apparently, and I did not know this, uppity also has a racist connotation. https://www.dictionary.com/browse/uppity ("*Uppity* means 'haughty' and 'snobbish'—an adjective for someone who *puts on airs*, someone who is self-important. But, this descriptor has a very racist past, used particularly to disparage Black people as 'not remembering their place as inferior.'").

one?" or, "Yeah, but does she have to be so shrill?" Sadly, much like uppity, shrill is a term that is often used to describe women. Along with bossy. And a bunch of other words like frumpy, high-maintenance, diva, and ditzy.[6]

Elizabeth relays that one male professor would be patronizing toward women in her class. When a woman would speak and use the word "like," for instance, he would mock them in his response back to them. For example, the female might say, "So, like, the marital assets would be divided 50%-50%." And he might say, "So, like, are you sure about that?" Maybe he was trying to be funny. Maybe he was trying to rid students of bad habits (filler words). But it's hard not to believe there was some weird gender stuff going on there.

Hearing all these stories made me realize that maybe the face of sexism hasn't changed all that much.

3. You Will Be Judged by the Clothes You Wear

In the "Getting a Job" chapter, I told you the story about my former student who got in trouble for wearing a sleeveless blouse to work. What I did not tell you is that the people who complained about her sleeveless blouse were the firm's female paralegals. Are you seeing a theme? Sadly, much of the sexism that women will experience is from *other women*.

Early on in my academic career, I would get comments on my clothing in student evaluations. In one of my first sets of evaluations, I had students say that the slit in my "plum skirt" was too high and that some clothing choices were "inappropriate and offensive." While I can't know for sure, I would bet money these comments came from female students. A male student would never use the word "plum." Incidentally, my plum skirt is part of a suit that I wore on my interview to the Supreme Court of Canada and to my law school graduation ceremony. It is a very conservative suit, but apparently, the slit was just too high for one girl's taste. I can assure you that my clothing could in no way be characterized as offensive—unless one thinks that Banana Republic and Ann Taylor are offensive.

It was bad enough I had to read these comments. They were petty and should not have seen the light of day. But what was worse was that all the evaluations, including the ones with comments about my clothing, went to the Dean. In my end-of-semester review, the Dean mentioned the comments

---

6. *See* https://togetherband.org/blogs/news/words-that-describe-women.

about my clothing. Not in a "this is a problem" sort of way. But more in a "there's some silly chatter" sort of way. Nonetheless, it was embarrassing to have the Dean see these students comments, which were not true and designed to take me down a peg.

The subsequent semester, a student in my class came to see me privately. He told me that he had been at a bar the prior weekend and that there were some girls in my class trash-talking me.[7] One of them said, "She is such a whore!" The student thought I should know that there was this anti-me sentiment among a cohort of female students. It was distressing to hear. *A whore? Really? Where in the world does that come from? Is this a new expression the kids are using?* I tried to move past the comment, but it was hard knowing that these things were being said about me by students in my class.

I met with the Dean again after the Spring evaluations. At this point, I had some context for the weird clothing references. I conveyed to him the story about the "whore" comment to get him to see how the original evaluations may have been part of some broader effort to undermine my authority or reputation. The Dean did not say much. Since the current evaluations did not have any references to clothing, the Dean concluded that we seemed to have "moved past that."

For three years, every time I met with the Dean, he brought up the initial comments about my clothing and how I had "moved past that." I genuinely believe he meant for this to be supportive. But I felt like the clothing comment imprinted itself in his brain as something legitimate that I had "overcome." This could not be further from the truth. I did not overcome anything. The statements were false from the beginning.

Because of my early experience with these comments, I became hyper-aware of how I dressed. Not too short. Not too tight. Not too low cut. Not to gape-y.[8] Not too high a slit.[9] Not too light colored.[10] Not too scoop neck.[11] How many male professors have this experience? None. I've seen male professors go to class in baggy jeans, in sweaters with holes in them, in skinny dress pants, in

---

7. Recall, law school = sieve.
8. Check blouse buttons and use clothing tape.
9. Learned my lesson on that one.
10. Or it could be somewhat transparent in some lights.
11. Or you might see a bit of a bra strap with the wrong move.

LL Bean puffy vests, in whatever they want. I suspect there's not a whole lot of "he's a whore" comments in those student evaluations.

What's the takeaway for you? Good question. I want to say: *Dress however the f**k you want.* But sadly, I think I need to say: *Be mindful of how you dress.*

4. There Is a Double Standard

Above, I talked about being judged based on the clothes you wear. I hope you realize that the passage was not about clothing choices *per se.* Clothing is a metaphor for all the ways that women must tread lightly. Not only in what they wear, but in what they say, and how they say it.

Quick example. I sent out an email to my class last year dealing with housekeeping issues. One student apparently did not like the "tone" of one sentence in the email, and he let his views be known to the administration. By contrast, a male professor around this time apparently "yelled" at his students when the class was not prepared.[12] Any fallout? No. The male professor could yell with impunity. I, by contrast, needed to be informed of my tone issues.

Another male professor sometimes deliberately schedules meetings so that students need to come in over the holiday weekend because "that's what lawyers do." This professor's students show up and respect him all the more for it. If I ever did that, I honestly believe that there would be a mass revolt.

I shared with you my experience of the double standard that exists in academia. I've told you that students hold me to a different standard than they do their male professors. They judge me on whether I am kind, caring, and compassionate. If I am not sufficiently kind, caring, and compassionate, you can sure bet I'll hear about it. *For f**king ever.*

The *Harvard Business Review* did a study on how gendered language is employed in leader evaluations. In complete "non-shocker" news, here's what it found:

> The most commonly used positive term to describe men was analytical, while for women it was compassionate. At the other extreme, the most commonly used negative term to describe men was arrogant. For women, it was inept. We found statistically significant gender differences in how often these terms (and

---

12. I'm hearing this second-hand, so I don't know whether "yelled" is an accurate term. Students *always* exaggerate.

others) were used (relative to the other positive or negative terms available for selection) when describing men and women—even though men's and women's performances were the same by more objective measures.[13]

So, you're telling me that the highest compliment for a man is "analytical," and the highest compliment for a woman is "compassionate"? Tell me something I didn't know.

It won't surprise you one bit to know that there are double standards when it comes to female lawyers. A male lawyer who is aggressive is called a "shark" (in a good way). A female lawyer who exhibits the same attributes is called a b*tch. But, wait, there's more! If a female is too quiet and meek, then she does not have "what it takes" to be successful.

As a female lawyer, you may find that you twist yourself into knots trying to be different things to different people. You may feel like you need to be kind and reassuring to the client; assertive, but not overly domineering, in court; and the right level of confident in meetings. I can tell you it is exhausting. While I don't currently practice law, I feel like I walk a fine line all day every day. Be nice, but not too nice. Be assertive, but not too assertive. Watch your tone. Try not to come across as intimidating or condescending.

You will see that I have the following advice for you later in the book: "Be Who You Are." I mean that. I do. But sometimes you should know that there are consequences associated with being who you are.

5. The Subtle Ways That Sexism Presents Itself

At the beginning of this chapter, I said that the face of sexism has changed. Today's sexism is usually quite subtle and often manifests in the form of things like talking down, patronizing, gaslighting, and mansplaining. All these things are difficult to pin down and to call anyone on, so you often end up just letting it go. But you shouldn't. The more you let this stuff go, the more it will happen.

Let me give you some examples of what I mean by *subtle sexism* (sounds like a good book title, right?).

My male boss once sent me an email asking me to "think about ways" I might have come up short in my interactions with a co-worker. *What?* Let's

---

13. https://hbr.org/2018/05/the-different-words-we-use-to-describe-male-and-female -leaders.

leave aside that he had made a completely incorrect assumption about what I did or didn't do. But "think about" is something a parent would say to a child. You're not my dad. Don't treat me like a ten-year-old.[14]

Another example. An announcement was made that I had been appointed as a Staff Editor of the *American Business Law Journal*. A co-worker wrote to me and proclaimed that this would be "such a valuable opportunity" for me. You might be thinking, *well, that's a nice thing to say*. It's not. When you're mid-career and are told this by a male who is about ten years your senior, it's patronizing. Like pat on the head patronizing.

A female co-worker of mine once got a message from a male co-worker telling her she got "carried away" in her comments at a meeting and that she was "angry" and "emotional." Way to play into the crazy, emotional woman narrative.

Then there's the male "hero" colleague. I brought up an issue at a faculty meeting about some male students in the class being belligerent. I explained that I did not think this was a matter of sexism but rather of entitlement and wanted to have a discussion surrounding that. One of my male colleagues said, "Send them my way. I'll have a word with them." Thank you. My knight in shining armor.

The worst, though, is the performative male colleague. The colleague who claims to be a champion of women but is *so* not. I received an email from one of these men about a year ago with a subject line indicating that he "esteem[ed]" me as a colleague. Is that even a correct use of "esteem"? He then proceeded to thank me for the wonderful work that I do as a scholar, teacher and member of the law school community. He noted that nobody worked harder for our students. The catch: He addressed the email to "Tina," not "Tanya." Yup, you esteem me alright.

The examples I've just given you have been largely from my time in academia. But don't assume practice is any different—it is probably worse. When I was a very junior lawyer, I was involved in some high-stakes settlement negotiations. I traveled to Florida with a senior male lawyer to meet with a prominent plaintiff's attorney (someone you'd probably recognize from television). I was responsible for laying out our legal position over a steak dinner. I was obviously nervous, and I guess I was speaking quickly. The senior lawyer interrupted me

---

14. This same gentleman suggested that I work on "self-improvement" and that he hoped I "ha[d] not given up on trying to improve as [I] get older." *Seriously, who says this?*

and said, "Take a breath, slow down and start again." I was mortified. *I mean, did you really have to treat me like a child in front of this other lawyer?* I'm sure he meant well, but I can remember how much I wanted to sink into the ground to this very day. Would he have interrupted a junior male lawyer and told him to slow down and start again? Don't know for sure, but don't think so.

6. Be Careful Leaning In

Leaning in was terrible f**king advice—at least in my case. Leaning in is a concept popularized by Sheryl Sandberg, the former CEO of Yahoo. The idea is that females should advocate for themselves and be assertive in demanding what they deserve. For instance, if you are asking for a pay raise, gather all the relevant information and approach the matter with confidence and from a position of power.

Problem is people don't like women like that. We just established this above. Leaning in is not very *feminine*. And, as we know, people do not respond well to women who deviate from their prescribed gender roles.

I used the lean-in approach to ask for a raise once. I spent months compiling all the relevant information. I worked with numbers (scary!) and I sliced the information every which way. I tried to show on paper how valuable I was. This is all classic lean-in stuff. You know what? My boss told me that I should bring more "humility" to the conversation and that I was engaging in unrestrained advocacy. *But that's what I thought I was supposed to do!* I did not get the raise I asked for. And the relationship with this boss became incredibly strained. He repeated to me on multiple occasions that I was not sufficiently humble. I don't know if it's just me, but that feels patently gendered, doesn't it?

Is there a lesson in here? Maybe. But I'm not sure what it is. Just be forewarned that leaning in may not always be the best approach. Leaning in may cause your boss to lean out.

7. Do Not Shoulder the Burden of Administrative Work

In the academic realm, there is a fair amount of administrative work. This is work like drafting reports and internal documents, organizing speakers, and serving on committees. The work is not usually very hard. But it is tedious and flies below the radar. No one calls you up to congratulate you on coming up with a new draft of the Honor Code. A disproportionate share of administrative work falls to women. It has been documented time and again, and I've seen it firsthand. I don't know whether this is true in the law firm setting—but I suspect that it is. Whether it's the perception that women are "better" at these things, or the view that men's time is more valuable, it's a real problem.

Last summer, I was asked to share my views on a new amendment to the Honor Code. I was not on the Committee that was considering the change, but I was one of the two co-proponents of the amendment. The Committee was composed of three men. When the time came to discuss who would work on re-drafting the amendment, one of the men suggested that I do it.[15] He said he was "too busy" writing law review articles and just didn't have the time. *Are you kidding me? You're too busy, and what, I'm not? And let's not forget, I'm not even *on* the Committee.* Some version of this conversation has played out in every law school in the country. And, like I said, I suspect that there is a lot of this in the legal profession generally.

What do you do if this happens to you? Don't stand for it. I didn't. And I won't. If it's clear that I am being tasked with a disproportionate share of administrative work or if I am being asked to do work so that a male can have "more time" for his research, I will politely decline. But I'm tenured. This is way harder for a newly minted attorney to do. I get it. However, it doesn't change my advice.

8. Imposter Syndrome Is Connected to Gender Dynamics

Several of the female students I reached out to expressed that they had not experienced sexism *per se*, but that their Imposter Syndrome was linked, in part, to gender dynamics.

Claire is a superstar 2L student. She relays that gender dynamics in law school "can sometimes lead you to believe that you're not as qualified or competent as your male classmates." She explains that "the combination of Imposter Syndrome and being surrounded by outspoken men can cause you to not even express an interest in opportunities you may be qualified for." She has the following advice for female law students: "Your male classmates' competence will be assumed. Yours will have to be earned. This is the ultimate frustration and the source of a lot of Imposter Syndrome, so just stick to the old saying—you have to be twice as good."

---

15. In case you're wondering, it was the "Tina" colleague who really "esteems" me.

Tasha, a recent graduate, also felt like her gender played a role in her Imposter Syndrome. In terms of advice for future law students, she says this:

> Do I have good advice for dealing with this? I don't know. I let one man's comment bother me for a solid week. But, my advice is to remind all the future female law students and attorneys that you belong. The little digs more often than not are jealousy or you threaten them. Law school brings out a lot of insecurity, and sometimes it causes people to go on the offensive. Don't be afraid to take up space. Don't be afraid to ask for the same opportunities being afforded to other male students.

Adriana is a little further along in her career. After graduating near the top of her class, she landed an amazing job at a top law firm (so proud!). Here is what she had to say:

> Most of the "secret" to success in law school and practice seems to be to act with confidence. You will notice that male students, especially white male students, will speak and act with a confidence that might not even be backed up with the right answer. This confidence continues into practice. I cannot even count the number of times I have been in meetings, in court, and in court conferences where I have found myself second guessing my facts and argument because of what opposing counsel is representing to the court. Nearly every time, my understanding was accurate and opposing counsel was wrong (I do not know whether these attorneys were misrepresenting facts intentionally or because they were not well-prepared).
>
> Learning to sound and act confident in every situation will get you very far in school and in practice, especially as a female. The male students and attorneys are already doing that. If you couple fake confidence with actual facts and law to back it up, you will already be far ahead of the male students who are just acting confident but are likely not as prepared as they sound.

Now, I don't want this section to come across as male-bashing. It's not intended to be. What these women have experienced is the same thing I've seen for the entirety of my legal career. Men *tend to be* more outspoken than women. They *tend to* come across as more confident and secure in themselves. They *tend to* "take up space," as Tasha says. And this *tends to* have spillover effects on women.

When I was a law student, the assertive male students intimidated me the most. They were the polar opposite of me, and it made me feel like I did not belong in law school or the legal profession. As a young lawyer, I felt the same way (remember my boss who told me I was reactive and not proactive?). Early in my academic career, the feeling continued. It even continues to this day.

Sometimes knowing that "it's not just you" is helpful. You may not change what you do. You may not try to "act and sound confident" as Adriana suggests. You may not bother trying to "take up space," per Tasha's advice. But having a framework for understanding what you may be feeling and experiencing is valuable in and of itself.

9. You May Get Comments About Your Appearance

I naively thought that law was a *professional* field, and therefore, people would be professional. I was wrong. At several points in my career, comments have been made about my appearance either to my face or in a forum where the comments made their way back to me. It's weird and uncomfortable and undercuts what you feel are your legitimate accomplishments.

Let me give you a few examples. I interviewed at a prominent Toronto firm during my first year of law school. I thought the interview went well. I felt like I did a good job and I enjoyed meeting the lawyers there. Then, a few days later, I heard from a friend of mine who was a paralegal at the firm that lawyers were talking about the "hot" girl who interviewed with them. She figured out it was me they were talking about and told me about it. She thought this information might be relevant to my decision on where to summer. It was. I opted to go to a different firm.

After my third year of law school, I summered at a top New York firm. I had been given an assignment by a senior associate, which I completed (and did a good job on). Several weeks later, he called and asked me to do another assignment, which I did. I brought the assignment up to his office and he had no idea who I was. He put out his hand and introduced himself. I was confused. *But, um, I did that assignment for you a couple of weeks ago. And you asked me to do this assignment.* I explained all that to him and some revelation suddenly dawned on him. He said, "But you were wearing glasses last time." *Okay, yeah, and....* He proceeded to say, "Well you can't expect me to recognize you when you no longer look like the girl next door." What the eff?! You remember me not based on my work product (or my name, for that matter) but based on whether I'm wearing girl-next-door glasses?

The glasses thing seems to throw a lot of men for a loop. It was my second or third year teaching. A professor thought that it would be a funny "class Jeopardy" question to ask which male and female professor was the hottest. Yes, he thought this was a good question to ask to a class of 80 1L students. A female student told me about this, thinking I would want to know (I apparently was the professor he had selected for the "female" category). I raised the issue with the administration, who in turn, arranged for me to talk to the professor. I explained to the professor that I was not angry or offended. I just had a hard enough time establishing my authority in the classroom, and stuff like this didn't help. His response was something to the effect of, "But you wear glasses. So, of course, students think you're a serious teacher." *F**k off with the glasses thing.*

Then there was the clueless colleague who once said to me, "You're not as dumb as you look." *Just wow.* I can't remember if I just froze or if I said something. But he clearly realized that what he said was inappropriate and offensive. He tried to walk it back. It got worse. He said, "It's not that you look dumb, but sometimes you act dumb." *Just stop.* This happened at a job where this man acted like he ruled the roost and where I already felt like an imposter. While the latter is clearly not on him, this comment has stuck with me for over a decade. *Is this what people think of me?*

I don't think any of these things were particularly ill-intentioned, even the latter comment. And I debated whether to even talk about this stuff in the book. *Cause, like, woe is me. People said you were pretty. Boo f**king hoo.* But ultimately, I decided to share some of these experiences because I don't think they are outliers. I think some of these sorts of things will happen to you (I mean, I hope not—but I'm realistic). And as a 24- or 25-year-old woman, it's really hard to know how to deal with comments like this. It's awkward and embarrassing.

But it's more than that. It makes you question what people see when they see you—a lawyer or a potential date. It takes its toll on your sense of professional identity and exacerbates whatever preexisting insecurities you may have already been carrying around. I wish I had some good advice here, but I don't know that I do. I guess all I would say is if stuff like this happens to you, try your best not to let it affect your sense of self-worth. Chalk it up as a one-off and move on. People are stupid and say stupid things. You can't control stupid.

10. When the Professional Turns Unprofessional

It is a hard truth that women sometimes face unwanted personal advances in the work setting. Sometimes this is just an awkward situation that ends up resolving itself with some time and distance. And sometimes a professional relationship is severed because of an unrequited overture. I feel like I'm writing for an 18th-century audience: "advance," "unrequited," and "overture." Okay, let me try to say this in language you'll understand. You may get hit on at work and it may f**k up some of your professional relationships.

I would not say that this happens a lot. But it happens. The first time I experienced something like this was early in my career. I was contacted by a partner I had met at a law firm dinner for Supreme Court clerks. He was the head of a practice group and well-known in his field. He told me he had an interesting project he was hoping to talk to me about. We met up for dinner to discuss. He told me that he was planning on writing a new casebook and was looking for a co-author. He asked if I would be interested. *Would I be interested?! Of course, I would!* I had no academic connections to speak of and thought this could be a way to get my foot in the door. I was on cloud nine for the rest of the dinner.

By dessert, however, I clued into something: this man wasn't just interested in me professionally. The realization was almost slow-motion. My excitement over the book slowly drained away. I extricated myself from the situation, which was not easy to do. And we never spoke again.

On some level, it was no big deal. It's not like I had actually started work on the book. He had just made me the offer a couple of hours earlier. But, nonetheless, it felt like something had been taken away. Or, more accurately, something had been given, but for the wrong reasons. I felt a sense of loss that stayed with me for a while. As someone who did not have any law connections, this felt like a huge blow to my future career. Fortunately, it wasn't. But I never fully recovered from feeling like I had earned something based on merit, only to realize I hadn't. Or—maybe I had—it's just that there were strings attached.

* * *

I told you that this chapter was a last-minute addition. Why did I originally decide to jettison it? And then decide to put it in? Other than because I'm an "indecisive woman."

I originally decided not to include this chapter because there are a lot of less-than-happy memories in here for me. I have presented you with a small snapshot of some of the ways that I have experienced gender dynamics in the workforce. But these stories are abridged, somewhat sanitized, and devoid of context. In other words, the reality is worse than what I've described. I did not particularly want to take a trip down (bad) memory lane. And I did not want this chapter to be about all the ways that I've been aggrieved (*Poor girl—people hit on you!*). *Ergo*, I made the decision to cut it.

But I've been experiencing more than my fair share of drama at work, and much of it involves male offenders. It's not all sexism stuff, but there is *often* a gendered undertone there. It's made these issues more prominent and acute in my mind lately.

Also, I recently received this email from one of my 2L students that stuck with me:

> Also, this is definitely pushing the professionalism line, but I hope it brightens your day to know that many of us women see you as a hero because you seem to be thriving in a male dominated world, and you are always dressed like a boss.

The email was sweet and sincere and made me smile. But I felt like female law students should know that appearances *can be deceiving*. I am doing my best to "thrive" in a male-dominated world. But it is not always easy, and I don't always thrive. I do not want you, my female readers, to be left with the impression that I am kicking a** in a male-dominated world. I'm just doing the best I can.

But I do agree with the student on one count: I am always dressed like a boss.

TWENTY

Namaste Sh*t No One Tells You About Law School

U have to go thru ur Elle Woods crying alone in a bunny costume phase to get to ur Elle Woods kicking ass at law school/life phase.

RANDOM GOOGLE IMAGE

1. Be Who You Are

My husband is a rock star. Not only is he the #nicestpersonintheworld (like "helps old ladies cross the street"[1] nice), he is also a kick-ass lawyer and world's most popular professor. My husband has been a visiting professor now for six or seven years. He has won the Adjunct Professor of the Year award four times. His acceptance speeches are legendary. He has now designated himself the Greatest of All Time Adjunct—GOATA.

He is amazing in the classroom. Students *love* him. I mean *looooove*. He starts and ends every class with cool music (other professors have to tell him to turn it down). He has "Class Sponsors" (usually funny YouTube videos). He provides a whole bunch of supplementary help in the form of "Coombs Cares" (emails, handouts, etc. to make students' lives better). He has been known to dance in class, do push-ups, and simulate the Rocky stair climb. He tells war stories—literally—because he is a war veteran. He plants fake cocaine on stu-

---

1. It's hard getting my husband into a store because he's too busy scouring the parking lot for older people who might need help getting things into their car.

dents in Criminal Procedure to ease the students into search and seizure law. He puts every student's name in his exams (he usually has 80 or so students). He has running jokes all semester about the same students ("Mr. Florida" and "Gold Chains"). He does a segment based on Jimmy Kimmel's mean tweets where he reads former student evaluations out loud. In the background, he will play "Everybody Hurts" by REM. Then he will read, in the most somber tone possible, the following: "Professor Coombs looks like Vin Diesel—if Vin Diesel lost 20 pounds of muscle mass and drove a crappy jeep."[2]

I think you all get my point. My husband is an awesome professor. Students love him. Nearly every course evaluation will say, "Best professor I've had in my life."

Alright, we get it. Your husband is awesome. And, so what? Well, I'm a little bit jealous. Okay, a lot jealous. A number of years ago, the *Associated Press* did a profile piece on my husband, where they quoted the then-Dean:

> [The] dean of the law school[,] praised Coombs and Monestier Tuesday. Coombs, he said, has been an extremely popular member of the faculty whose "deep expertise in litigation has informed his teaching." He described Monestier as high-performing.

My husband is "extremely popular." I, by contrast, am "high-performing." Now, there's a back-handed compliment if I ever saw one.

I want to be like my husband. I want to be popular, funny, approachable, relatable, and "the best professor" students have ever had. Every year, around student evaluation time, we have pretty much the same conversation: *How can I be more like you? Why do students love you so much? But I'm relatable, aren't I? How can I be less scary?* Every year, he gently tells me, "You are who you are." And then suggests we order pizza to distract me from the conversation. Pizza is my kryptonite.

I am not the funny professor. I'm not the professor who wants to play music in class. I once played "The Gambler" by Kenny Rogers to explain settlement dynamics in my Civil Procedure class, and it was the *longest* three minutes of my life. I'm not the professor who will run up and down the aisles getting high

---

2. By now, many of you are wanting to look him up for sure. I'll save you the trouble of a protracted google search: David Coombs, www.armycourtmartialdefense.com. *Yup, he's hot too.* I didn't think that was appropriate to write in the text, but no one reads the footnotes, right?

fives from students. Not only would this be difficult to do in my Calvin Klein Gayle pumps (which I own in eight colors), it's just not me. And it never will be. I am the professor who knows her stuff cold, who spends countless hours making sure everything is organized for optimal presentation, who has high expectations, and who gives tough love. That's who *I am*. When I try to be soft and cuddly, it just doesn't work. It feels inorganic. One of my students remarked to me once, "You don't strike me as someone who has pets." *Ouch.* True, but still, ouch. I'm reminded of an interaction with a student from about seven years back. It was in my Sales class. I told the class that we would be having an open book exam and that half of it would be multiple choice. John, a student in my class, looked deeply perplexed. I asked him if everything was okay. John said, "Open book, multiple choice? I feel like *I don't even know you anymore.*" Open book, multiple choice is not typically my style. But then John said, "And now I'm really worried. Because what you're telling us is that the exam will be so hard that not even our notes will be able to help us." I can't say he was entirely wrong. One student lamented to me that he wished I could be more like one of his other 1L female professors. The student relayed that this other professor was more personable and started every Zoom class with a "How's everyone doing? Thumbs up!" (or something like that). I tried to picture myself being the peppy professor. It's not me. I'm the "Okay class, let's get started" professor. No nonsense. Let's get down to business.

I *wish* I could be the "thumbs up" professor. I *wish* I could be like my husband. But I'm not. And no amount of wishing will make it so. When I've tried to adjust my style too much, it didn't work for me. I'm not saying that there aren't changes to be made around the margins. And I have made those changes, where I can. I am proud to say that I now occasionally *step away* from the podium when I teach. One student who had me as a 1L and then had me again as a 3L remarked, "Oh my God. You have legs!" But my point is that you can't fundamentally change who you are. So, instead, you need to embrace who you are and be the best you possible.

Even though I will never be my husband, students do appreciate who *I am*. Students know I am a straight shooter. Students know where they stand with me. Students know that I care deeply about their success and know that, with hard work, they can achieve. Students know that I give 100% to my teaching. And, not to brag or anything, but more than a few students have said that *I* am the best professor they have ever had. Maybe because they haven't taken my husband yet. One student even invited me to her wedding in New Jersey, which I attended, and made me the honorary Rhode Island[3] godmother to her daughter. *Take that,* GOATA.

This is obviously a lot of navel-gazing, and you might be wondering, "What does this have to do with me?" Everything. You are who you are, and you cannot fundamentally change that. If you are a quiet/shy person, you will not magically become gregarious. Don't wish you were someone else. Don't try to be someone you are not. Don't think you are deficient in any way. You are *you.* And being you is enough.

Remind me about this advice after I read my next set of student evaluations.

2. You Are Not the Only One Who Doesn't Have Their Act Together (They Are Just Better at Pretending)

Earlier in the book, there was a chapter about Impostor Syndrome. I want to transition to a bit of a different, but related, topic: Why does it feel like I'm the only one in law school who doesn't have their sh*t together?

Everyone else seems to have understood the reading. My eyes glazed over at the mention of "promissory estoppel," and it was all downhill from there.

When the professor asked us about the policy implications of the case, I didn't even know what she meant by that. But, Arjun answered, like usual, and of course got it right. I mean, I don't even understand the question. Not only does Arjun understand the question, he also knows the answer.

The professor asked us today what the definition of an offer was. We did that weeks ago. Literally, how am I supposed to remember that? But, like half the class put up their hands and the student the professor called on got it right. Are all these people just sitting at home memorizing definitions every night?

Katelyn walked into class today with her typical picture-perfect hair, trendy jeans with the coolest suede boots. She looked like she just spent a weekend at the spa. I, on the other hand, threw on an Old Navy hoodie that has a tiny soy

---

3. Now that I'm living in New York, we're going to have to revisit this label.

sauce stain from yesterday's dinner. I felt like it was an effort to brush my teeth. How are these people managing to do law school and look like that?

I overheard two students in my class talking about how they are going to start studying for the exam soon. It's October. Exam? What? Are you kidding me? How do I compete with that?

A kid in my class already got an internship for next summer. A paid one! Should I have been applying? Where do I even begin to look for internships?

I pulled into the parking lot today and parked next to Natasha. She drives a brand-new BMW SUV. I have a beat-up Honda Civic that may or may not last through the winter. Which reminds me, I need an oil change. Cause I have time for that.

There's a spot on the second floor where the cool kids hang out. They are always drinking their Starbucks and joking around. They never seem to be doing any work, but they are rock stars in class. They always have their hands up and get the right answer. I, on the other hand, spend day after day in "my" library cubicle and barely understand anything I read.

It is likely that some, if not all, of these resonate with you. Remember what I've told you before: Law school is a complete mindf**k. Law school is like Instagram in real life. You are seeing a snapshot of your classmates' personas. The snapshot they want you to see. What you don't see and what you don't know is that, on some level, they are just as scared and overwhelmed as you.

Appearances are deceiving. It could be that Katelyn (the one with the great hair) suffers from severe anxiety, and dressing up makes her feel like she can get through the day. It may be that Arjun (the policy answer guy) is good on his feet but can't write an exam to save his life. It may be that the girls who are studying in October don't really know what it means to "study" and so they are doing it all wrong. It may be that the cool kids on the 2nd floor are all going to get C's.

Just because things look a certain way does not mean that they are that way. Law school is a time when you feel incredibly vulnerable. Not only because it's new and scary and overwhelming for you, but because you compare yourself to other people. Which makes it so much worse. Please try your best not to fall into this trap. Do not read into things and then use those things to beat up on yourself. Stay focused and grounded, and don't let the "noise" of other people get in your head.

3. Get Out of Your Own Way

Many law students suffer from a serious affliction: self-doubt. The smallest thing can send them into a tailspin. They tend to over-think things, leading into a spiral of "what ifs" and "is this a bad decision?" The same skills that are useful as a lawyer (analytical reasoning, arguing both sides, seeing logical connections) can be harmful to your mental health.

Let me give you an example. I first got the idea for this book in the summer of 2021. For the first couple of months, I went back and forth on whether it was worth pursuing. I went from "This is an awesome idea," to "This is so stupid," to everything in between. *What if my school doesn't like something I say? What if something I write gets me in trouble? What if this is not helpful advice? What if the book is cheesy? What if colleagues view me as not "scholarly"?* You get the picture.

Self-doubt is normal. Especially among law students. It is healthy—in moderation. When self-doubt stops you from doing what you want to do, from making good decisions, from succeeding, then it becomes a problem.

I had a student once, let's call her Ruby. Ruby was very smart and very conscientious. But she had trouble getting stuff done on time because she spent so much time worrying that it "wasn't right" or she "just wasn't sure." Her self-doubt was getting in the way of her success. Here's how she describes it in her own words as a 1L:

Anxiety and over-attention to details were big struggles for me. I am hyper aware of my own errors and imperfections and not nearly as aware of my strengths or deficits in relation to those of my peers. I had no idea that some of your general critiques and criticisms may not apply to things I was doing. I tried really hard not to worry so much, and to let some of my details and hang ups go, but in the end, I'm still handing in outlines that I am terrified will not live up to your expectations. I still struggle with the balance between what needs to be in the outline and how it should be in the outline for turning in to you, versus what needs to be in the outline so that I remember the material and can study from it. I tried to put a time limit on my work but still far exceeded it each week. I also tried to remind myself that done is better than perfect, but at the end of the day, done isn't always good enough and submitting outlines has made me doubt whether or not I should be in school.

Ruby struggled with these challenges a great deal in her first, and even into her second, year. Eventually, she got much better about managing her self-doubt and proceeding even in the face of it.

There's an expression you're probably familiar with: Get out of your own way.[4] Sometimes, when we're experiencing self-doubt, it is helpful to remember that advice and just move forward in spite of that doubt.

Back to me: Even as this book went to print, I struggled with whether it was a good idea to have written it. It didn't help that one week before submitting the manuscript for this book, a student wrote in an anonymous evaluation that "[Prof. Monestier] turns to her embarrassing blog to write posts complaining about her insecurity that everyone likes her husband better than her and how she is obsessed with validation from students.... [She is the] most whiny and unprofessional professor I have ever had. She seems to only care about receiving personal validation from her job." Wow.[5]

Sometimes, the self-doubt does not go away. Sometimes you just must accept that you will never feel 100% about something, but you just have to make the best decision you can under the circumstances. In my case, my husband, my Research Assistants, and my publisher were all telling me that that book was a worthwhile endeavor. Being someone who needs more reassurance than that, my husband also said the book was funny, well-written, not cheesy, relatable, useful, and all sorts of other stuff. I had to trust that some of these people were better positioned than I was to make this assessment. If it turns out that they were incorrect, well then, I have other people to blame (which is always nice).

4. Trust Yourself

One of the hardest things I've found about being a law student, and a lawyer, is developing the ability to trust yourself. You are always looking at what other people are doing and assuming that they are right. It is hard to do what *you* think is right...because, after all, who are you to know what's right?

When I was working as a lawyer before I became a professor, I wrote academic articles in my spare time. Not for fun. But because that is what I needed to do to break into the academic job market. I wrote an article called *A*

---

4. If you're looking for another expression to capture the same thing, you might use what my husband calls me: "an impediment to progress."

5. I guess my "Be Who You Are" message didn't land with this student. As if that weren't enough, another student posted an anonymous comment that I "suck" and that this book "will say the same sexist, outdated bs." I'm not sure what the sexism comment is about—am I sexist against men or against women? But, yes, the book does contain "outdated" advice about how people used to study in the olden days.

"Real and Substantial" Mess, where I critiqued Canadian courts' approach to personal jurisdiction. I felt pretty good about the paper. Then I gave it to my friend, Mike. Mike went to Columbia and had been a practicing attorney at a prominent New York firm for about a decade. He could write motions in his sleep. Mike liked the paper...sort of. He thought I needed to "restructure" the article and make it more forceful. Like "The court erred" instead of "Arguably, the court was mistaken in its approach." I was gutted. But I understood what he was saying, and I changed the paper to reflect his comments. I then submitted it to a law journal for consideration.

The journal had a double-blind peer review process, so they sent it off to three anonymous reviewers. Two of the reviewers liked the ideas in the paper but thought that it needed to be "restructured." Although they didn't know it, they wanted me to go back to the version I had before. The third reviewer did not think the paper made an original contribution to the scholarship.[6]

The journal made me a conditional offer of publication. The condition was that I re-work the paper to make it reflect the comments from the two reviewers. I submitted the "revised" (i.e., original) paper to the journal the next day. They were floored: *How did you get this done so quickly?* It was what I had originally written, but I didn't have enough confidence in to submit.

Two years later, I was at a conference. The Ontario Court of Appeal was deciding a key jurisdiction case. A professor from the University of Toronto came up to me and said, "So you're the one who put a bee in the bonnet of the Court of Appeal." My article apparently was the catalyst for the Court of Appeal to revisit its approach to jurisdiction.

Three years after that, the issue made its way up to the Supreme Court of Canada. Whose journal articles were all over the briefs submitted to the Court?[7] You guessed it! Who did the Court cite in its judgment? Yup, that's right.

---

6. I dug through all my old emails and found the review: "After all these years, I would expect to see a new take or a new argument drawn from or based on jurisprudential developments since then. While the paper submitted is well written and displays obvious familiarity and ease in dealing with the subject-matter, it mainly restates many of the already published arguments and critiques of *Muscutt* and the *Morguard* progeny (most of them are referred to in the footnotes) without offering anything new or advancing the discussion. Given that courts seem not to have noticed the many doctrinal objections to recent case law, it may be that one more voice will have an incremental effect. That may [be] reason enough for you to publish it—but if so it should be with full appreciation that it will not be an original contribution to Canadian scholarship on this question."

7. By then, I had written a second article on the topic. Eventually, there would be a third.

But that's not all, folks. Shortly after the Supreme Court's decision, I was contacted by a professor who was editing a two-volume book on "Personal Jurisdiction and Private International Law." The book was intended to be a compilation of the most influential articles on personal jurisdiction in the common law world. My article was selected as one of eight articles featured in Part I of the book dealing with "Fundamental Questions." Almost every other author in that section taught at a fancy law school (Harvard, Oxford, Chicago) and was four decades older than me. I guess, contrary to the one reviewer's thoughts, there was something original and interesting (and "fundamental") about my article.[8]

I wish I could say that I learned my lesson after this and that now, I always trust myself. But that wouldn't be true. I am better at trusting my instincts, but I still probably place too much weight on what other people think and do.

But even writing this section has helped crystallize for me that I need to take the advice that I'm giving. In the months before publication, I sent the introduction of this book to a colleague so he could get a flavor for the book. To be clear, I was not seeking commentary or feedback. But, of course, I got it. He suggested making a bunch of changes. *Maybe eliminate the part about the law review screwing you over? Consider omitting the descriptions of each of your articles and talk more about your academic writing in general.* And so on.

Thanks, but no thanks. I wrote it how I wrote it and that's how it will remain. In years past, I would have stewed over this message for days and wondered if there were other portions of the book that should be tweaked. Not anymore. It's my book, not yours. I'm going to write it the way I want to write it.

As a law student, I would urge you to try to develop confidence and trust in yourself and your abilities. And work on this skill as you progress throughout your career. In my case, it's still a work in progress—but, as you can see, I have made great strides.

5. Your Grades Do Not Define You

Law school grades, particularly 1L grades, are very important. So important, in fact, that one of my students, Leticia, insisted that I make a public service announcement to you. Instead of me making this announcement, I asked her to put it in her own words:

---

8. And the article did not have an "incremental" effect as the third reviewer predicted. It changed the law. Put that in your pipe and smoke it, anonymous reviewer.

One thing that I was not aware of prior to the start of my 1L year is the significant role that first semester grades play in securing a 2L Summer Associateship, internship, and many other opportunities. Going into law school, I knew I would need to adjust, but so did everyone else, right? However, some people did not take quite as long to adjust (which was a wakeup call in and of itself). I thought I had more time to adapt to law school, familiarize myself with professors' teaching methods and material, tighten up my outlines, and be ready to crush law school exams. This was not the case. Law school exams quickly approached, then passed, and eventually I received my first semester grades. They were nowhere near as good as the grades I earned in undergrad, and I honestly thought I did well on exams, so I was expecting much better grades.

I tried to remain positive and tell myself that I could improve next semester and even the semester after that. However, despite receiving much better grades in my second semester of 1L year, my GPA did not increase *that* much—at least not to where I wanted (and needed) it to be. I felt as though I dug myself a hole that I could not get out of. I quickly realized that I had really screwed myself over by not getting it together sooner and performing well on first semester exams.

The realization that I could perform at a higher level was almost more frustrating, and I beat myself up for not doing so sooner. Immediately after 1L year, it is time to start applying for summer internships, associateships, and other coveted opportunities. This being said, there are only two semesters worth of grades on rising 2L's transcripts. As I began to apply for positions, I found myself reflecting back on my first semester of 1L year, and really wishing I had been aware of the great impact it will have on my future. If I knew this sooner, I would have approached it much differently.

I agree with Leticia that grades are very important. Grades have a snowball effect. For example, when I was in law school, 1L summer jobs were based exclusively on first semester grades. I had straight A+'s, so I got a 1L summer associate position. Based on *three* grades. Then, 2L summer jobs are based on about eight 1L grades, plus any other relevant experience (read: 1L summer law firm experience). I was offered a permanent position at a New York law firm really based on my 1L grades. Plus, I guess I made a good impression. All of this to say that I 100% agree with Leticia.

But I also want to say that grades aren't everything. Definitionally, not everyone will be at the top of the class. If you're not in the top 25% of the class (or top 50% or 75% for that matter), does this mean you throw in the towel? No. Your grades are not the measure of who you are. They are a measure of how you performed on one particular day on one particular exam.

Grades do not necessarily portend[9] how successful you will be, what job you will get, and what kind of lawyer you will be. There's an expression you might have heard before: The A students become professors. The B students become the best lawyers. The C students make the most money. There is some degree of truth to this. I have seen students who were nowhere near the top of their class turn into fabulous lawyers. They are top-notch criminal lawyers, partners in law firms, and in-house attorneys at Fortune 500 companies. B (or even C) grades in law school is not a death sentence.[10] It might mean you have to work a little bit harder to get a job. It might mean you really need to work on improving your grades (employers love seeing forward progress!).

Also, once you graduate from law school and get a job, no one will ever ask you about your grades ever again. Grades are really only ever an issue in getting your first job. Once you get that, you can parlay it into something else...the snowball effect I mentioned above.

You are not the sum of your grades. Do not go through your law school career feeling that way.

6. Self-Criticism Is Not Helpful

We are our own worst critics. If you spoke to your friends the way I'm sure you sometimes speak to yourself, you would have no friends. Law students are a particularly critical bunch. If they get the answer wrong in class, they will rake themselves over the coals for it. If they fail to spot an issue on the exam, they will ruminate for days. If they flub an oral argument, they will replay the embarrassment in their minds over and over again.

None of this is helpful. Mistakes happen; that's why pencils have erasers. That was another inspirational quote I came across. There is really no use dwelling on your mistakes and beating yourself up over them. I know this is easier said than done.

---

9. Nailed it!

10. A reality check: If you have B and C grades, you may not get jobs that tend to be reserved for the tippity-top of the class, like clerking for an appellate court.

I was the person who dwelt for weeks on my mistakes. After every exam, I did the worst thing you could probably do. I opened my outline and went through every page to see if there was perhaps something I missed in my answer. Invariably, I would catch a potential issue that I could have discussed. And I would be really hard on myself. My mom would come into my room and gently pry my outlines away from me. She was concerned that I was a reviewing material a little too intensely for an exam that I had already taken. Good call, Mom.

I'm not the person to let herself off the hook. I'm still mad at myself for hiring a terrible wedding photographer. My wedding was 13 years ago.[11] And let's not forget the time I backed into the giant rock at school and scratched the back bumper of the car. I still cringe every time I see the scrape on the bumper. Oh, and there's the bad call on the Barely Beige paint in the upstairs bathroom. I knew I should have gone with Montgomery White.

This is definitely a case of "do as I say and not as I do."

7. Your Parents Will Love You Anyway

A lot of students, particularly first-generation students, feel an enormous amount of pressure to succeed. They feel like their parents came to this country to give them a better life. And if they don't do well in law school, they will have let their parents down. I understand the feeling. I do.

Your parents love you and support you regardless of whether you "succeed" in law school—using whatever definition of success you've set for yourself. They will love you if you have B's and C's on your transcript. They will love you if you get a crappy-paying public defender job. They will love you if you don't make law review. Do not feel like you're letting your parents down by not getting straight A's and the most prestigious jobs out there. If you are genuinely doing your best and giving law school your all, they will be proud. I guarantee it.

Case in point. I told you before that my brother, Dennis, was not academically oriented. He did not do well in school. He ended up going into sales, which is a perfect fit for him. He currently sells garbage cans. No, not Oscar

---

11. Not only were the photos bad, but the photographer almost got into a physical altercation with my husband at the wedding. My husband asked the photographer to take a photo of him dancing with his mom and sister, and the photographer got mad that he was being "told" what to do.

the Grouch garbage cans.[12] The garbage and recycling bins that you put out on the curb each week. He sells those to big cities across Canada. You think my parents love Dennis less than me (the academic golden child)? I mean, they should, given all the crap Dennis has put them through. But they don't. They love us equally. At least they say they do. In my household, we know that Mom loves Dennis more and Dad loves me more. But my point—which got away from me a bit—is that you are not letting your parents down if you are not a superstar in law school. So please take that pressure off yourself.

I feel like you've heard a lot in this book about my dad. He's definitely a character. And his life lessons, however unorthodox, make pretty good sense. You haven't heard that much about my mom. Probably because she's pretty normal. But my mom has always been my Number 1 supporter and has done everything in her power to help me succeed. So, I wanted to give her a special shout out here. Since there were only a few stories in this book about my mom, I thought I'd share one now to show you how sweet she is.

The year after I got my LL.M., I got several interviews for a full-time faculty position in Canada. One of these interviews was for a position at the University of Windsor, a school that is about four hours from Toronto, where my parents live. My parents kindly offered to drive me to the interview.

The school had put me up at a hotel the night before the interview. There were two queen size beds. My parents took one; I took the other. Unfortunately, both my parents are, how can I say this, not quiet sleepers. They snore. It's annoying. And it's particularly annoying when you're trying to get some rest the night before a big job interview. I hushed them several times, and eventually dozed off.

I got up in the middle of the night to get some water. I walked into the bathroom, and I heard a quiet whisper coming from the bathtub. *Don't be scared. It's just me. Mom.* WT*************? I nearly had a heart attack. Why was my mom in the bathtub in the middle of the night? I look over and see she's there with a pillow and blanket. Yes, she was sleeping in the bathtub. Seriously? *Mom, what in God's name are you doing in the bathtub?* She replied, *I knew the snoring was bothering you and I didn't want to wake you up. So, I slept in the bathtub.* Now that's love.

---

12. Who would have thought there would be two Oscar the Grouch references in a law school academic support book?

8. It's Okay to Not Be Okay

Many law students struggle with anxiety, depression, and other mental health issues. Before I go further, I want to be clear what I mean by anxiety. I mean clinically diagnosed anxiety. Every law student says, "I have anxiety over my grades," "This exam is giving me major anxiety," and "Cold calls ramp up my anxiety." Sure, these things might cause you stress and worry and discomfort. But I am talking about more than that. I'm talking real anxiety—like a psychiatrist assessed you and determined that you suffer from anxiety. Why it is important to distinguish between the two? Because I think that for students who have real anxiety, it minimizes their experiences to have others constantly refer to their anxiety as if it were the same thing. It's not.

For you, law school can be a real struggle. If you have depression, for instance, it can take all your effort to just get out of bed in the morning. And even when you do, it's hard to force yourself to care about classes and studying—because, well, you don't. It just all feels empty.

And for those of you who have anxiety or panic attacks, it feels like the world can come caving in at any moment. Your amygdala is on turbo-mode, constantly monitoring for any danger and keeping you in a perpetual state of angst. I have had some students whose anxiety was so bad that it made them physically sick. One girl developed severe migraines and another developed stomach problems because the anxiety was so acute. For these students, law school is treacherous. They are not only navigating this whole new world, but they are doing so in a constant state of disquiet that can turn into fear at the drop of a hat.

It is difficult to go through law school if you have a serious mental health condition. But difficult does not mean impossible. I have seen students with anxiety get much better with time. The girl who had stomach problems due to her anxiety graduated with Honors. And, get this, she tried out for (and made) the trial team! By the way, trial team involves speaking in front of lots of people, which is probably the most nerve-racking thing a student with anxiety can do in law school.

How, specifically, should you navigate law school if you are struggling with a serious mental health condition?

For starters, you should realize that you are not alone. There are many other students (and professors and lawyers and other professionals) who struggle with mental health issues. Having a mental health condition does not mean you are broken or unworthy.

Second, you should get help. You need to get professional medical help to help you manage your condition. This might mean therapy, this might mean medication, this might mean some combination of the two.

Third, you should let select people at the law school know about what is going on. Who those people are will be up to you. Every school will be different. Usually there is a Dean of Students who deals with issues like this, and perhaps liaises with your professors. Alternatively, you might want to let your professors know if your mental health condition is particularly serious and impacts something in their class. Use your discretion here. As I've said before, your professor is not your psychologist. But sometimes it is helpful to keep them in the loop if you are really having a hard time.

Fourth, you should let a friend or family member in. A therapist and a professor knowing you have anxiety or depression is not a substitute for having a close friend or family member by your side. It may be awkward or embarrassing to bring it up, but it will be worth it. Most of the time you'll be greeted with more empathy and understanding than you think.

Ultimately, my message to you is this: You are not alone, and your mental health struggles don't define you. You are much, much more than your hardest days.

9. Things Will Work Out in the End

Law school is full of ups and downs. You may not get the grades you want. You may not get the summer internship you want. You may not get a summer internship at all. You may not know what type of law you want to practice. You may not get a job right away. You may not pass the bar. You may not even end up practicing law. All these things happen. But things do work out in the end.

I had a former student named Sophia. Sophia was a very good student; she graduated at the top of her class. But she was very shy and introverted. The thought of going to court made her sick to her stomach. Sophia ended up at a prominent litigation firm. And, as you might guess, litigation firms *litigate*. There is an expectation that you actually go to court and speak. Sophia made as many excuses as she could to avoid court. And she woke up every day dreading going to work. Sophia applied to several corporate law firms because she figured there'd be less of a chance she'd have to speak in front of people. But she didn't get any of those jobs.

I was hoping this was all just a phase and that Sophia would eventually become more comfortable with public speaking. But after two years at the litigation firm, Sophia was adamant that this was not for her. She debated leaving the law altogether. This period was really hard for her because she loved aspects of the law—just not the speaking aspect. As luck would have it, a position as a permanent law clerk opened up and she was hired. To say that Sophia was thrilled was an understatement. She is now working for "her" judge and couldn't be happier.

Moral of the story: Things will work out in the end.

TWENTY-ONE

Student Reflections

have learned that despite my best intentions, you are only going to believe what I say *to a degree.* You will discount some of the advice I give you because: (1) I'm a professor, so you think I'm deliberately not giving you the true skinny on law school; and (2) I'm of a different generation, and you think "the kids" do things differently now and I am out of touch. I get it. Which is why I brought in trusty reinforcements!

I reached out to several current and former students and told them about this book project. I nixed anyone who did not seem sufficiently impressed with my masterpiece. For the rest of them, I asked whether they would consider writing a "reflection." Most of them were like, *what *exactly* are you looking for?* To which I responded, *write what you want to write.* I told them that they should feel free to share their story, provide advice to incoming law students, or say whatever they wanted to say about law school. I did not want to impose any parameters on them.

Below, you will find very thoughtful reflections from real students who have been exactly where you are right now. Some of these stories and experiences will resonate with you; others will not. I don't necessarily endorse all the advice and thoughts that these students provide, but that is beside the point. Read though the narratives and take what is helpful and jettison the rest.

1. Matteo's Advice: "Don't Be an A-Hole"

I want to begin by saying thank you to the author of this book and the best professor that I have ever had, Professor Tanya Monestier. Professor Monestier, thank you for being an excellent professor, advisor, and overall person. I can honestly say that I do not think that I would be where I am today if you were not my professor. So, for that, I thank you.[1]

Now, I want to change directions and focus my attention on the readers of this book. I think it is important for you, all, to know a little bit about me, so you can understand my law school perspective a bit better. Simply put, I am not your classic law student. For starters, my parents are not lawyers or doctors, like the parents of many law students. I have tattoos, I curse a lot, and I do not use big fancy words. Like Professor Monestier, my parents were both born in Italy and immigrated to the United States. That being said, I am the first one in my family that attended and graduated from law school.

I was born and raised in New Jersey. Chances have it, if you met me, your first guess would be that I am from New Jersey. Professor Monestier and her husband (another great professor) enjoy poking fun at my gold chains and Kappa tracksuits. I entered law school directly after graduating from undergrad, which I believe was a great choice. So, if you are asking yourself if you should take a year off, I highly recommend that you don't. Now, I think you know enough about me. Rather than writing about the typical B.S. that any law school graduate would tell you, like take good notes and attend social events, I am going to give you a different perspective. I will give you four points that I think will help prospective law students succeed in law school and the legal profession. I was going to give you "four rules," but then I would come off like the law school a-holes that I will speak about later on.

Point 1

The grind. The grind is a word that I use to describe law school and what it takes to make it through law school. As I am sure you have heard, law school is difficult, demanding, and requires massive amounts of time and effort. The only way to thrive in a setting such as law school is to grind. Simply put, you

---

1. I debated eliminating this since it really has nothing to do with you. But ultimately, I decided that if that's what Matteo wanted to say, *who am I* to edit that out?

need to get your priorities straight and dedicate your full attention to law school. What does that mean? You need to prepare for class, attend every class, and spend time with the subject matter of the material. When I say attend class, I do not mean that you are physically present and possibly still drunk from the night before, like some of you did while in undergrad. I do not judge. What I mean is that you need to have read the cases, thought about the cases, and be prepared to get called on. Back to giving your full attention to law school. Make sure that your family and significant other understands what you will be going through. You will not have time to entertain bullsh*t arguments about not having enough time to talk or enough time to go grab dinner. Trust me, I have seen how this can affect a law student, and I can tell you that it will only drag you down. One little tidbit, if you use tobacco or nicotine products, I suggest quitting before law school because law school will only further this addiction.

Law school is not comparable to undergrad. I graduated undergrad with a 3.98 GPA and was one of the top 30 students out of almost 4,000. I am not saying this to flex or show off, because honestly, I believe that grades can only get you so far. Specifically, if you do not know how to communicate with people, I think that you are going to be at a disadvantage in your legal career. Anyway, the reason I am mentioning this is to highlight the difference between law school and undergrad. If you did phenomenal in undergrad, do not enter law school and think it will be easy. You will need to put in 10x more effort just to break into the top ranks of your law school. Honestly, I can say I worked significantly harder in law school in comparison to undergrad and that placed me in the top 25% of my law school class.

Point 2

Many people enter law school with the intention to make a ton of friends, participate in study groups, and be "social butterflies." On the other hand, some people enter law school and think they do not need any friends and they can make it through law school alone. Based off of my experience, I think it is important to have one true friend. Of course, I was friendly with many of my classmates, but I can honestly say that I had one real friend throughout my three years. To this day, I am still very close to him. As a matter of fact, we got matching tattoos in law school. Naturally, we got the tattoos in Garamond font, which is Professor Monestier's favorite font. I am sure that she speaks about Garamond somewhere in this book.

Having one true friend is important for many reasons. First off, this friend will likely be a person to complain to. You will do a lot of complaining in law school. I don't care how mentally tough and driven you are, you are going to get frustrated with professors, other students, and school in general. That being said, you will need someone to complain to. Trust me. Not only will this friend serve as a person to complain to, but you can also turn to this friend for opinions, help, and overall advice. Importantly, if you have a real friend, you can confidently talk sh*t about other people with the confidence that they will not open their mouths. As you will learn, many law students have big mouths and like to gossip. I recommend staying away from all of the gossip. I am sure that you are thinking, "wait he was just speaking about talking sh*t, but now he is saying not to gossip." There is a difference; a conversation with a trusted friend is not the same as the talk going through the hallways about who hooked up over the weekend.

Point 3

Don't be an a-hole, it is simple as that. Before moving on, I just want to say that as I am writing this, I am getting the feeling that a lot of you reading this think I am a hater and bitter. Truly, I am not. Like I said in the beginning, I am going to tell you the things that many former law students would not say, but they are thinking. Anyway, the reason I say don't be an a-hole is because many law students are. You are likely asking yourself, "what does he mean?"

First, many law students try and use big complex words to sound smart. Whether it be in conversation with other law students or in response to a cold call, there is simply no need for this. Of course, I do not recommend speaking like I do (f-bombs every other word), but just get your point across in a simple and succinct manner. Once you begin your legal career, you will notice that judges and lawyers want information in a concise and easy to understand manner. In concluding my rant on this point, I just want to say if you are one to try and sound smart by using these "big words," you will likely rub people the wrong way and simply come off like an a-hole.

Another thing that you will notice while in law school is that a lot of law students will compare themselves to their peers. This is how this typically plays out: law students are sitting down before class having coffee and chatting. One law student begins telling the others how much he or she studied that weekend, how long their outline is, or how many pages their brief was. The other students begin questioning their work ethic in comparison that one student. Now that you are done reading that "hypo," (hypothetical situation that many law professors use to teach a concept) I want to say that situations like that are never good. It leaves your peers feeling bad about their work product. That being said, I raise this point to say that if you ever find yourself in a situation like this, do not feel bad or feel like you need to do the same thing as your peers. Move at your own pace and have confidence in your study methods and practices.

Point 4

My final point, the importance of outlining, is a dedication to Professor Monestier. Outlining is a very simple, but also a very complex, concept. You will hear this word a disgusting number of times. Many law students spend all semester preparing for class, going to class, and taking notes. Unfortunately, many students take it no further. Specifically, they will wait until the end of the semester and then spend hours upon hours trying to create an outline. DO NOT DO THIS. What you should be doing is the "Tanya Monestier Method," as I like to call it. This "method" is very simple; when class is over, sit down and type your notes into your outline. Simply, all you are doing is creating your outline as the semester progresses, so your outline is done when finals roll around. I would literally go to the library after every class and type my notes into my outline. Not only will your outline be complete for finals, but you will absorb the material and realize what you understand and what you don't understand. I won't belabor this point because I am sure Professor Monestier speaks about this in some other section, but I strongly recommend that you do this.

The last thing I want to say is, use Garamond font. You have probably never heard of it, but there is a strong likelihood that this book is written in Garamond. Even if the final product is not in Garamond, I can guarantee you that Professor Monestier wrote her drafts in Garamond. Professor Monestier swears by this font and even asserts that it is backed by scientific research. Specifically, Professor Monestier believes that readers will take a stronger liking to the written document and the writer if it is in Garamond font. Who knows if that is true, but Professor Monestier has convinced me of this. I can confidently say that I have not typed in any font besides Garamond since Professor Monestier's Contracts class.

I want to thank Professor Monestier, one last time, for asking me to write this contribution. I am truly honored to have written this. To the readers, I want to wish you all the best of luck. Though law school is likely one of the most difficult time periods of your lives, it is one of the most enjoyable and rewarding experiences. Stick to the grind and graduate; you will not regret it.

2. Olivia's Story: "I Was Truly Falling Apart at the Seams"

I am, and probably always will be, what Professor Monestier once termed "skittish." I sit quietly in the back rows of lecture halls and sink in my seat hoping to avoid eye contact with the professor. I would rather skip a class and teach myself the rule against perpetuities than have to answer a cold call in Property. And, most illustrating and devastating, I would miss out on free pizza 9 times out of 10 just to avoid social interactions (that may not sound like a big deal, but free pizza is one of the few doses of serotonin in law school).

During my 1L year, I abruptly became extremely aware of these characteristics, and I began to question my capabilities because of them. I felt silly for thinking that I, this quiet anxious mess who can't even handle the Socratic method, could become a lawyer. It didn't matter that I was offered a 90% tuition scholarship in the honors program, or that after my first semester I received great grades; I still didn't feel good enough. This feeling of inadequacy took a hold of me, and suddenly everything spun out of control. I lost twenty pounds over just a few months because I had so much anxiety and was so busy studying that I would forget to eat. I had sporadic full body panic attacks that required my boyfriend to drive four hours just to hold me until I calmed down. I entered pits of depression, feelings I had never experienced and didn't know what to do with. I was truly falling apart at the seams, and it was scary.

Finally, I did what felt like the absolute end of the world: I talked about it. I was floored when my mentor at my public service placement, whom I idolize because she is all the things I aspire to be—confident, intelligent, seemingly unfailingly composed—told me that she has struggled, and still does, just like me.

What I want you to take out of this passage is this: your mental health struggles are not predicates to failure in law school. Just because you sometimes feel broken or overwhelmed by anxiety doesn't mean that you can't be at the top of your class, or clerk for the highest court in your country, or zealously advocate for your client in court. Anxiety, depression, self-doubt—these feelings make us human, and in many ways, they can make us better students and advocates. Law school is hard enough already, so if you feel yourself slip into dark places, don't be afraid to ask for help. You would be surprised by the people around you who know what you are going through, I promise.

P.S. this passage is dedicated to Zoloft, Spotify Calming Rain sounds, and my dog Ace. Couldn't have done it without you three.

3. Grant's Decision to Go to Law School: "It Was the Right Decision for Me"

I had a difficult start in life. For a time, I probably held the record at the local hospital for the youngest and smallest premature child born at 1 pound, 9 ounces. Although I was born in July, my parents did not share the joy (or relief) of my coming home to my older brother until mid-October. In preparing to write this chapter I reviewed a letter that my mother wrote to unborn-me about one week prior to my birth where she summed up my chances as "not optimistic." Children born as small and as young as I was often died because their bodies could not produce an enzyme that allowed their lungs to expand, or, if they did survive, they would have life-long chronic disabilities. Yet, both of my parents were determined to bring me into the world. I survived and survived well.

I grew up in a small, rural town in the Northeast. My mother was a hairstylist with a high school education and my father had some technical school as an electrical engineer after he came home from serving in combat in Vietnam. He was the breadwinner and when the recession hit, his company laid him off right as I was applying to school. My parents were not poor, but we were never wealthy, either. Prior to my brother and me, no one in our extended family had gone to college. We were the first generation with the opportunity to earn an education.

I spent four mostly fruitful years in college, dabbling with a bachelor's degree in history and a second in political science. I graduated from undergrad in 2013 as a mostly A and B student in the midst of an economic downturn.

You're probably saying, "Oh yes, economic downturn, I read about this somewhere in X paper or from Y website." But what does that term *mean* to real people? What it means was that someone with student debt coming from a good school with a decent academic pedigree relied upon the kindness of his neighbor to get a minimum wage job assembling widgets in a makeshift warehouse. I did get to drive a forklift and boss high school kids around—that was fun. Yet, as that temporary summer gig turned into two long years, my hope dwindled that I would ever get that blessed administrative job making, God I hope, at least $30,000 per year. The world grew a little darker. Then, a thunderbolt: I interviewed for, and accepted, a job working as a bottom-level paralegal at a boutique firm in the city. From 2015 to the end of 2018, I advanced my way rather quickly to the top of the paralegal hierarchy at the firm. Long gone was the guy rumbling around with a forklift talking to delivery drivers moving palettes. In his place stood a more confident, slightly richer but let's not kid ourselves, youngish professional. I never grew any taller in the interim, much to my chagrin.

The thought of becoming a lawyer and going into law school did not materialize until I was burnt out three too many times at the firm. Day in, day out, week in, week out, me and a handful of others began to realize what was glaringly obvious to anyone who bothered to give it consideration: we could do as good a job (sometimes even a better job) than those who reviewed our work. Yet we were paid half as much because we did not have the right letters after our name or the all-important bar admission.

And so, still knowing nothing about law school or the LSAT or what the Socratic method even was, I began to apply to several different schools in the New England area. In time, a school accepted me and I put in my time. I rose not only to be a prominent member of the law review, but I also managed to sneak into the top ten in the class through sheer determination of will.

I relayed this experience to you because I always found most answers to the generic water cooler question of, "so why did you come/go/want to go/ to law school?" so boring. Do not be that person that gets a professional degree because it "just felt like the next thing" right out of college, or because "you want to change the world." Once you're out of college, the "next thing" for you to do should be to get a practical job learning practical skills. Doing so builds character, a modicum of wealth, and an ability to deal with *pressure* in life that academics simply can never, ever give you. It worked for me. But for my struggles prior to law school, I would not have ended up so high at the end. In short, go to law school to become a lawyer if you want to practice law and if you enjoy long hours of research, writing, and argument. Some sectors in the profession will be blessed with very high salaries while others will not, but if you enjoy the practice of law, then the money will follow in time.

Getting back to that *pressure* for a moment—most of law school is just showing up to class and taking quality notes. Hell, studying is not all that difficult it is just *time-consuming* and *boring*. You'll read throughout this book about the "dos and don'ts" that the author recommends. I agree with some and disagree with others. That isn't my focus. If you wanted a succinct summary of my time in law school it was (1) get up at 7AM; (2) drive 45 minutes to school; (3) sit in class and be either bored or confused; (4) study in the library until 9PM; (5) drive 45 minutes back home; and (6) repeat six days a week, or seven if it was finals season.

Instead, the worst parts about law school for me were the tertiary things. Three years is a long time to go without a paycheck when it's something you're used to. It is a long time to put friendships and relationships effectively on hold because, as much as you would love to continue your weekly trivia nights or going out with colleagues for drinks on a Friday, most of the time you will not have the time, the energy, or the money to do so. That doesn't end upon graduation, either. Hell, I took my bar examination in July of 2021 and did not find out that I passed it until mid-November of that same year. It is only now, in November, that I feel like my life is truly flowing forward, steadily again. Even that has been disrupted by personal tragedy in my last year of school.

After a severe fall, my mother had been sick on and off for about five years. She would plateau for a time, and then decline, plateau, decline, plateau, and so on. Throughout my life I was blessed to have her as my mother because she was one of my strongest, most vocal cheerleaders. She supported my decision to go to law school and while she never quite understood all of what that entailed, she never ceased to tell me how proud it made her feel that her sons were doing well in life. I could do no wrong in her eyes… unless I didn't give quite as nice a card to her for Mother's Day as my brother did. Right around her 66th birthday in March of 2021, she fell for the final time. I drove her back home from the hospital with my dad, we helped her back into the house, and then I came by with my girlfriend to check in on them not long afterward. Our conversation only lasted for a few minutes, but it was the last time I spoke with her. I told her and my dad that I had applied for the bar exam, finally, and that I was excited to graduate in May. Only a few days later, she passed away overnight.

When I received the news that nobody is ever prepared for, I was working on a motion for the judge I was interning with and took the rest of the day off. Life can be cruel in strange ways because while I was sitting in our sunroom with my dad and my brother trying to absorb what had happened, I received an email from the bar examiners rejecting my bar application due to a technicality. You'll probably read about court cases that were decided because of a "misplaced comma" or some such nonsense, and it was no different for the bar exam application, it seemed. I was ready to burn the whole building down. Thankfully, I calmed down and went through the motions of living for the rest of finals, the semester, and graduation. I concentrated on balancing my grief with my desire to see my semester through to completion. My judge offered to let me end my program early in light of what happened, but I was determined to finish what I had started. I owed it to my mother (and to myself) to keep myself together and satisfy my obligations. I then battled grief long enough to barrel through bar preparation and, it turned out, succeed beyond my wildest dreams.

Despite the ups and downs that my life has taken up to this point, one thing I do not regret at all is taking the big risk to apply to law school and making it my life's career. I have no way of knowing what that career will look like in the medium to long term. However, it was the right decision for me.

4. Jasmin's Journey: "Sh*t Does Not Go the Way You Expect"

I started law school during a pandemic. Yep, one of the most challenging experiences in my life started while the entire world was brought to its knees. I guess "go hard or go home"? You probably can't tell, but I can sometimes be...dramatic. Although, in my defense, it doesn't get more dramatic than living through a pandemic. One minute we thought we would only press pause for two weeks because of a weird virus, and the next minute we were all quarantining for over a year. Needless to say, me and everyone else who started law school in 2020 were navigating uncharted waters. This is my story. *Law & Order sound effect.* I told you I bring the drama.

Due to COVID-19, my entire first year of law school was remote. We were the Zoom babies, as a friend of mine likes to call it. We went to class on Zoom, had office hours on Zoom, and even met each other to socialize on Zoom. Despite the challenges that this brought, there were three major things that helped me survive, and actually thrive, throughout my law school journey (which is now in-person, btw!).

My Support System

I have a support system of friends and family who understand that I'm taking a big step toward something I've wanted to do for as long as I could remember. They understand that my law school journey requires my time and dedication. The captain of my cheer squad is my mom. Her support is unwavering, and it gives me the confidence I sometimes need when I question my capabilities. You see, my mom is an opinionated woman. She never shies away from a moment to tell you how she really feels. As you can imagine, that leads to some "passionate" conversations between us, because she also raised an opinionated daughter. My mom is the one who gives it to me straight, no chaser. She grounds me and adds so much perspective to my life. Find the person who can head up your cheer squad, and you'll make it through those moments of doubt that law school tends to bring.

Sh*t Never Goes the Way You Expect

This one was a hard pill to swallow. I'm a planner. I plan almost everything, down to the outfit I will wear to the Barristers Ball two months away. I have always lived by the mantra, "If you fail to plan, you plan to fail." Plans are good, but I've come to terms with the fact that they are not set in stone. They are more like guideposts to keep me on my path.

I had a completely different vision of what my law school career would look like. I would be in a different city than I currently am. I would have a different part-time job than the one I currently have. And I would have a different lifestyle than the one I currently have. I chose my current school, in part, based on the fact that it would allow me to live in New York City for at least my first year of law school. After that, I planned on transferring to a school that was physically in New York City. Well, the universe wanted to teach me a lesson, so none of my transfer prospects came to fruition. I would need to hightail it to a different state that I had been to once in my life and where I literally knew nobody. Are you getting used to my dramatics yet? I dreaded every moment of it. I was going through a really tough time in my life, and now I had to leave home and everything that felt safe and stable to move away and face the unknown. I dragged my feet but eventually went, huffing and puffing. I didn't have a place to stay. I had never seen the law school's campus. I didn't even have friends that I could look forward to seeing. In my eyes, this was the universe conspiring against me.

Ironically, what I had seen as negatives were also disguised positives that would completely enrich my path in ways I could never predict. During my transition to Rhode Island, I connected with one of my law school professors who has made me feel immensely grateful that I did not transfer. I've met wonderful friends and built relationships that I hope to foster for a very long time. I've also had an opportunity of a lifetime, one that I would've never had if I transferred to another law school (emphasis on, and thanks to, said Professor).

I've learned that even though sh*t does not go the way you expect, it can still work out—maybe even better than you anticipated.

Finding My Voice

Most people's first impression of me is that I am shy and reserved. If you spoke to my family, they would find this laughable. I have multiple family members who describe me as "feisty," and I did admit to being opinionated at some point earlier. *Well, which is it? Am I shy and reserved, or feisty and opinionated?* Yes, yes, yes, and yes—I'm all of the above.

For the longest time, I thought I had to be one or the other, because, unfortunately, I usually see things as black or white. I'm learning to embrace the "grey" much more. I'm all these things because I'm a multi-dimensional person. I adapt to my surroundings based on my comfort level. For example, as much as I'm somewhat used to being in law school, it's still quite unfamiliar. Unfamiliar in the sense that I'm constantly learning new things, things I am not an expert in. In these environments, I tend to be more reserved. But don't mistake my reservation as me shying away. It's just my way of processing and adjusting. I still have a voice and will speak up when I feel compelled to.

On that note, as a Black woman, I sometimes feel conflicted on matters of activism and the purpose of my voice in law school. While I believe in the importance of activism, I also believe you don't need to have the loudest voice to make a difference. I say this to mean that I don't necessarily need to take a bully pulpit in order to fight for the things I support. My voice can still be impactful, even when I'm not publicly outspoken. I'm sharing this element of my voice, not for you to agree or disagree, but simply for you to understand that we all play different roles and play to different strengths. I've learned that in an environment where we face implicit pressure to be *everyone else's* version of courageous, we need to practice empathy and understand that we all have our own voices.

5. James's Experience: "I Was a Total F**k Up in High School"

I was a total f**k up in high school. The look of disappointment on Professor Monestier's face when I told her this was truly soul crushing. But I somehow made it into law school where I am ranked near the top of my class and am a member of both Law Review and Moot Court. Not only is that intended to be a humble brag, but it is also intended to send you this message: you can do well in law school even if you were not always a star student. I also have two other messages for you. First, law school costs *a lot* of money. And second, it *is* possible to work and be successful in law school as long as you are a fanatic about time management.

School was never a big priority in my family. Both of my parents are immigrants and neither finished high school. I was raised by a single mother whose native language is not English. While she can speak English, her language skills were not quite good enough to be able to help me with schoolwork growing up. I had to get through school with little to no help from any adults. I never particularly struggled with schoolwork, but I just did not care enough to try to do well in school. And my family never really pushed me to do well in school. I even failed freshman science in high school. As I said, I was a f**k up. But, by the time I reached my junior year in high school, I realized I had to get my sh*t together. Most of my friends were planning to go to college and I figured I should probably go too. I managed to get into college despite my sub 3.0 high school GPA.

During my first semester of undergrad, I realized I needed to take responsibility for my education and put my best foot forward. After all, I was the one on the hook for my student loans. With that said, my first semester was a difficult adjustment. I seriously contemplated dropping out and working full-time at the local grocery store. But, since I had already paid for the semester, I decided that I should at least see how my grades panned out before making the decision. I worked hard that first semester and, to my surprise, did really well. At this point, I decided maybe school *was* my thing. I applied, and was admitted, to my school's honors program.

During undergrad, I worked pretty much full-time while taking a full course load. Working that much while in school was not ideal, but I really had no other option. I had no one to turn to for financial support. Looking back, I am thankful for this, as it prepared me for the grind that is law school.

During my last semester of undergrad, I decided that law school was the next step for me. My plan was to take a year off in between undergrad and law school. I began working at a law firm full-time, while *also* continuing to work at two part-time jobs. I worked sixty to seventy hours a week while studying for the LSAT. I managed to do decent enough on the test to get into most of the schools I was planning on applying to.

Due to family circumstances, I ended up taking three years off before I finally started law school. The time I spent working at law firm really helped solidify the decision that I wanted to be an attorney. I do not think law firm experience is a "must" before starting law school, but the experience is worth it if you are not 100% sure that you want to go to law school.

Before I made the decision to go to law school, I crunched the numbers, and I realized that I either needed to work part-time while I was in school, or I had to take out a crushing amount of student loans. I opted to work while in school rather than taking out loans. Everyone I knew who went to law school said I was insane for working while in law school, especially during my first year. But I figured life could suck for the three years while I was in law school, or it could suck for forty years while I paid off student loans.

I entered law school feeling like I was at a disadvantage compared to my peers who did not have to work, but this only motivated me more. My first semester was very difficult, not only because I started law school during a pandemic, but because I also had to figure out how I would squeeze in two part-time jobs. Being this over-extended made me have to hyper-focus on school. I spent just about every waking hour during the week doing schoolwork, except for Friday nights when I worked. I then spent most of Saturday working, and the entirety of Sunday doing homework. Time management was key because I really did not have time for anything outside of school and work. It was miserable and I did not get to see most of my friends during my first year of school. But I knew I really wanted to be in law school, so the sacrifices were worth it.

Working during law school is not ideal, but it is manageable. It is possible to do well in law school even if you are working, despite what many people may say. The key is time management and having enough time to dedicate to schoolwork and then work-work. But you have to use the school time to the most productive extent possible. I found that my phone was a major distraction, so I set my phone to silent which helped, but I also decided to leave it somewhere, like my locker, car, or a separate room, so that I would not get the urge to take a break and scroll for a few minutes.

For me, time management and organization went hand in hand. At the beginning of the week, I sat down and organized all of my syllabi and emails to make a list of the readings and assignments I needed to do that week. I then tentatively allocated time throughout the week to get everything done. Keeping an organized email inbox is important to me and helps keep me on track. I keep emails in my general inbox for things I need to act on, and I file away emails once I have completed what is required of them, so I still have them on file if I need to reference them at a later date (pro tip: make sub folders on your email for filing away emails, such as a sub folder for each class and sub folders for non-class things).

Because of COVID, the social experience I had at law school my first semester was probably not the typical experience. I pretty much went to school for class and then went home. This was probably for the best for me personally because, quite frankly, there were fewer distractions. By the end of my first year, though, I became good friends with two other students. We call ourselves "the tripod." Both students are hardworking, and school is the top priority for all of us, which is probably why we get along so well. It is important to choose your friends wisely in law school and to surround yourself with people who have similar goals and drive. Otherwise, they may just become a distraction. This may come as a surprise, but not everyone at school is highly motivated to do well (and there is nothing wrong with that!). But these individuals can end up steering you in the wrong direction and take away your focus from what matters.

Law school is a sacrifice. There are some days when I just want to quit. And other days when there is no place I would rather be. What keeps me going is the end goal of becoming an attorney and of being an example for my younger family members that they can achieve whatever they put their mind to despite any roadblocks they encounter.

6. Beth's Epiphany: "Attorneys Are Not Perfect"

If I knew then what I know now....

When I first started law school, I was overwhelmed and intimidated. I wasn't the typical law student. Law school was never part of my life plan. I was an introverted single mom returning to school after seventeen years, hoping to create a better life for myself and my two kids. I had a merit-based scholarship, and while that should have been a source of confidence, it made me worry even more about being able to keep up with my classmates. I have always had the mindset that I need to be satisfied with "doing my best," but for the first time, I had to make peace with knowing my life circumstances placed real limitations on what "my best" would look like.

As the first week of orientation and first classes unfolded, career services, academic support, and each professor reviewed their expectations for us as students. Over and over, we were told things such as, "Emails to professors must be free of errors," "I will know if you are unprepared for class, so you need to read everything three times," or "Do not submit any draft assignment unless you have proofread it multiple times." I began to think that everything needed to be perfect even though I was supposed to be learning! I received positive feedback from professors, but with each good grade or compliment, my anxiety increased, and my perfectionism became more paralyzing.

Thankfully, I had two major epiphanies during the summer between my 1L and 2L years. The first occurred when I worked part-time for a small transactional law firm doing legal research and drafting. One of my first assignments was to research an issue for a client who had received a demand letter from her ex-spouse's attorney. The first thing I noticed was that the attorney's letter had several typos. Later that summer, I had to amend a company's operating agreement. The company was a new client because its previous attorney had retired, and again, I noticed several oddities with inconsistent language, grammatical errors, and fonts and spacing changing throughout the original document. I began to realize that practicing attorneys are not perfect and as such, I did not need to be perfect to make it through law school.

The second occurred when I took Professional Responsibility as a summer class. My kids were visiting their dad for four weeks, so I had plenty of time to focus and complete my readings, outline, and even study! Law school was so much easier when I didn't have to pack school lunches, read on the floor of my son's karate dojo, or draft memos by the pool during my daughter's swim classes. I earned one of the top three grades in that class, which boosted my confidence tremendously. Even though I was in law school, my top priority was still taking care of my kids. My summer success helped me realize that I was having a hard time during regular semesters not because I wasn't smart enough, but because I was doing my best despite competing priorities.

Now that I have graduated, passed the bar, and am working, I believe even more strongly that what I learned that first summer is true: success in law school (and beyond) doesn't depend on whether you possess some mythical genius capabilities. It really boils down to identifying your priorities and working diligently towards setting and achieving your goals. Study smart, pay attention to small nuances and details, and most of all, believe in yourself.

7. Ryan's Take: "It's Not Rocket Science"

My goal in this reflection is to demonstrate to you that there is no "magic trick" or "secret" to being successful in law school. Law school is often viewed as a place where only the super smart, wealthy, and/or privileged students can succeed at a high level. While this view may be the general rule (as my dear friend, Phil, would say), there are certainly exceptions. I learned things in law school from Professor Monestier that allowed someone like me to not only get through law school, but to graduate second in my class. Let me be clear, this reflection is *not* a "you got this!" motivational speech. I only wish to share how following a system (or as I like to say, "Monestier's Method") can help someone who wasn't always top of their class and who doesn't come from money not only succeed in law school but do so at a high level.

As I just alluded to, I do not come from money. I grew up in an inner-city area where most of the people around me did not go to college and where most relied heavily on state-provided financial assistance (including my household). Both of my parents are physically disabled which meant that my household's primary source of income growing up was SSDI and food-stamps. My parents also got divorced when I was nine, which further impacted our financial situation. Academically, I was never the top of anything. I would always copy homework off a friend or simply wouldn't do it. I also struggled significantly with reading and writing—which are essentially the two pillars of the legal profession. I had reading and writing tutors, special assistance from school, and was even in remedial-level math and English classes. School simply wasn't my thing growing up. I cared far more about sports or whatever I had going on in my life at that time. Even when I got to college, I struggled with reading and writing. For example, I failed my undergraduate university's graduation writing requirement on my first attempt.

With this background in mind, it is likely not a surprise for you to know that law school was completely foreign to me. No one in my immediate family had gone to college other than my dad. I really had no idea what I was getting myself into when I decided to go to law school. I had no idea how difficult law school was, what it entailed, or how expensive it was—all I knew was that I wanted to be a lawyer.

When I started the application process, I recall my college professors would always stress to me how difficult and competitive law school is—not to mention the bar. Once I got accepted to law school, I was very unsure of myself. I knew I had weaknesses and was entering a complex and highly competitive profession. This meant, in my mind, I would have to work hard just to be able to compete with my colleagues. I should also mention that I was participating in a "3+3" program, which allowed me to earn my bachelor's degree in three years (instead of four) and go to law school a year early. Because of this program, however, I did not have my bachelor's degree throughout my 1L year. This meant that if I didn't pass, I would not receive my degree *and* would not be able to remain in law school. The combination of not knowing what to expect in law school, my own academic insecurities, and the fact that if I failed, I would not have any degree to show for it (and still be on the hook for a bunch of money), led me to want to do whatever necessary to pass.

I became known as the guy who essentially lived in the professors' offices—which was, in all fairness, an accurate assessment. In my mind, the professors were a resource I could utilize to improve and overcome my academic shortcomings, so I had *no shame*. Sure, I may have spent too much time visiting my professors but hey, at least I got a mug out of it…[2]

Through my many, many meetings with Professor Monestier, she explained to me how she succeeded in law school and what steps she took to graduate top of her class (hence the name, "Monestier's Method"). One of the most important lessons I learned was that what was necessary to be successful in law school is not out of anyone's reach and is not rocket-science. Law school success, however you subjectively define that term, does not require you to be super smart. It just requires attention to detail, consistency, and self-discipline. "Monestier's Method" focuses on basic skills such as taking good notes, outlining for every class regularly, completing class assignments in advance, and beginning to study for finals at least one month early. With that said, it should be clear that "Monestier's Method" involves more work.

Professor Monestier always urged everyone to outline on a weekly[3] basis for every class. Outlining on a weekly basis would force me to go over material while it was still fresh in my mind, identify my areas of confusion, and have a better overall understanding of the material through spaced repetition. Outlining, however, is not simply copying and pasting your class notes into another document. This requires you to sit down, work through all the material, and organize it into a logical and coherent document. Professor Monestier explained that your outline should have good macro and micro-organization. To be honest, I did not know what "macro" and "micro" organization meant. When I asked, Professor Monestier explained that a useful outline has a good macro or overall structure (such as starting each new topic on a different page and using consistent formatting) as well as a good micro or sentence-level

---

2. Professor Monestier played a game with the class (the Ultimate Contracts Challenge—the U.C.C.) where she gave out mugs as prizes. There were some prizes left over after we played the game so she asked students to vote for who should get them. One of the categories was, "Spends the most time in office hours." The class unanimously agreed that I should get that prize.

3. Author's note: Actually, it's daily.

structure (such as writing in full sentences, explaining a general rule and then the exceptions, etc.).

After a long week of classes, reading assignments, legal practice assignments, and other law school obligations, the LAST thing I wanted to do was sit down and outline for all my classes at the end of the week. But I did it and it made a tremendous difference! I found that I would have things memorized mid-way through the semester because this system forced me to revisit the material on a consistent basis and identify my areas of confusion before it was too late. And again, what Professor Monestier was suggesting was not earth-shattering. In fact, what she was suggesting was basic and required only a little more time and effort.

As for studying for finals, I learned that it was all about consistency and spaced repetition. When I had first started law school, the idea that 100% of my grade would be based on one, maybe two exams (if there was a mid-term exam) really concerned me. So, I went to Professor Monestier, and she explained that what I had to do was simple: start studying early and study consistently. Professor Monestier explained that starting to study for finals about one month before finals began would provide me with an opportunity to identify any weaknesses and time to address those weaknesses. She also explained that if I studied consistently for that period, I would be able to recall the information better and have a more solid understanding of it too. However, Professor Monestier stressed that having a good study routine is only half of it—I also needed to use my time productively. Professor Monestier suggested things such as re-writing my outline sections at a time to better retain the material, speaking aloud the material as if you were explaining it to another person, and studying the material in an order different from how I learned it.

While this sounded like a lot of work (and it certainly was), I did exactly what Professor Monestier suggested. For nearly every final I took in law school, particularly during my 1L and 2L years, I began studying at least one month early. I would create rotating schedules so that I could make sure that I hit every class a certain number of times before the final exam. Having this system ensured that I gave each class the same time and attention, and again, helped me figure out what I didn't know. I would also break up my outlines, which were usually anywhere from 70 to 115 pages, into three or four chunks and would re-write each chunk, speak each chunk aloud to either myself or a friend (or my dad), and would study each chunk in a different order every session. This method of studying helped my ability to recall the information so well that for most courses, I did not need to physically see my outline to study the material in the days leading up to the exam. I would be able to recall my outline in the chunks that I studied and would walk through all the information all based on memory. If I missed something or forgot something, I would refer to my outline. This method largely took away the stress of worrying whether I would be able to recall the information and allowed me to focus more on the actual issues presented on the exam. So, while Professor Monestier's method of studying was time-consuming and required a lot of work, for me, the time and work was worth it and helped me feel like I did everything I could to do my best.

The key takeaway from my law school experience (and I hope yours after reading this reflection) is that small things like attention to detail, providing yourself with a system, and being consistent (all of which are relatively basic) can help you achieve anything you want, and even exceed your expectations! I'm confident that I would not have performed as well in law school without Professor Monestier and her guidance. I'm very thankful for her and everything she has taught me.

Conclusion

Truth be told, I hate writing conclusions. It's like, I said what I want to say. I'm done. I don't need to re-say what I already said just to wrap it all up in a bow for you. But I'm fairly sure that the editors are not going to let me off the hook and just write "The End." That would be nice, though, wouldn't it?

Maybe I'll do a little inspirational stuff here, which I've told you before I don't do. I don't do it because, well, I'm not your life coach. And I kind of suck at inspirational. But I've got some space to fill up, so let's give it a try!

You may come away from reading this book a little overwhelmed. Over 300 pages on things you should know before you go to law school. It's a lot. This book may cause you to panic, to lose sleep, and to spend day and night researching self-regulated learning (one can only hope!). Okay, students: *Chill the f**k out.* Oops, that's not super inspirational, is it?

Let's start over. I promise you: It will be okay. You will find your way throughout law school. And you will probably graduate.[1] And you will likely pass the bar exam.[2] *F**k it,* I give up. The End.

---

1. A fairly high percentage of students who matriculate end up graduating from law school. Probably well over 90%. So, you should be good. And note to self: You are turning into your dad with the 90%.

2. Unless you go to school in California. Also, the New York bar is really hard too.

Acknowledgments

Before I get to my "acknowledgments" I have to tell you what I hate about acknowledgments: they tend to be corny, over-sharey, and cring-ey. They tend to read something like this:

To my husband. Without you, my life would be empty. You are my rock, my part-ner in crime, my everything. I cannot imagine my life without you. I thank God every day that you came into my life.

Yuck, yuck, yuck. I literally have a visceral reaction when I read something like this. It's all over Facebook whenever anyone has a milestone birthday or ac-complishes anything significant. I often have to stop reading halfway through because I am *embarrassed* for the author. One of my favorite comedians has a television special called, "Aren't You Embarrassed?" That's exactly how I feel.

Now that I got that off my chest, I proceed to my non-effusive, non-over-the-top acknowledgments.

To my husband. Thank you for setting up a Wix site and getting my blog rolling. Without that, this book would never have been written. And thanks for proofreading the book and adding a double space after every period (I know that's your pet peeve; what you don't know is that the editors remove that extra space).

To my family, Mom, Dad, Dennis, and Yvonne. Thank you for keeping me grounded. And refusing to let me talk about the book for more than five minutes. Cause we know it's never about "me" in this family.

To Emilia and Charlie. Here's hoping you grow up to be just like your Zia. Always remember, your good looks and beautiful blue eyes can only get you so far. Mind you, it might be quite far...I hear it's called "pretty privilege."

To the students who helped me with this book, Neisha, BJ, Maddy, and David (squared), and to the students who provided thoughtful reflections about their law school experience. Students like you are the reason I do what I do.

To all my former research and teaching assistants. I am so proud of all that you have accomplished. You are proof positive that what I say in this book works.

To all the students I have enjoyed teaching over the years. You know who you are. If you are not sure if I "enjoyed teaching" you, I didn't. You have made turning down the big bucks worth it. Sort of. Mainly.

To the folks at Carolina Academic Press who saw my vision for this book and made it a reality: Scott, who green-lighted my use of the words sh*t and mindf**k. Carol, who (clearly) is amazing at spotting talent when she sees it. Ryland, who gracefully shepherded a high-maintenance author through the publication process. And Steve, who indulged my request for five different sans serif font sample layouts (Futura, Quiche Sans, Filson Soft, Dusk and Freight Neo, in case you're wondering).

To the legal publisher that thought this book was too "edgy" and not the "right fit" for them. Once this book becomes a big success, I'd like to say, "How do you like 'dem apples?" If it doesn't become a big success, then "Good call."